T0114390

John O'Brien

At Home in the Heart of Appalachia

John O'Brien earned a B.A. in English at West Virginia University, held writing fellowships at the University of Iowa and Stanford University, and was the recipient of a National Endowment for the Arts fellowship. His work has appeared in *Hudson Review*, *Massachusetts Review*, *TriQuarterly*, *Iowa Review*, *Country Journal*, *Harrowsmith*, and *Gray's Sporting Journal*. He was diagnosed with a rare cancer in 2002, and died in 2004 while living with his wife, Becky, in Green Bank, West Virginia.

*At Home
in the Heart of
Appalachia*

At Home
in the Heart of
Appalachia

John O'Brien

ANCHOR BOOKS
A Division of Random House, Inc.
New York

FIRST ANCHOR BOOKS EDITION, AUGUST 2002

Grateful acknowledgment is made to the following for permission to reprint previously published material:

HarperCollins Publishers, Inc.: Excerpt from "Chimneys" from *Searching for the Ox: New Poems* by Louis Simpson, copyright © 1971, 1973, 1974, 1975, 1976 by Louis Simpson. Reprinted by permission of HarperCollins Publishers, Inc.

Alfred A. Knopf: Two brief excerpts from "Metaphors of a Magnifico" by Wallace Stevens from *The Collected Poems of Wallace Stevens*, copyright © 1954 by Wallace Stevens. Reprinted by permission of Alfred A. Knopf, a division of Random House, Inc.

The Library of Congress has cataloged the Knopf edition as follows:
O'Brien, John, 1943–
At home in the heart of Appalachia / John O'Brien
1st ed.
p. cm.
ISBN 0-394-56451-0
1. O'Brien, John. 2. Mountain whites (Southern states)—Appalachian Region, Southern—Social life and customs. 3. Appalachian region, Southern—Biography. 4. Appalachian region, Southern—Social life and customs. 5. West Virginia—Biography.
6. West Virginia—Social life and customs.

CT275.O24 A3 2001
2001089765

Anchor ISBN: 978-0-385-72139-4

Author photograph © Shelly Turner
Book design by Virginia Tan

www.anchorbooks.com

In memory of my father,
James Patrick O'Brien
and
for Becky, True North

Destiny fits, always,
There's no such thing
as a life not meant
for the person living it.

From "Chimneys" by Louis Simpson

I shall never forget what the Queen of Bhutan said when I was a boy in India. She said, "We want progress, but not so fast as to leave the human soul behind."

Dr. Henry Taylor, brother of Dan'l Taylor-Ide,
director of Woodlands Institute

Gatsby believed in the green light, the orgiastic future that year by year recedes before us. It eluded us then, but that's no matter—tomorrow we will run faster, stretch out our arms further . . . And one fine morning—

So we beat on, boats against the current, borne back ceaselessly into the past.

From The Great Gatsby *by F. Scott Fitzgerald*

Contents

*At Home
in the Heart of
Appalachia*

Prologue

IT IS the hottest day of summer and I have started for my father's birthplace in Piedmont, West Virginia. Sometime today they will bury him in southwest Philadelphia and I will not be there. The flurry of phone calls two days ago made it clear that my presence would only add to family stress. My father, at long last, is beyond caring about anything I might or might not do, and so I see no point. Still, after two sleepless nights, I find myself desperate for a formal gesture, and driving to Piedmont is all that I could think of. For reasons not entirely clear, I want to hear stories from someone who knew him as a boy. If it's possible, I will locate Grandfather O'Brien's grave, something I have put off far too long.

After traveling around the country for fifteen years I left Oswego, New York, and came home to West Virginia in 1984. For the last ten years I have lived in Franklin, the seat of Pendleton County. Piedmont is two hours north through the mountains. Leaving the town of Franklin, Route 220 ascends a hill, then gently rolls along the bottom of the South Branch Valley. Meandering as whimsically as the small river that it follows, the narrow road weaves beside the water for several miles, veers upward into shady hardwood forest, then glides down to the river again and again. I lose myself to this dance.

I have been trying to remember good times with my dad. In some of my best memories, we are fishing rivers like the South Branch on my right—the two of us wading through knee-deep water as dusk comes on. Since coming back to West Virginia, I have haunted the South Branch. Subsistence fishing—bass and trout for the table—has

3

been the closest thing to religion in my life, and my father gave that to me.

Up one mountain and down another, I roller-coaster in and out of shadowy forests, passing small farms where drowsy cattle and black-faced sheep stand in steep hillside pastures, past village-size towns with names like Upper Tract and Smoke Hole. I lose my sense of time. I am fifty-two and have been driving through Appalachian landscape like this since I was three years old. I could be a boy staring out the window of my father's ancient Plymouth; an adolescent on his way to West Virginia University; a lovestruck young man driving toward Green Bank to ask Jamie Sheets for his daughter's hand in marriage; or a middle-aged man coming home to the mountains with two children of his own. I have spent my life leaving Appalachia and coming home again; if I belong anywhere in the world, it is here. Despite fifty years in southwest Philadelphia, my father belongs here, too.

Between small towns, late-summer flowers crowd the road shoulders. My father loved the names of wildflowers, and driving along he would often say them out loud. I do this in his memory now: "Queen Anne's lace, black-eyed Susan, ironweed, teasel, yarrow, joe-pye, vetch."

At Keyser, five miles down the Potomac from Piedmont, the smell of sulfide seeps into the car. I stiffen and grip the steering wheel—the mill.

Entering Piedmont makes my chest tighten. It's like driving into a movie—the scenery outside the window does not seem like the real world. I know but do not know this town. The spidery metal bridge across the Potomac that made me think of a gigantic erector set as a boy has been replaced by a low concrete structure as featureless as a highway overpass. In my memory, Piedmont will always be a gritty mill town bristling with working-class energy: people loaded down with parcels rushing in and out of downtown stores; humpbacked cars cruising up and down while packs of children chase each other down narrow side streets. It floats in my mind like something painted by Léger.

Now the shops are closed. Storefronts have been crudely boarded up, and the windows have been smashed. Shattered glass glints hard from the sidewalks. The only person on Main Street is an adolescent girl in a T-shirt, cutoff jean shorts, and shower flip-flops. Looking angry and bored, she stops to light a cigarette, cupping both hands around the match despite the absence of the slightest breeze.

Across the weedy railroad tracks, Piedmont High, where my father played the clarinet and met my mother one winter afternoon in 1935, is now an ancient ruin. The roof has caved in and vines climb up and over the crumbling walls. Turning down a side street, I discover a blue jay tire-flattened into the hieroglyph of a bird, a pulsing cloud of flies above it. My father has died, and his town is dying as I drive through it.

Piedmont seems more like a ruined village than a town. The small streets I remember from childhood visits look like alleys. The Potomac, a bulling river in my memory, is now a shallow stream that I could wade. But up this steep cobblestone street, my father's house has not changed. A wood-frame structure covered with tan, sand-specked tarpaper, it sits near the top of the steepest hill in Piedmont. I remember it as small and so it remains. The O'Briens no longer own the house, that much I know. I only hope whoever lives here now will not come out to find me staring at their front door. I could not explain, at least not quickly.

Something flickers in the rearview mirror outside the car. Glancing that way, I see the face of an old black woman, like a soft brown owl in the mirror. She is sitting on a porch down the street and leaning forward on her chair to watch me. Black people live in my father's neighborhood now. If a black family owns his house, he would have been troubled. In southwest Philadelphia racial tension that often erupted into violence made my father bitter about "the coloreds."

Eighteen years of silence stand between us now. I made the break, but whether the fault is mine has never been clear to me. Over the years, I have often thought of myself as too self-centered to make room in my life for my own father. At other times, I have convinced myself that I had to create distance between us. In my mind, this has become, as Wallace Stevens said, "old song that will not declare itself." An image often comes to mind: I am under murky water struggling toward the surface while my father holds my ankles. But here is another image that I live with: my father is on fire and

My father, James Patrick O'Brien, 1976

reaches for me, but I will not reach back. I have missed him for eighteen years and miss his presence now. And I have never blamed him for anything.

I don't know how things broke down so badly between us, or when the trouble started. I don't know how it's possible to miss someone but deliberately keep them out of your life. I want to believe that there are reasons for these unruly emotions and that if I look back over my life carefully enough I will find them.

For me, remembering is like looking into a kaleidoscope. Each look back turns the cylinder and another pattern appears. Some things do remain fixed—Piedmont, leaving and returning to these mountains, subsistence hunting and fishing, the heartache my father and I share, and the reverberations that his father sent through both our lives. It's meaning that will not hold still. The biggest part of the mystery is Appalachia itself; where does that strange, sad place begin and end? What has being Appalachian meant to my father, to my grandfather, and to me? Trying to understand is like picking up a bead of mercury—something is clearly there, but I cannot grasp it. But these people are real and these events did happen. I'm not certain I fully understand a good part of what I am going to tell you but will start with a trip to Piedmont forty years ago.

Slipping a Bach tape into the car's cassette player, the Concerto in C Minor for Oboe and Violin, I wait for the second movement, which my father might have liked. Let Bach make his case for grace and order here in Appalachia and in my life.

1. My Father Takes Me Home

AUGUST 1952

ON THIS sweltering day, I'm sitting on the front steps of our house on Greenway Avenue, in southwest Philadelphia. Through the screen door behind me, I hear my two brothers and two sisters complain about the heat. We have spent the afternoon filling paper bags with clothing, picking ripe tomatoes from the garden down the block, checking doors and windows, and scrubbing up. As soon as my father comes home from work, we will leave for Piedmont. I have filled buckets of water for Richard and Lady—my father's prized rabbit hounds that will stay here in the alley—and now all that's left to do is wait for him.

Beyond the curb, the blacktop has become as soft as fudge. Up and down Greenway Avenue the oven-hot air shimmers, turning the colored girls jumping double Dutch into a wavering mirage. Waiting has always been hard for me, but waiting for my father is the hardest. At last he rounds the corner by Mazy's closet-sized grocery store, brown lunch bag in one hand and that tattered, oil-stained cap perched on top of his curly red hair. Once brown, the cap has faded into beige. He does not want a new cap; he brought this one from Piedmont when he moved to the city. As always, when he thinks he is alone and unseen, he frowns and stares into the middle distance—a worried man. No one in the world walks like him; each foot flares out wide to either side, ducklike. My father is a sailor on a ship at sea.

Jumping up I shout, "It's him," and everyone flies around—double-checking windows and doors, turning the water off, unscrewing fuses. After one last look at Lady and Richard we stampede to the old box-turtle Plymouth. Inside the car, my younger brother David begins a litany of good-bye. It's "Good-bye, house, good-bye, porch, good-bye, Beauty"—the striped cat on the porch—"good-bye, Richard, good-bye . . ."

Then older brother Patrick snaps, "Shut up, you idjit." And the first in-car fight begins.

"You're not the boss of this car."

"Oh yeah? Well I'm older and that means . . ."

In the front seat, my father clears his throat and says, "Listen up once." I see his pale blue eyes in the rearview mirror. My father is a gentle, soft-spoken man, but when his voice takes an edge, we listen. He says, "We're gonna start this trip friends and end this trip friends. Right?"

"Right!" we all shout, but my brothers glare at each other.

The peace restored, my father goes through a series of small physical adjustments. He squares his shoulders, adjusts and readjusts his cap, shifts around to find a perfect position in the seat. When everything seems in order, he places a hand on the dashboard, then lowers his head like a priest whispering a prayer. I'm not sure, but he could well be praying. Our old Plymouth is a fourth-hand car, and making it all the way to Piedmont is not certain. At last, he slaps the dashboard and starts the engine. Pulling away from the curb, he shouts, "Off like a dirty shirt!"

On the road after dark, we play buzz, a math game he has taught us. Then he leads us in song: "Good Night, Irene," "In the Cool, Cool, Cool of the Evening," and "Swing Low, Sweet Chariot." We all sing loudly and happily like campers around a fire, but at odd, mismatched moments I hear only my father's voice. He means it when he sings, that's the difference. There is something sad about the way he holds long notes. At times, even happy songs seem touched with melancholy.

Passing through small Pennsylvania towns, we children fall asleep on top of one another like a litter of kittens. I momentarily wake up when my father toots the horn to say, "West, by God, Virginia," as we cross into the state. Hours later, sensing the loss of motion, we all wake up and untangle. Gaping and yawning, we tumble out into the dark town. Across the street from my grandmother's house, a door opens and light pours out. A woman in padded housecoat and hair rollers—at least this is how she appears in memory—calls to a small dog down the block. She does not seem to notice us in the dark. David, who is not quite awake, thinks Grandmother O'Brien is calling him. He runs across the street and through the open door while the woman stands gasping as a perfect stranger rushes in: the O'Briens have come back home.

BOTH SIDES of my family, the O'Briens and the Bells, came from this small town. Piedmont, which means foot of the mountain in French, is a paper-mill town on the banks of the Potomac River in northeastern West Virginia. The mountains crowd in tight and houses sit at strange angles on impossibly steep hills. (The cobblestone street on which my Grandmother O'Brien lives is so steep, it occasionally appears as an escalator in my dreams.) Train tracks split Piedmont down the middle. Long lines of open cars, loaded down with coal from the southern part of the state, rumble through town at odd hours of the day and night. Across the Potomac, in Luke, Maryland, the stupendous chimneys of the world's largest paper mill, Westvaco, spew out yellow sulfide smoke. When it rains in Piedmont, the water turns to mild acid that eats the paint from cars and homes. The rank smell has worked its way into furniture, rugs, clothing, pet fur, and women's hair. God knows what it does to human lungs. When I was a boy, the river was dishwater gray. Below the mill, all of the native fish had died and so had the vegetation along the water's edge. On some days, the Potomac smoldered acid fog and the smell of rotten eggs was overwhelming.

My relatives worked at the mill. Each weekday morning my grandparents, aunts, and uncles drove across the metal bridge to work their shift and then drove back home at night. Families paid their bills, fed their children, and kept their homes in good repair. On summer evenings after work, couples sat on porch swings to take the cool night air. In the fall men like my Grandfather Bell and my Uncle Jimmy—a legendary outdoorsman—hunted the woods and fished the streams that were unaffected by the mill's runoff. On Saturday nights beer joints filled up and on Sunday mornings so did the churches. Women like my Grandmother Bell, who was tall and handsome, walked to church in their finery. Their husbands, scrubbed free of the week's mill grime, wore their "go to meet'n" suits and escorted them, walking on the curbside as chivalry required. The high point of the social year was the mill picnic—one day for white people and another for black. My relatives, like most residents, thought Piedmont was special, a good place to live. Concerning the ever-present smell, Grandfather Bell quoted old Mr. Luke, part-owner of the mill, who always said, "It smells like *money* to me." My grandfather invariably chuckled when he said this.

My own feelings about the mill, even as a boy, were more ambivalent. It was true, most of my relatives worked there, and on some level, I understood how important that was. But my Grandmother O'Brien stacked paper all day long and came home with razor-thin cuts on both hands. To ward off infection, she soaked them in hot bleach water each night. I can remember seeing her at the kitchen table, hands suspended above a steaming dishpan. The treatments were painful, and Grandmother had to master herself each night. After holding her hands above the pan for half a minute, she closed her eyes, then slowly let her hands sink. A wince of pain was replaced by an expression of acceptance that made me think of saints on holy cards. In my mind, the mill was like purgatory: terrible things happened there.

That vision aside, I have pleasant memories from those Piedmont visits—kitchens crowded with relatives, uncles dropping into a boxer's stance by way of greeting, the sense of being related to half the town. Grandmother Bell had a refrigerator on the back porch filled with small bottles of Coke—"pop," she called it. She kept a wooden bowl on the kitchen table filled with fresh fruit and told us to help ourselves; this was opulence beyond imagination. We spent long afternoons at the town swimming pool a few blocks from the Bells' house, and I dreamed about this all through winter. One of my uncles had a small dog that did wonderful tricks on the sidewalk beside the Bells' house. As I recall, it was a small pug-faced dog that would sit, shake hands, roll over, and play dead on command. The dog's big trick, the "piece of resistance," was to sit on its haunches wearing spectacles with a toy smoking pipe in its mouth. With a flourish my uncle would say, "Winston Churchill!" On every visit, Grandfather Bell told me the same joke: "Oncet there was a sheep born without a nose. How do you think he smelled? *Awful*, just like all the other sheep." He laughed every time, his pipe clicking against his false teeth. My grandfather was a one-joke man; if you've got a good one, stick with it. I laughed along with him, even after the only thing that was funny was the fact that he was telling the same joke again.

For me, coming home always had to do with language. My mother's ancestors, like most of the people who settled this part of Appalachia in the 1750s, came from Ulster, England, or Germany. Appalachians have always been conservative speakers. For the longest time people in the southern mountains resisted the homogenizing influence of middle-American speech and kept the distinctive accent that developed in the early 1800s. The Scotch-Irish lilt, along with a delight in rich metaphor, prevails. My Piedmont relatives used words like "reckon" and "yonder." People spoke about feeling "poorly" or "dauncy"—worse than poorly, I think. A paper bag was a "poke." Cast-iron frying pans, those old black ones that weighed a ton, were "skillets" or sometimes "spiders." Young lovers went "a-court'n." My Grandfather Bell might say, "The porch needs a-paint'n." Or, "By jacks, look who's a-com'n through the door," placing the "a" before verbs to keep the rhythm in his talk alive. Since the 1950s, television and popular music have weakened Appalachian speech, but it's still here. Mountain talk is highly inflected; it rises and falls like spoken poetry. The only national figure who sounds like my Piedmont relatives is Loretta Lynn, the country singer from Butcher Hollow, Kentucky. (Lynn not only sounds like one of my relatives, she also looks something like my mother.) To my ear, Appalachian speech is music.

Despite pleasant memories, what remains most vivid about those visits, at least now as I look back on them at fifty-six, is the strain between the Bells and the O'Briens and my father's anxiety about being home. The families did not get along, and in fact refused to recognize each other's existence. They never exchanged harsh words—in my presence anyway—but I cannot remember anyone from one family referring to someone from the other by name. It was always, "Will you be having dinner up the hill then?" Or "How long will you be down at the other place?"

I remember driving to the Kroger store with Grandmother O'Brien. My mother sat between my father, who was driving, and

Grandmother O'Brien on the passenger side. On the way back, my mother had to speak to her father about something, and so we pulled up beside the Bells' house. As Grandfather Bell approached her window, Grandmother O'Brien became as stiff as a mannequin, staring straight ahead without blinking or making the slightest movement. For some reason, I thought she was attempting a magic trick; if she sat absolutely still and held her breath, she would become invisible. The trick seemed to work because Grandfather Bell spoke to my mother right through Grandmother O'Brien's face, as if she were not there.

The Bells lived in a pleasant brick house in the valley bottom, in a part of town called The Orchard. Like most of Piedmont's quality folk, they were prominent Presbyterians. The O'Briens lived "up the hill"—sometimes "up the mountain"—not far from where the "coloreds" lived. Even as a boy I understood that "up the hill" indicated more than direction. The expression carried unpleasant weight.

My father's ancestors, Catholics, had come from southern Ireland as a result of the first potato famine in the nineteenth century. Catholics were, and still are, a rare and suspect breed in Appalachia. (There was no Catholic church in Piedmont. To attend Sunday mass, we drove across the erector-set bridge into Westernport, Maryland. Catholics from small towns up and down the river did the same.) When my father was a boy, Catholics were also at the bottom of the socioeconomic ladder, and so it is difficult to determine where religious intolerance ended and imaginary class distinctions began. In any case, the families could not abide one another.

Class difficulties played out at mealtime. At the Bells', we sat down at a table covered with a linen tablecloth. Grandmother Bell, who had her white hair tinted blue each week, came to dinner in a housedress that made me think of the *Donna Reed Show* on television. My Grandfather Bell wore a fresh dress shirt to table each day. There were two forks—a mystery to me—a fancy butter dish, and those odd, fat butter knives. We only occasionally made conversation, rather than talked, and those meals were so quiet the only sound that I remember clearly is the clicking of forks against china.

My father's profound sense of inferiority overcame him at times like that. The fear of saying or doing something that would shame his family terrified him. Sitting stiffly on the edge of his seat, he nervously watched my mother's hands from the corner of his eye. I don't think he ate anything at the Bells'. Once, when I asked my mother why he seemed so frightened, she told me about the first time he came to dinner at her house. My father, a skinny, freckle-faced boy, had taken a slice of butter for his dinner roll but ended up with too much on his knife. Frugal as always, he scraped the excess back onto the butter dish while Grandmother Bell watched in horror. My father flushed deep red and began to stammer apologies, which only made things worse. Oddly, I cannot recall any of the food at the Bells'.

I do remember meals at the O'Briens', but not fondly. At the bare kitchen table "up the hill" we ate fried cornmeal mush, "hamburgs," green beans boiled with fatback, and stewed tomatoes mixed with gooey lumps of Wonder Bread. It was the kind of food "hillbillies" ate, and that distinction lies at the heart of the family strain. Like middle-class Americans anywhere, the Bells needed to establish clear distance between themselves and what they saw as the lowest social rank. In the southern mountains, this normal human impulse can be more intense and therefore more damaging.

Working-class Appalachians who want to enter the middle class, or to make it clear they have arrived, at times imagine the gene-deficient monstrosities of James Dickey's *Deliverance* or the cartoon-ish dimwits from the *Beverly Hillbillies* on the "other side of the tracks." There is more to escape and more to deny in these hilly towns. The fact that hillbilly stereotypes make as little sense as black or Native American stereotypes is of no consequence to the people who struggle to escape them. The O'Briens and the Bells were decent, hardworking people, but neither family understood the social pressures that affected them, which only made the imaginary distance wider.

For most of my life Appalachia confused me. When I met people around the country and said that I was from West Virginia, they would sometimes say, "Ah, Appalachia" in a peculiar way. They seemed to think that I had come from—or perhaps escaped—some exotic, dreadful place, but for the longest time I did not know where Appalachia was exactly or what it meant to be Appalachian. As a boy, I don't think I ever heard the word "Appalachia." My parents and relatives thought of themselves as West Virginians. Years later, when I went to college in Morgantown, West Virginia, I began to hear the word in reference to the state and region, but I never understood what it had to do with my family. My parents and Piedmont relatives, like most West Virginians, shared this confusion. If someone had asked Grandfather Bell what Appalachians were like, he might well have said, "Beats me, by jacks. Never run into one." In time I would learn that Appalachia was an imaginary place and that being Appalachian was imaginary but terribly damaging. If the subject had a discernible starting point for me, it was on these early trips to Piedmont with my relatives trying to dodge the hillbilly identity.

Beyond family tensions, my father's feelings about coming home always seemed mixed to me. He was happy and excited as we piled into the old car in Philadelphia. Crossing the state line, his ceremonial horn-toot was heartfelt; he was a West Virginia boy coming home. Driving around Piedmont, he pointed out the homes of people he knew and occasionally told stories about them. Once, driving past Piedmont High, he sang part of his school song. He liked being with his younger brother, Phillip. (Watching the brothers walk down the street was a revelation: someone else in the world did walk like my father.) Both brothers had red, curly hair and pale blue eyes. I can remember my father clowning around with Phillip, and even laughing out loud, but a good part of the time on those visits he seemed anxious and preoccupied.

One day at the Bells' comes back: My father and I are waiting in the living room. My mother is in another room talking with her parents. I sense that the talk is serious, perhaps about money. My brothers and sisters are at the town pool for the afternoon, but I can't go. A day or two before, I opened the back door of my Uncle Jimmy's car as he rounded a sharp turn on a steep mountain road and went sailing out. Impaled on a fence post, I woke to find my father kneeling in front of me whispering, "Please, please, don't be dead." The wounds at the back of my head and base of my spine were superficial but required a lot of stitching up. I have been walking around with my head in a turban of white bandages like a very young war veteran. No swimming pool for this boy.

My dad has never been comfortable in this house but today he seems to be trapped inside a burning building. He sits down in an armchair, jumps up, walks to the window, pulls the curtain back as if expecting someone, walks back across the room, and sits down again. Something happens in the next room. Voices rise up in anger. Moments later, my mother walks into the living room and whispers to my father. Mother hurries out of the living room. I follow my father out of the house.

Now we are on the sidewalk in front of the Bells'. Across the street, there is a small firehouse—little more than a large garage— and the men are washing an old red truck with rags and buckets of soapy water. Passing, I see the two of us distorted in the truck's gleaming brass bell, a dwarf father and son with enormous round heads.

Down the street, we walk into a small drugstore and sit facing one another in a plywood booth. The chubby man in an apron brings me a fountain Coke—the first and last soda my father will ever buy me. Sucking on the straw I notice the chubby man staring. Now his face lights up and he comes over to stand right beside my dad.

"Ah-ha," he says.

My father flinches and looks at him, puzzled.

"Red O'Brien," the man says. "You old Red Devil you."

When my father squints, the man says, "It's me, Red, Patty Amarosa all growed up."

Then, in a gesture that will always remain vivid, Patty puts both hands out, palms up to the ceiling, wiggles his head with his eyes closed, and tells a story about the two of them stealing cherries from a tree in someone's backyard. They had climbed a fence and run from a dog. I have forgotten the other details.

As the man talks, my father shakes his head no. But Patty will not back off. "Don't try and kid me, Red. Don't kid a kidder."

My father bolts out of the booth and almost runs to the door. I hurry after him as Patty stares at us.

I have told and written this small story many times. When I was young, the point seemed to be an encounter with a small-town eccentric. In my thirties, the point became a father's embarrassment when confronted with a frisky story in his son's presence. In my memory, the colors and shapes have not changed—me, my father, Patty, stealing the cherries—but now the story is about my father's desperation in Piedmont.

According to the family's unofficial history, or at least to the stories I have heard, my father left Piedmont in the early 1940s because the mill was not hiring. This may well be true, but I am convinced that there is more to the story. There was something painful about being Red O'Brien in Piedmont. Other memories confirm this. My father never looked up old friends on those visits home and, as far as I know, never spoke to anyone outside the immediate family. I can remember him becoming nervous in store aisles when he saw someone who seemed to recognize him.

One evening that week, I walked out onto the back porch at the O'Briens' to find my father chain-smoking on the old porch swing. This remains fixed in my memory because he rolled his own cigarettes back then, which made me think of cowboy movies. He kept his "make'ns" in a small cloth bag that closed with a red drawstring, and his "homemades" were as shapeless as a marijuana smoker's first joints. He was not a heavy smoker normally, but that night I watched him pitch one misshapen butt after another over the porch rail. Staring into the dark yard, he was lost in heavy thoughts. When I said something, he snapped at me. "Go on back in," he said in anger, which was not like him.

In Philadelphia, his life was never easy. With a family that kept growing—ten children, all born at home—and an assembly-line-worker's salary, we were the poorest family in a very poor neighborhood. Money was always running out, and when people in the neighborhood whispered "layoff" house to house, my father could not sleep. When the bottom dropped out we lived without power or water by the light of a coal oil lamp. I can remember eating mush and thin soup cooked on a camp stove. Once, the bank threatened to evict us and would have if Sy Tarensky—who employed my mother at his discount store on Woodland Avenue—had not made the mortgage payments. Through hard times, my mother was the family metal; history has made women from the Appalachian Mountains determined survivors.

My mother was strong-willed and always knew precisely what she wanted. If a neighbor raised an eyebrow about the number of children in our family, she looked straight at them and said, "Every last one was my idea." I have never been sure about that. But my mother was a strong woman. She was never "Mom," but always "Mother." We were not allowed to use pronouns when we referred to her. If Mother overheard one of us saying "her" or "she," she snapped, "Who's 'she,' the queen's cat?" As a young woman, in the old black-and-white snapshots that I have seen, she does look, as I said, like Loretta Lynn. With long, wavy black hair, high cheekbones, and bright eyes, she was pretty in the natural way that women from the southern Appalachians often are.

My mother met my father (or at least this is the story she tells) in the hallway at Piedmont High. She had stopped to drink from a water fountain. Apparently it was between classes, and students were streaming past. As she bent over, someone stumbled into her hard enough to bump her face against the faucet, causing a spectacular nosebleed. Schoolbooks went sprawling all over the hallway. Turning to give whoever it was "what for," she discovered Jim O'Brien, a red-headed boy with freckles and pale blue eyes.

As my father dropped to his knees gathering her books, he kept repeating apologies and seemed to be in more pain than she was. His remorse was so genuine my mother fell in love with him at once. She has always said, "I knew right then; I told myself, I'm going to marry this boy." Two years later, she did just that.

Through the worst of times, that steely determination kept the family from going under. Without power or water, hanging on by a thread, my mother became a general in a bunker under siege. She turned adversity into proof of virtue; the world was a hard place for good people, and the fact that the O'Briens struggled meant that we were good. We would make it through if she had to knock the world flat.

We children did not suffer through times like that. We were always warm and dry, and no one went to bed hungry or, for that matter, unloved. My mother kept her worst fears to herself and, like children generally, we had our own world. Living by coal oil lamp and cooking on the Coleman stove was like camping out. Decades passed before I understood how desperate we were at times.

I do not mean to say that my father's life was joyless or that he was constantly troubled. While money was always a serious problem, those rock-bottom times were rare. My father came home from work to a family that loved him. On winter evenings, he sat on the couch to read the *Philadelphia Evening Bulletin* while one of his children sat on the floor massaging his feet. Before supper on steamy summer nights he drank a bottle of Ortlieb's beer, liberally sprinkled with salt, in the cool alley near his rabbit hounds. With his green work pants rolled up to his freckled Irish knees, he soaked his feet in a dishpan of bleach water and relished every sip of icy beer.

My mother was an exceptional cook, and although meat was scarce, the food was invariably good and there was always enough to go around. We ate stews, soups, navy beans, spaghetti, and fish on Friday. It's amazing what a truly good cook can do with very little money. These were formal, sit-down meals. My father sat at one end of the table while my mother anchored the other. All of the children crowded in between and every meal was a family ceremony that my father presided over.

A cup of tea formally closed his day. Toward the end of the meal, he told one of his children to put the kettle on. Whoever it was—me as often as anyone else—waited in the kitchen until the water boiled, then poured it into his china pot. My father was quite fussy about his tea. If the wait stretched out too long, he would snap, "Bring it here to me," and rap his knuckles on the table. Then again, if the tea had not steeped long enough to develop character, he made a sour face at the first sip and impatiently dumped it back into the pot.

Properly steeped, the tea settled my father. We could not leave the table until officially excused, and he often took the hour after dinner to teach us things. He loved language. Taking small sips of tea, he would sometimes spread the *Evening Bulletin* on the table and advise us to listen up as he read a sentence containing a new word. I can still see him repeating, "Periphery, periphery—P-E-R-I-P-H-E-R-Y. What's it mean, you think?"

After a few wild guesses, he might send one of us to get the battered, coverless dictionary from the closet floor. I can remember sliding a magnifying glass down the page as he spelled the word again. At last, there it was—huge, inky-black letters bleeding off in rainbows under the fractured light. We learned not just new words but the names of flowers, small towns, state parks. Watching my father repeat a word he had fallen in love with was like watching a man sample exotic cheese; he savored the taste and feel of it on his tongue.

At table, he told us parables about the world, using knives, forks, and salt and pepper shakers to illustrate his tale. The salt shaker might become the white man, the pepper—obviously—the "colored." Spoons turned into women and knives into men. God, Catholics, Protestants, boss, worker, everything had its counterpart on the dinner table. I once saw a bottle of Hunt's ketchup turn into Pope Pius XII. My dad was a magic realist long before any South American writer.

He prayed every day and filled his house with icons—plaster praying hands against the wall with last Easter's blessed palms behind them and pictures of Christ exposing his heart of flame or knocking on the handleless door to the human heart, which could be opened only from inside. A two-foot-high, plaster-of-paris Mary sat on the television set. The statue had tumbled over once, chipping the nose from Mary's face. Someone had glued the nose back on but slightly out of line, giving our Holy Mother the appearance of a featherweight boxer who never learned to duck.

At mass on special Sundays, we children filled one pew and part of another. My father was proud of having what the nuns called "a good Catholic family"—parish code for married couples who did not practice birth control. His religion sustained him. He was overboard in a wild sea, and the Church was his life preserver. I see him sitting in the old stone church where I was baptized, dressed in his threadbare pinstripe suit and his floral tie wider than a kite. Redolent of Old Spice aftershave, he has a tiny speck of toilet paper stuck to his neck where he nicked himself shaving.

In my father's mind, there was no clear distinction between fundamental Catholicism and Appalachian subsistence life. He took his sons rabbit hunting outside Philadelphia each winter and eel fishing on a sluggish stream on summer nights. At ponds and lakes we caught sunfish, perch, bass, catfish, and a strange small fish that he called a mill roach. There was a small Catholic convent at the end of our block on Greenway Avenue, and the mother superior gave us permission to dig a garden on the grounds. Each spring we planted beans, tomatoes, radishes, lettuce, corn, and cucumbers. We tended the garden all through summer and in the fall put up jars of beans and tomatoes. At least one year, my father found an orchard outside the city that would let him pick up windfall peaches, and we canned those as well.

There were eels fried crispy, catfish, sweet sunfish, rabbits, pheasants, squirrels—which my mother cooked into wonderful potpies—and venison when he was lucky enough to shoot a deer in the Pocono Mountains. Groundhogs, which he called "whistle-pigs," were better than chicken in his opinion, though I cannot actually remember eating one at his table. Each fall he gathered black walnuts from somewhere in Cobb's Creek Park. He shucked them out and let the nuts ripen up on the roof of the "back shed."

These memories come back: I follow him down the wooden steps into the dirt-floor cellar, greeted by the smell of mushrooms, with quart jars of canned tomatoes in my arms. At the bottom of the steps, he has turned an old wooden door into a shelf by propping it up on poles against the crumbling foundation stones. The door is almost covered with jars of tomatoes, peaches, and peach preserves. He places his jars on the door, then takes mine. Standing back to look at the jars of red and gold gleaming gemlike in the stair light, he claps his hands in pure delight and says, "Money in the bank. Money in the bank."

We are by the grape arbor, another of his failed experiments, in the small backyard. The sky is pale, washed-out, and the neighborhood is oddly quiet. It feels like Sunday in my mind. He will teach me to skin eels. I stand beside him like a nurse at an operating table, holding small nails, a hammer, and his needle-nose pliers.

Reaching into a bucket of eels caught the night before at the mill-run, he lifts one out. It shines wet and satin-black. Two feet long and as thick as his thumb, it writhes a little in his hand. Pressing the narrow head against the wood of the grape arbor, he extends his free hand and says, "Nail." He pushes the nail through the eel's tiny head and holds it pinned against the wood of the grape arbor. "Hammer," he says. Three quick taps and the eel hangs suspended.

"Now the tricky part," he says. With a single-edged razor blade, he gently cuts a complete circle around the eel's neck. Gripping a speck of eel skin with the needle-nose pliers, he pulls down slowly. It sounds like tape being pulled free from a wall. Going inside out, the black satin skin magically turns lapis blue. A small sound escapes my mouth.

As poor as we were, my father's attempt to create subsistence life in southwest Philadelphia had nothing to do with poverty. Food caught or shot or found was better than anything "store bought." More to the point, God had put wild foods in the world for a man to find. Eating fish from the rivers, game from the fields, was taking communion.

One lucky morning in the Poconos, he shot a stunning eight-point buck and somehow found the money for a full head-mount. We called the deer Oscar. The trophy was much too large and far too regal for our small dining room, but night after night Oscar stared out over my father's word lessons and parables like an antlered god. Sitting down to a meal of wild food, while Oscar kept his watch, my father felt part of some large design.

But for all of this, he may have been the most thoroughly defeated man I have ever known. His after-dinner parables, or most of them, were designed to teach us not to get our hopes up or to expect good things to happen—at least not in this life. Ultimately his message was: Keep your head and expectations down, and you might slip by unnoticed. Don't be making too much of yourself in your mind. Pride cometh before a fall. Self-praise stinks. You can't just go and do whatever you want. That's wild thinking. What pipe *you* been smokin'? Don't say things can't be worse. Pray they don't *get* worse. When they do, pray harder; it's all you got. I cried because I had no shoes, till I met the man who had no feet. My father was convinced that hope created disappointment and that ambition invited tragedy, and his pessimism included his children; we would never amount to anything because he was our father. I worried over this long before I understood what I was worried about. My mind jumps back to scenes that feel like lacerations.

We are walking home from the plant one winter day. There has been a truck drivers' strike in Philadelphia, and the *Evening Bulletin* has not been delivered for several weeks. Enterprising men and older boys have been driving down to the *Bulletin*'s printing building to buy stacks of newspapers for five cents each. They sell the copies outside of factories for a quarter. This has proven dangerous in some cases; the union goons occasionally rough people up and take their newspapers. My father has done without his *Bulletin* for days, but walking home, we pass two boys selling newspapers in front of the Fels Naphtha soap factory on Island Avenue. Mumbling, "What's the difference? What's the difference?" he buys a copy and jams it up under his arm as if angry at the newspaper. As we continue walking down Island Avenue, a car glides up behind us and slowly follows. Two men inside begin to yell things, "Scab! Fucking scab! Hey, Red on the head, like the dick on a dog! Peckerhead scab!"

Down Island Avenue out to Woodland Avenue, they keep at it. Walking backward, I turn to watch them. My dad's face turns bright red, but he says nothing. He studies the ground in front of his feet and walks faster.

I remember other scenes like this, though most of them were less painful. Anyone in a suit or uniform made my father stammer, blush, and look at his feet. I wanted him to stand up for both of us. But I loved my dad. He took me hunting and fishing, taught me to love language, to watch birds, to cook, and that it was all right for a man to be gentle. None of my friends did anything with their fathers. Most neighborhood men were cold and more or less ignored their children. A number of them often got drunk and abused their families. My father did not get drunk. He never cursed, took the Lord's name in vain, told off-color jokes, or struck his children. When he lost his temper and yelled at me, he would show up at my bedside to apologize. Standing in the dark room, a mass of ticks and gestures as he agonized with great remorse, he would mumble, "I shouldn't of done the way I did. Yelled like that. I'm sorry I did that. Sometimes I get things on my mind. I was thinking maybe we ought to run the dogs here soon." The abject humility that made me wince at certain times made him saintlike at others. I loved him and desperately needed his approval, but he had none to offer.

My father's despair, I would decide in time, resulted from his acceptance of the hillbilly label and from his own father's public suicide. It also had a great deal to do with what has been called Appalachian fatalism—a profound sense that you are fundamentally inferior and that life is absurd and hopeless. And so I was caught in a paradox even as a small boy. I was desperate to escape the despair that was my father, but wanted to keep him in my life.

In Piedmont, there was no moment of epiphany about Grandfather O'Brien. On our visits, no one ever mentioned him, and his absence was such a given I never thought to ask. But in the doglike way that children sense things about the adult world, without understanding, I began to feel his presence in that house. At the O'Briens', the family women sometimes sat at the kitchen table talking until late at night. My father or Uncle Phillip might sit with them for a time, but as the evening wore on, the men drifted away. The women spoke in lowered voices and even bent their heads toward one another to whisper at times. If I strayed too close, the conversation stopped, and my mother or an aunt would shoo me off.

Later, in bed, as the house settled into quiet, I could hear the soft buzz of their voices in the kitchen. I only heard bits and pieces and now even those fragments have worn thin in my mind. I do remember a tone very clearly: The O'Brien women were making moral pronouncements about the world and specifically about men. They whispered things like: It's just like some men to . . . That was him every time . . . What I think he did was . . .

I cannot remember a transition between ignorance and understanding. It's as though I woke one morning just knowing that the disembodied pronouns—the "he" and "him"—in the late-night talk referred to my grandfather. One afternoon I spent some time looking through Grandmother O'Brien's family album. Someone had removed pictures from a number of pages, leaving a patch of dried glue that made me think of a giant's thumbprint. I thought, They've taken his pictures out.

Now a small photograph hovers in my mind. Oval, twice the size of an egg, it's one of those color-tinted black-and-whites from the early 1900s. My grandmother, a robust young woman, smiles at the camera. It may be a wedding picture; she wears a long, formal dress. My grandfather appears distracted and stares hard to his right at something beyond the picture frame. Like my father, he is a short, redheaded man. But the color in the photograph is not right; my grandfather's hair is pink. Do I remember this? Or has my memory conspired with imagination to fill a gap? The photograph has been in my mind for at least forty years, but I cannot remember where or when I saw it.

I still remember the day—and even the moment—when I was told about my grandfather. I was twenty-six and visiting my parents in southwest Philadelphia. My father had gone to bed one night, but my mother and I sat up late at the kitchen table drinking shots and beers. A day or two before, I had asked my dad about his father, and after looking frightened, he turned around and ran into the cellar. Now I can't remember if I asked my mother or whether she volunteered the story. Grandfather O'Brien had been an angry, troubled man who drank too much, she said. Drunk or sober, he lived his life in fits and rages, terrorizing his family. One day at the mill, he argued with a foreman and cursed the man. Fired, he went back to his tarpaper house on the hill, drank whiskey, then went out into the backyard. In a burst of manic energy, he drank poison, cut his throat, and shot himself, all within a minute. I still remember the way the hair on the back of my neck stood up as my mother spoke and the strange sense that I had always known this story.

THE PIEDMONT visit winds down. It's an overcast day, and I'm on the back-porch swing at the O'Briens'. It must have rained during the night because everything looks wet. Patches of mist hang here and there on the steep mountainsides and the smell of the mill is overwhelming. Behind me in the kitchen, the adults fumble with good-byes. They begin sentences but do not finish. "Well, if you're planning to . . ." and "I just thought you might . . ." They are trying to say something that refuses to be said. Looking back, I realize I have felt this all my life, an anxious feeling that the point of being alive is about to become clear and that it will be dreadful.

I do not want to leave this town. In part, it's the swimming pool and the Cokes in Grandmother Bell's refrigerator. But it's also the sense of extended family, of belonging to something larger in Piedmont. More than anything, I do not want to leave the mountains. Sometimes, when my father talked about hunting and fishing in West Virginia as a boy, I thought he was talking about paradise and a time before despair was the center of his personality. A landscape of deep forest filled with white-tailed deer, wild turkeys, whirling grouse, speckled trout, and ice-cold streams grew in my mind. My dad was happy there, somehow whole, and so was I. That vision of Appalachia became my dream life.

Inside the car, it's all heavy weather. There is no fine edge of excitement or extended litany of good-bye. Instead of spirited in-car fights, a sullen impatience weighs us down. Starting down the dreamlike hill, my father has nothing to say.

2. The O'Briens
Go Home Again

I OPEN my mouth and my father's voice comes out in mine. "All right now, we're gonna start this trip friends and we're gonna end it friends. Right?" I have never commanded the respect that my father did, but my son and daughter, after exchanging menacing glares, do stop arguing.

My daughter, Shelly, nine; my wife, Becky; and my son,
Christopher, fourteen, on the day of his eighth-grade
graduation, 1984

There are four of us—Becky, my wife of eighteen years; Christopher, who is fourteen; Shelly, nine; and me. I am forty-one. We are ready to leave Oswego, on the shore of Lake Ontario, and start for Franklin. Everything we own—not much in the end—has been packed into a three-quarter-ton rental truck.

Chris and Shelly have been arguing about which tape will play as they start the twelve-hour trip. Christopher prefers Sting and The Police—"Every move you make, every step you take, I'll be watching you"—the hymn to paranoia that I have been hearing from behind his bedroom door for weeks now. Shelly prefers ABBA, something about a dancing queen.

Shelly flares up: "You always get your way. Always."

Christopher fires back, "And you always say that. You think leaving Oswego is my big idea?"

I raise my hands as if surrendering and say, "Please!"

Christopher flashes an angry look and turns away. He will leave his first love in Oswego—a girl named Angel—and does not understand why he must. My son is a terrific kid and we have been good friends. He and I have argued about a lot of things, and have even become angry with each other, but never like this.

As always Shelly bounces back at once. "Coochy," she says—adolescent Oswegoese for "Hey, no problem."

I have been using my father's expression about starting and ending trips as friends for years now. It's strange but I may have said it a dozen times before realizing where it came from. Becky often says, "Your dad's coming out in you again." I make outrageous puns and jokes, seem a living network of ticks and gestures, and walk with my feet flared out. I sing around the house and in the car. There are things about him buried so deep they are an unconscious part of who I am. It's as if my father and I share a single personality. We have not spoken for twelve years. It seems a cruel joke—moving farther and farther away as I become more and more like him. That's as strange as poetry.

When Becky talks about my dad, she smiles and sometimes touches my face, hoping to gentle me back toward him. My wife—a small, blue-eyed woman with honey-blond hair—is from a farm village in West Virginia and is caught between an Appalachian sense of family and her concerns for me. I am often lost between ideas and emotional states, often unsure. Becky knows her mind.

It is hard to think about twelve years of silence if only because I cannot resolve the heartache. I write letters and throw them away, pick up the phone and put it back down. Sometimes I wonder if my father struggles over our separation as I do. He has nine other children to worry about, so our distance might be easier for him. This is what I tell myself.

We will make this trip in two vehicles. Becky—with two children and two sedated cats—is in the Oldsmobile. I will drive the rental truck, accompanied by a monstrous fern that almost fills the cab. I wanted to give the fern to a friend, but Becky put her foot down. I bought it after receiving a National Endowment fellowship and in her mind the plant has something to do with good fortune. In mine, it adds to the lunacy of twelve hours in a truck I can barely drive.

Becky and the children start for the car while I check out the apartment, empty and vaguely ominous now. My footsteps ring in the high corners of each room. Some scenes pass through my mind: It's the middle of the night as a blizzard howls like an Arctic beast around the house. It is snowing sideways, in my mind the snowflakes as big as tennis balls. Filleting a gigantic pike on the kitchen table while Christopher watches. At three in the morning an insane TV evangelist lashes the stage with a bullwhip—"And they whupped Him, and they whupped Him." A silent movie of Becky yelling at me because I drink too much and let my family down. How could these small, ordinary rooms have contained all of that? I am a ghost come back to haunt myself.

I will miss certain things about Oswego. It's this small, forgotten town on the edge of a lake that Walt Whitman dubbed "Blue Ontario." The "good, gray poet" came to Oswego after the Civil War, and I like to think of him walking by the water having tender thoughts about everything in sight. Like my old Philadelphia neighborhood, Oswego is working-class and ethnic. There are family-owned Irish bars on every other block. A bar called Yam's, by the Oswego River, sells shots of Bushmill's whiskey and keeps the Chieftains on the jukebox. It will always be my favorite bar. Small Italian grocery stores offer the earthy fragrance of oregano and smoky provolone the moment you open the door. The proprietor in his white apron talks Italian to a round, old woman dressed in black. You can buy homemade sausage, imported prosciutto, a dozen kinds of olives, cannolis, crusty rolls baked that

*Myself on left, with Dave Harbert, my existential-
phenomenologist friend, on right*

morning, baccalà, and, on rare occasions, tartuffe—that wonderful
white truffle. I worry that my cooking will become less interesting in
West Virginia.

The fishing has been exceptional along the lake. From late April
until mid-October, I fished three or four evenings a week, catching
trout, salmon, catfish, perch, pike, and smallmouth bass. I fished
through the ice in winter but less often. I will miss my fishing partner,
David Harbert, an existential-phenomenologist with a Ph.D. from
Yale who is as passionate about subsistence fishing as I have always
been, though we came to it from entirely different directions. Heidegger and Saint-Exupéry were David's masters. He wanted to get
back to "authentic experience"—whatever that is—and thought I was
a natural phenomenon, something like a dancing bear. In his opinion,
I had arrived at the accurate existential view by instinct rather than
proper analysis. When I told him my "existentialism" was most likely
Appalachian fatalism dressed up for town, he laughed and said,
"What a card." He thought I was making a joke and maybe I was.

David wanted to fill the gaps in my philosophy. Drifting down a
stream in his canoe—a bizarre variation on Huck and Jim—he would

start on Heidegger or "St. X." Most of it passed well over my head, but this never troubled David. Once started he would go on and on—at least until I began to sing "Settin' the Woods on Fire," that Hank Williams song, loud and horrendously off-key. We would end up laughing at our own foolishness. Dave filled in for my father, I think. But I will never again hear about Saint-Exupéry's Little Prince while jerking a plastic frog along the lily pads, waiting for the explosion of a pike—that sweet absurdity is gone for good.

I have been through every room twice. Taking one last look around, I close the door on five spent years.

The immense steering wheel in the truck cab belongs on a tugboat and there are too many gears. I just hope I can make it to I-81—which I should be on for twelve of the fourteen hours—before stripping the transmission altogether or crashing into something. On the interstate, I will drop into a cruising gear and stay there. As Becky pulls away in the Oldsmobile I glance toward the monstrous fern—the longest fronds just inches from my face—and say, "You ready for this?" With a series of grinding noises, I lurch down the street to a reggae beat.

We leave town by different routes. Christopher wants to drive past Angel's house. Angel will be on the front steps and the presence of a garish rental truck—Chris has assured me—would "ruin the whole thing." I'm all right with this arrangement. Leaving Angel is easily the hardest thing Christopher has ever done and I'm worried about taking a bright adolescent into a small Appalachian town. I pull off beside the Oswego River south of town to wait. As I'm watching the river my mind begins to drift. It comes to me that this time and place is a bookmark in my life; the narrative, or what passes for narrative, has come this far and is about to change direction.

AFTER THOSE boyhood trips to Piedmont I graduated from West Catholic High in Philadelphia and made up my mind to go to college. I don't know where the idea came from. College wasn't something O'Briens did, or even thought about. We graduated from high school, found a factory or unskilled office job, "did a stint" in the service, and married other Catholics. When I told my father of my intentions after dinner one night, he laughed. He was not being deliberately cruel, but my announcement, coming out of the blue, startled him. To be honest, he had every reason to be startled. I was at the bottom of my high school class, and the family lived from one paycheck to the next. I had no money and my parents had none to give me. More than that, the thought of one of his children going to college made my father anxious. We had our place in the world, and trying to change that was dangerous. No good would come of it.

In the weeks after I announced my plans, he would cautiously approach the topic: Had someone told me I should go to college? Where did this big idea come from anyway? I cannot remember what I told him. No one had ever encouraged me and I knew nothing about college. But I had watched him walk to General Electric every day, his head and hopes held down just to keep going. I hated everything about GE—even the building. It was an enormous twenty-story complex that took up an entire city block, easily the largest building in southwest Philadelphia. It was rust-red with windows that gave off an oil-slick sheen at sunset. Elmwood Avenue, in the factory's shadow, was in constant twilight. I remember: my father's constant fear of being laid off or fired; a foreman named Kern—an archvillain in my boyhood fantasies—who was on my dad every day, calling him a hillbilly, redheaded hick; my father weeping in his bedroom. There is no narrative here.

This scene comes back: At twelve or thirteen, I am at the Cyclone fence surrounding the factory parking lot waiting for my father. The lot is filled with old cars baking in summer heat. Way across the lot, a loading dock at the bottom of the building opens like a black mouth. Men are jammed inside the mouth. The distance and wavering air makes GE a monstrous hornet's nest in my mind. A Klaxon sounds. A roar goes up, and the men swarm out.

And this from my senior year at West Catholic High: My father and I are rabbit hunting in November. After a morning following Richard and Lady through stubbled fields and thickets we eat lunch in the old station wagon: sandwiches of some kind, steaming tea from his thermos. We are parked on a gravel road between fields and woods. At the edge of the woods across the road, there is a small stepdown transformer behind a Cyclone fence. Pointing his sandwich at it, my father says, "I make them."

I must have looked confused because he went on, saying, "Circuit breakers. That's the line I'm on."

Half-eaten sandwich still in hand, he goes through a series of robot-like motions and says, "Same thing all day." A moment later he adds, "It's what I dream about." He closes his eyes and repeats the motions.

Until late in my last year of high school, I had thought very little about my life. I must have assumed that I would find a factory job or end up in the service like my older brother, Patrick. Then, with high school graduation months rather than years away, I began to lie awake at night and worry. The thought of living like my dad depressed me. I wasn't afraid of factory work, or of poverty, but of being trapped the way he was. He knew he was on the bottom because men like him— hillbillies? Appalachians? O'Briens?—belonged there and that conviction was unshakable. I thought college might help me escape his life, but that was really all I knew. I would never have said this for fear of hurting him.

My father's skepticism about college could not have been more obvious, but his concerns were genuine. I had been a wild kid, and he was convinced that college was another "wild idea." He did not want to see me "build up this pipe dream and come crashing down." To his credit, he never said you can't do it or don't go. And I did go. In August 1961, I took the 11 trolley to Penn Station in downtown Philadelphia and boarded a train for West Virginia.

During that first year, I lived with my Grandfather and Grandmother Bell and attended Potomac State College in Keyser, just a few miles from their home in Piedmont. In the fall of 1962, I transferred to West Virginia Universitiy in Morgantown. My first semester there was a disaster and I dropped out in January. I didn't know how to study or live on my own and I made a mess of things. Broke, emaciated, and struggling with clinical depression, I tried to hitchhike back to Philadelphia only to become stranded in a town outside the city. I spent the night in a small police station and called my dad in the morning. When he came to pick me up, the first thing he said was, "You don't have to feel bad. You stuck it out longer than I ever thought you could." For the first and only time in my life, I yelled at my father.

For the next nine months, I lived at home and worked in a tent factory on Woodland Avenue. What I remember most about those months are mood swings. I would become angry with my father for having no faith in me, then become angry with myself for feeling that way. At times I convinced myself that he was right; college *was* another wild idea. Then I could not stand the thought that he was right, and that would start the anger again.

We had not talked much during my senior year of high school, but now we said only "hello," "good morning," and "pass the sugar." When I walked into the living room, he would duck behind his *Evening Bulletin* or suddenly remember an unfinished job and hurry off. I would hear my parents out in the kitchen talking seriously about trouble at GE or about money, but the moment I appeared the conversation abruptly stopped. If I asked my father about work, or anything important, he looked anxiously at my mother, who delivered a diplomatic non-answer. Everything was fine. My father loved his job at the plant. They had no worries. It was like communicating through an interpreter. I had become a stranger.

When I went back to college and found my feet, it felt right to me. I had no money or direction but felt easy and unencumbered most of the time. As long as I had a place to sleep and enough to eat, I did not feel trapped, and that's all that mattered then. I had escaped my father's despair, or thought I had. It would take some time before I saw the irony of moving back to Appalachia to escape Appalachian fatalism.

It took six years to get my first degree from West Virginia University. I worked every semester and changed majors three times. I started out in forestry because I thought foresters lived in the woods. Hunting and fishing with my dad were the best times growing up and that's what I wanted, a life in the woods. When forestry didn't work out, I switched to biology because biologists studied animals. In a required American literature course, I discovered that I liked to read.

It was hand-to-mouth for those six years. I lived in one seedy room after another and held a series of dead-end jobs: dishwasher, pot scrubber, food-service worker, model-car salesman, phone jockey in a collection agency—easily the strangest job, bellhop, library assistant. At times it seemed as if I was going to school so I could work, rather than the other way around, but that was all right. The students and adults I worked with had come from failed farms or nearby coal towns. They were like my relatives in Piedmont, and I liked being around them.

I also liked living in West Virginia. Morgantown, despite hosting a university of 25,000 students, remains blue-collar and decidedly Appalachian, or at least Appalachian as I understand the word. Like Piedmont, Morgantown is an extremely hilly town surrounded by mountains. Walking to class on October mornings, I sometimes heard shotguns from the ridges as hunters shot gray squirrels. In November, cars with buck deer strapped across their roofs passed the university buildings. I even managed to hunt and fish from time to time. Two blocks off campus and I was in a working-class neighborhood full of boxy houses on impossibly steep streets. People parked their dated cars with the front wheels turned in hard against the curb—just like my relatives in Piedmont—in case the "hand-brake was to give."

I probably spent too much time in beer joints, funky places with plywood booths and fat jars of pickled eggs on the counter, a cheese-cake calendar of some mountain beauty in short-shorts sitting on a tractor. When I walked through the door, it was 1947. Appalachian beer joints—the good ones anyway—are working-class pubs. The same characters walk in day after day. You come in to find out what's going on in the neighborhood and nurse a Stroh's beer.

Becky and I met on a blind date in late December 1964. That year I was sharing, with three boys from a small West Virginia town, an apartment above a store that sold bathroom tile, and we had a Christmas party planned. At the time I was dating a slender, attractive girl named Laurie. Laurie and I argued on the day of the party and broke up. One of my roommates was dating a Kappa Delta girl named Mary, and someone had just dumped one of her sorority sisters. Mary put us together. I can still hear her saying, "Becky's this really cute country girl from way back in the mountains. The sweetest thing. You two are . . ."

I had stopped asking sorority girls out by then. I told myself they were vain and shallow, but the truth is they made me feel inferior. I did not have the money, clothes, or social confidence to date middle-class girls, but more to spite Laurie than anything else I called Becky.

The next few months play like a Frank Capra movie in my memory. Becky walking across the frozen lawn in her country-girl wool coat and Jackie Kennedy pillbox hat, so blond and pretty. We were so wonderfully mismatched. I remember our first kiss in the glow of the Goodyear tire sign. We traced hearts in the snow and whispered during phone conversations until three in the morning. After a night out with friends, I would end up in the alley beside the sorority house throwing pebbles at her window. It was pure American corn and the best months of my life.

Becky Sheets, my wife-to-be, 1963

I went to visit Becky's home in Green Bank, Pocahontas County, a village in a beautiful alpine valley. It was mountain farmland surrounded by hardwood forest. In the cold, clean air I fished for native trout behind Becky's house and in time hunted deer with her relatives. We took long walks in the woods and picked out spots to build a house. Within a month there was no turning back for either of us.

We decided to get married in St. John's Chapel on campus because there was no Catholic church in Pocahontas County. If a Protestant minister married us, we would not—in my father's view— be married at all. The relationship between my dad and me had become distant and hard to understand. We never wrote to each other during those six years and almost never spoke on the phone. When we did talk, our conversations were brief and oddly impersonal. We were always polite, even deferential, but it was like talking to one of my roommates' fathers, and he was always in a hurry to hand the phone to my mother. Each time I hung up, I felt confused and off-balance.

I understood part of this back then. My behavior as an adolescent and the idea of stepping out of his fatalistic Appalachian script by going to college worried and frightened my father. By the time I met Becky, relations had become more strained. I had started to read and to change, not always for the better, and had become a fiery liberal ready to lecture anyone less noble than I imagined myself to be. Struggling to escape my own bigotry, I wrote a long tirade about our family's racism and sent it to my parents. I cannot remember exactly what I wrote, but I'm sure it was insufferable. I had easy, untested compassion for everyone except my own family.

On visits home, I would get into arguments with my brothers about GE and about the Church. I never argued with my dad. We could hardly argue since we never talked, but I can remember turning away from my brothers after an exchange to catch sight of him staring at me in shock. The difficulty arose from both sides. My arrogance and ignorance—the same thing, at least in me—stretched the distance between us.

I wasn't angry with my dad, though I did feel that I had somehow let him down, and I don't think he was angry with me. I should say that we were both busy with our own lives. When you look back and try to sort things out, there is a temptation to forget that there were other things going on. My father was still walking to work every day, still worrying about money, and still trying to raise small children. I had school, work, money problems of my own, and I was dizzy in love. I don't think either one of us had much time to worry about our relationship.

Then in 1965, about a year before Becky and I married, my parents came to Morgantown for their first and only visit. They had been to Piedmont on family business, and as it turned out, the trip coincided with semester break. One of the apartment bedrooms would be empty. Driving back to Philadelphia through Morgantown did not involve much more time, so why not stop to visit? My father kept talking about going to work on Monday morning and how it seemed like a lot of bother, but my mother made the decision; they would visit me in Morgantown.

Since we rarely spoke, my parents knew nothing about Becky. When I introduced her as the girl whom I would marry, I startled them yet again. I can still see my dad standing in the apartment kitchen looking from my face to Becky's, blinking in bewilderment.

We spent the weekend driving around campus, making clumsy small talk. I cooked dinner and made tea for my dad. A few students in an apartment down the hall were having a bachelor party, which made the evening awkward, but we managed. My father and I had one very strange moment. I had gone out into the kitchen for some reason, and he followed me. Ducking behind a cabinet, he urgently gestured for me to come over. When I did, he whispered, "That little girl, she's not . . . I mean she won't . . . That Becky Sheets will sleep in her own bed tonight?" I assured him that she would.

My parents left on Sunday afternoon. Neither of them had said anything about our plans, not good luck or congratulations. I was a little disappointed and once again felt off-balance. If anything, my dad seemed worried. Still, I thought the visit had gone well enough.

Then a few weeks later my father sent Becky an unsettling letter. Beginning with "Forgive this idle chatter, I'm not a good writer," he went on to say that I had "other girlfriends," which wasn't true, and that marriage was "serious business," adding, "It's never too late to change your mind." There was a strange obliqueness about the letter. My dad seemed to be tiptoeing around some dark truth and hinting at a later revelation. He ended with a request: "Please answer this idle chatter."

The line that stopped me was "Everything that's wrong with John comes from me." I had been hearing and feeling this all of my life and here it was again. Some dark flaw had passed from, or perhaps through, him to me. We were linked in failure, and he was apologizing for both of us. My dad had just met Becky and knew nothing about her, but now he was advising her not to marry me.

But what had he passed on? I cannot remember whether I thought about my grandfather in conjunction with the letter or not. At that time, I didn't know his story, but I had uneasy suspicions, if only because no one ever talked about him. Becky liked my dad. They were both unpretentious and felt drawn to each other. She did not write back because she didn't know what to say.

The letter stung, but I recovered quickly. At the time Becky and I were too excited about our lives to worry. I didn't know what to call the relationship between my dad and me, but wanted to keep whatever it was and this was all the more reason to get married in St. John's Chapel.

We were married two days after Christmas in 1966. Becky wore white velvet, and the altar blazed with poinsettias. My parents came down from Philadelphia. My dad wore the blue pinstripe suit he had worn to mass for years. I cannot remember what my mother wore. What stands out clearest in my memory is the two of them walking into the reception at the sorority house. My mother, always a tough customer, seemed to be at ease, even to swagger a bit—put'n on the dog—but my dad kept looking furtively left and right with his eyes wide open. His face was fiery red and he became a mass of tics and gestures, shifting foot to foot like a little boy who had to go to the bathroom, scratching at the back of his neck. There was an imitation Renoir above an imitation French Provincial divan. There were elegant, heavy drapes and a plush carpet on the floor. It seemed as if my father feared that someone would suddenly realize that Red O'Brien had slipped past the doorman and come to throw him out. I noticed something on his shoulder—dog hair, perhaps—and I brushed it off. This was the first time we had made physical contact in years. Whatever I felt about the letter had passed and my heart went out to him. My parents wished us well and meant it.

Becky had completed her undergraduate coursework a few days before our wedding, but I needed one more semester. During that time, we began to talk about trying to find teaching positions in Alaska. As a kid, looking through my dad's outdoor sporting magazines, I had daydreamed about living in a wilderness area where the hunting and fishing would be spectacular. Becky and I went to the WVU library and a librarian helped us locate a book with the addresses of all of the school districts in the United States. We sent letters of inquiry to all of the districts in Alaska and received applications and packets of information from most of them. The Native American schools in the Alaskan bush appealed to both of us, and we were overjoyed when Kodiak Island Borough offered us a two-teacher school in Ouzinkie (pronounced You-*zink*-key, as we would learn), an Aleut fishing village on tiny Spruce Island just off Kodiak.

In May 1967, we loaded our possessions, including a Siamese cat named Frodo, into a small Oldsmobile and started west. In the next fourteen years, we lived in nine locations, including the Alaskan bush, Iowa, California, Virginia, West Virginia (twice), and New York. In my mind, those years run together like a jumbled movie.

I can remember seeing Ouzinkie for the first time from the deck of the Tustamena ferry. The gray company store made me think of the mill in Piedmont. Small, unpainted houses surrounded the onion dome of a tiny Russian Orthodox church. Round-bellied salmon boats nodded on their tethers in the bay while gulls and kittiwakes mewed in counterpoint to the slosh and drag of the waves. Beautiful black-haired Aleut children ran down the beach waving to the passing ferry.

In season the small bay boiled with pink salmon, Dolly Varden trout, and tomcod. Sitka deer grazed like flocks of sheep on Kodiak across the narrows. Brant's geese, goldeneyes, pintails, and old-squaw darkened the sky like smoke each fall. An eighth-grade boy taught me how to catch octopus in the tidal pools, how to net Dungeness crabs, dig cockle clams, and hunt ducks from the shore. I filled my freezer and was as close to my father's subsistence dream as I have ever been.

We liked Ouzinkie and would have stayed longer, but halfway through our first summer an Aleut woman became convinced that her husband was "blond sick" over Becky and began to watch us through the scope of her husband's rifle from a second-story window. We could never see her there, just the gun barrel with its mounted scope protruding from below a shade. It inched slowly along as we walked the village path.

A conversation with a state trooper in Kodiak sent us back to West Virginia: "Well," he said, "she hasn't actually threatened you or done anything illegal, has she?"

"You mean, we can't do anything until she shoots one of us?"

"I wouldn't put it that way, Mr. O'Brien."

I didn't know any other way to put it and so we left the island.

After a year of graduate school in Morgantown, we were broke and expecting our first child. I took a job in a community college in Virginia. One of my students, whom I will call Tom Andrews, became my fishing partner. Floating around in a small, car-top boat on his bass pond, he told me about his father's suicide. After listening to his dad threaten to kill himself for years, one day Tom told him, "Go on then, kill yourself and quit drive'n the rest of us crazy." An hour later his father did just that. Pointing his fishing rod toward the shore, Tom said, "Found him over there in the pasture." My son Chris was born that year.

For the next two years Becky, Chris, and I lived in an Iowa farmhouse in the middle of an endless cornfield. I was on a fellowship from the University of Iowa, and Becky taught fifth grade in the small town of Oxford. Crossing the stubbled cornfield with a shotgun one November day, I was terrified by the wild stutter of a rising pheasant. I had been having trouble—panic attacks that made my heart race and froze me into a statue; an obsession with suicide—and then I plunged into clinical depression. I stayed in a psychiatric hospital for a brief time.

After I completed my master of fine arts we loaded our pickup and returned to the Alaskan bush, the interior this time—the Athabascan village of Nondalton, where I served as a conduit between the Uni-

As I looked in Iowa, 1970

versity of Alaska and four very bright Athabascans in a teacher-training program. In part, my job was to decode the doublespeak of textbooks and college professors into English. Becky, Chris, and I lived on moose, caribou, salmon, trout, and grayling. Once a week, a bush plane flew in mail, pilot bread, powdered milk, and canned goods from Anchorage. During the winter, we slept on the floor of a tarpaper shack in high-altitude flight suits from an Army-Navy store and used an outhouse at thirty below. Becky liked village life more than I did. It was like removing the clutter and fluff between us and the world. We worked hard to get winter meat and fish, but left almost everything else unplanned.

Those two years revolve around this episode: I am walking to the post office in my flight suit like a moon walker. Virgil, my drinking and poker-playing friend, steps out of his windbreak naked from the waist up to wave a whiskey bottle at me. I stop for a drink in his kitchen. Virgil has a new 300 Savage that he must show me. Standing at the kitchen window, several sheets of clear, heavy plastic rather than glass, he throws the gun up against his shoulder to shoot an imaginary caribou in just the way my father shot imaginary deer in the alley back in Philadelphia. The muzzle swings past my face and explodes an inch away, knocking me sideways. Virgil says, "Hole-la, I didn't know a bullet was in dis ting." He sits down on the floor and becomes preoccupied with the intricacies of his new rifle, working the bolt back and forth, peering into the breech. He has forgotten all about me. I decide that life outside the Appalachian Mountains is arbitrary. You live, you die—it's the same. God examines the breech.

I spent a year, 1974/75, at Stanford University as a Stegner Fellow, starting a novel, and running around with Ray Carver and Chuck Kinder. Ray, a writer of enormous power, told me stories about hunting and fishing with his dad; I told him mine. Here was another man shadowboxing with his father's memory. My daughter, Shelly, was born that year.

In the summer of '75, we returned to West Virginia. More than anything, I was hoping for a grant to finish the novel. While we were visiting with my family in Philadelphia, my parents took us to my brother Patrick's place in New Jersey one evening. Driving home—in fact, crossing the Delaware River on the Walt Whitman Bridge—I made the mistake of talking about my hopes for a grant. My father thought I was talking about going on welfare. Driving along, he erupted in anger: "Das rat, boss, let them dumb white folks work. The guv'ment takes care of us coons." He had never spoken to me like that.

We spent the next two years in a beautiful farmhouse in Pocahontas County. Instead of finishing the novel, I taught seven classes a day in a junior high school for a year. There was also early bus duty, late bus duty, and lunchroom duty. It was the most difficult job I have ever had. The fact that people manage to do this all of their lives awes me. Luckily, one of my students, a backwoods boy whom I will call James, took me hunting and fishing and taught me more about the woods than I had learned in all my years of hunting and fishing. For all practical purposes, James lived in the woods. My parents came to visit in the farmhouse and our relationship continued to deteriorate. Becky had taken a position as a first-grade teacher, and by then I had quit my teaching job at the junior high to write for a year, which my parents found immoral.

For the next two years I taught at Hampton Institute in Virginia. I took bluefish, flounder, spot, and crabs from the nearby bay. As always, I had the sense that what I was doing for money was just killing time before I got back to hunting or fishing. Then we moved to Oswego.

During all those years, two things remained constant: my pursuit of subsistence life and Appalachia as home. No matter where we ended up, Becky and I were always *from* West Virginia. Outside the southern mountains, we felt like Appalachian expatriates in some foreign but familiar country. Our lives could be going well or poorly, but we would begin to miss the way West Virginians spoke and saw the world. Landscape without rolling green mountains, no matter how spectacular, never felt right. Outside, there was always something missing.

For what it's worth, Native Americans sometimes fumble around in this same way trying to explain their attachment to the village. They will leave home for a decent job somewhere, feel empty and out of place, then return to the village again and again just as Becky and I always returned to Appalachia. After coming back to Nondalton for the fourth or fifth time, an Athabascan friend named Dennis Trefon told me, "It's like outside everybody lays this trip on you. Nobody knows you out there. You're always somebody's idea of an Indian. Stay

In Yellowstone National Park with Becky in June 1967,
playing at the subsistence life

out long enough and you start acting like that idea. All that phony stuff goes away when you come back to the village."

For Becky and me, coming home to West Virginia has always been like that, bringing to mind Gertrude Stein's wisecrack about Oakland, California: "There's no there there."

This last time, Becky made the decision to leave New York State and come back to West Virginia. Since Iowa I had been deferring to her judgment more and more if only because she knew her mind better than I knew mine. More than that, Becky's life would change dramatically if we moved and mine would not. She was teaching at the high school in Oswego and would have to find another position. Moving meant a new system, a new school, a new principal, and new students. I was writing every day—freelance articles, stories, and poems. My working life had become a small space cluttered with manuscripts and books, and it would stay that way. At that time I did not miss the

mountains as much as Becky did. I was writing about West Virginia—
family reunions, wild greens, fishing in the mountains with my dad or
friends—and it was like being there. Appalachia, at least the place
that we longed for, had moved into my mind.

But Becky's grandfather had died in 1977. Farmer had been the
family patriarch and she felt his loss keenly. Her grandmother, Gran
Sheets—from her dad's side of the family—died in December 1983,
and we drove home for the funeral. When we returned to Oswego,
we would be driving back from some shopping trip and I would see
her wiping tears away. At other times, late in the evening, she would
stare off into the middle distance. Losing her grandparents made
Becky realize how short our own lives were. We were in our forties,
which meant less time ahead than behind. In Oswego, when Becky
talked about going back, I sensed a kind of desperation; if we were
going to make it home by dark, we had to start back soon.

We both worried about Chris and Shelly, who were growing up
away from family. As a girl in Green Bank, Becky had been surrounded by uncles, aunts, cousins, and grandparents—even her
great-grandparents when she was small. Every Sunday morning they
had gone to Liberty Presbyterian, a small white church in a grove of
oak trees just down the road. Becky played the piano while the congregation sang. The walls of her mother's house were covered with
faded black-and-white photographs, some of them dating back to the
Civil War—stern old fathers in black, scowling through their beards;
dour ladies in long, heavy dresses; people made of oak. Becky knew
her ancestors in the same way she knew the uncles and aunts living
around her.

My father became part of the decision to go back. The estrange-
ment between us had always troubled Becky. You did not break family relations no matter what was said or done or who was at fault. In
fact, the idea of fault did not apply when it came to family. After
Farmer's death, she worried about my father. The thought of my dad
dying before we reconciled made her desperate at times. She would
say, "But he's your father, John. Your father. Some awful thing will
happen and then it will be too late. I'm afraid it will put you under,
and you won't come up again."

Since Iowa, the depressions have come and gone like fever. I don't
want to make too much of this. Everyone struggles. It's what people

have most in common, I think. But depression gets in the way. Because I am always straining to gain my emotional balance, the time never seems right for the added stress of reconciliation. Becky and I never argued about this. I always knew she was right and she understood that I was stumbling around. Somehow, in the back of my mind, I thought that going home to West Virginia would offer a way back to my dad. I would fish the streams and hunt the woods that he loved. I told myself that I would go to Piedmont, walk around his hometown, and find my grandfather's grave. Somehow this would open a door and I would find my way back to him.

Life in the southern mountains has a deep, rich center, but there is a downside to Appalachian culture, just as there is to any culture. The gender roles are narrow and people hold limited views about what does or does not constitute real work. These provincial people naturally have provincial opinions about food, sex, and dress styles and ideas. An anti-intellectual current runs through mountain towns just as it does through rural communities anywhere in the world. As deeply as we felt about Appalachia, there has always been a push away as well as a pull toward home, but we finally concluded that there was no perfect place to live and began to pack.

BECKY BLOWS the car horn as she drives past and I pull in behind the Oldsmobile. It's good-bye blue Ontario, good-bye Irish bars, good-bye Italian grocery stores and existential fishing friends. Come hell or high water, we are off like dirty shirts.

3. Reentry

TWELVE hours on the interstate passes like an extended hallucination—the constant roar of the motor, the strangeness of looking down on passing cars, and the foundation fern lashing itself to near-death. Up ahead Becky puts her hand out of the Oldsmobile's window and waves it in a circle, meaning everything's OK. I return the gesture. We have been signaling back and forth like this all day. When we are close enough, Shelly makes faces out the back window. I make faces in return. Christopher has not turned, which makes me uneasy. I tell myself he's just being "Cool Chris," the character he's been inventing for about a year.

At long last the signs appear for Harrisonburg, Virginia, and Route 33 West. Harrisonburg is small and southern. As with most of the country, the commercial energy has shifted from the downtown to a mile-long strip of fast-food restaurants, chain-store outlets, motels, and service stations just beyond the city limits. Downtown Harrisonburg, two blocks of family-owned stores surrounding an old courthouse, has become an exhibit in a museum—"The American Small Town." Slowing feels like a drug, the humid air as thick as syrup. The downtown square is deserted, and each building shadow stretches long and blue. It's the mood of De Chirico's *Mystery and Melancholy of a Street*. A flock of pigeons wheels past the shoulders of blind Lady Justice on the courthouse dome. In the distance beyond her scales, the blue wall of the Alleghenies blocks the sky. Home lies behind that wall.

Route 33 West is a narrow road that passes through Mennonite farm country. Large, well-kept barns are surrounded by pastures filled with dairy cattle. I think they are Holsteins, those black-and-white cows. This is gently rolling country, still fresh and green despite the summer drought. The yellow caution signs along this road feature black silhouettes of horse-drawn carriages. And sure enough, a buggy appears in the turn up ahead. As the distance between us shortens, I can see the driver, a middle-aged man with a salt-and-pepper beard but no mustache. His hat is very black and very round. He stares straight ahead as if transfixed. His plump wife, in a flowered dress and lace cap, sits beside him as complacent as a cat, an enigmatic smile on her face and both hands folded demurely on her lap. In passing, I am lost to the syncopated clip-clop and rich aroma of horse. For a second, it's another century.

I like to think Mennonites live simple, uncomplicated lives— though I know that no one lives that kind of life. Mennonites came into the Appalachian Mountains from Germany in the 1750s. Becky and I both have German ancestors who came here then. As I watch the buggy grow small in the rearview mirror, it comes to me that we may just have passed distant relatives.

We start up Shenandoah Mountain. The state line is at its top. Honoring my father, I toot the truck horn and say, "West, by God, Virginia." Starting down the mountain, the rock station I have been listening to wavers in and out with country music, advertisements, and a holiness preacher. Every time I have come back to Appalachia, I reach this point, the moment of reentry. There are too many mountains crowded close together for good radio reception back here, so with a certain amount of satisfaction, I cut the radio off. It's like saying good-bye to the American white noise outside the mountains.

Weaving around the S-curves and switchbacks, I pass through patches of hardwood forest so deep and shadowy the temperature drops. The mountain air is laced with the gingery smells of early fall. In the first wide turn ahead, Becky puts her hand out the window and points emphatically several times. My heart jumps. There it is: home. Lush green mountains shoulder tight together and roll off in all directions and the dark green hardwood forest is broken by the lighter green of pastures in a checkerboard pattern. Black cattle and cloud-colored sheep are painted on the landscape. Small white farmhouses sit half-hidden in the creases between hills. Smoke rises from chimneys. Turkey buzzards float above one small hollow like a dark mobile.

I smile and wave at Becky. She waves back. We have been to Grand Teton National Park, Yellowstone, and Glacier; camped in Banff, Canada; and lived in the Alaskan bush, but for us, this remains the loveliest landscape in the world. These are old mountains, weathered down to gentle mounds. The overall appearance is soft and green. Now, with dusk coming on, the ridges are turning blue. It's as delicate as a Japanese print.

At the bottom of Shenandoah Mountain, we glide into the village of Brandywine—two gas station/stores and a dozen small houses. The stores are closed now and, for all practical purposes, so is Brandywine. I pass an old couple on a front-porch swing, drinking what appears to be iced tea. In the parking lot of the second store, two girls—fourteen, maybe fifteen years old—hover around a shined-up truck. Inside the truck, two shined-up farm boys listen to ZZ Top, that raucous buzz.

Farther on, a boy walks across the grade-school playground toward the river with a yellow dog at his heels. Over the small bridge that spans the South Fork River, we enter open country again. At the edge of one pasture four deer, still in summer red, inch along the treeline. I have come back home.

WE HAD come to Franklin earlier in the summer while the children spent the day with their grandparents. Becky accepted a teaching position with Pendleton County schools, and we rented a yellow house on top of Anderson Hill in Franklin. The fairly new house had three bedrooms, two bathrooms, a small kitchen, and a living room— not lavish by any means, but clean and more than adequate. At $250 a month and with woodstove heat that would cost about $200 a year, the price was more than right.

We pulled in near dusk, then walked around exploring the place. Shelly was excited. She ran from room to room looking out the windows, announcing, "We got these mountains all around us." The view from several windows was lovely. Christopher looked around each room balefully and would not hold my eyes.

We set our two cats free. Albert, the large gray-and-white neutered tom with a head like a softball, belonged to Christopher. The small smoke-gray female was Shelly's cat Sugar. Both had come from a litter born of their Grandma Beaty's farm cat Ronnie, which made us love them all the more. The cat sleeping pills had worked until two hours north of Harrisonburg, and then Albert and Sugar both began to carry on. They wanted *out*.

Shelly carried the portable "pet hotel" in from the car and set it down in the middle of the empty living room. We all stood behind it to witness the big moment. When Shelly opened the door, Albert and Sugar tumbled out on top of one another. They began to run, stop, cry out, and run again—all through the house. This was not home, and they were as distressed as Chris was.

We ate pizza from a place downtown, then carried in the essentials from the truck—mattresses, bedclothes, bathroom stuff. Shelly's room was down the hall from ours and she tucked in surrounded by her favorite stuffed animals: a unicorn, a white baby seal, various teddy bears, and an oversized gorilla, as I recall. Christopher's room was in the basement, but he decided to spread his mattress in the living room.

Becky lay down beside me on the mattress in the white cotton gown she wore in summer. She turned to me and whispered, "Are we really home?"

"Looks like it," I said.

"Let's you and me have a deal," Becky said. "Let's stay here where we belong."

Becky was so happy to be home. Her feelings were clear and true. I said, "Deal," and hoped this was true.

I may have slept an hour before bolting up wide awake. The house was dead quiet. I walked down the hall to check on Shelly, sound asleep and dreaming. I knew she was dreaming because her face looked busy rather than composed. After straightening a few of her stuffed animals, I went out to check on Christopher. His head, as always, was buried under the pillow. That's how I slept as a boy, and I stood there for a moment wondering how things like that worked out. Where exactly is the head-under-the-pillow gene? What do we acquire and what gets passed along?

We had left all of the furniture in the truck, and so I had no place to sit. I paced around a bit, then went outside to sit on the concrete steps. The yard was ringing with crickets. Katydids, those pale green night bugs, were winding their sprockets in the trees. The night air was moist and cool. Looking up, I could see the tar-black silhouettes of mountains against the lighter dark of the night sky. It was like being down inside a bowl, tucked in and safe. That's what I remember feeling as I tumbled out of my father's car in Piedmont as a boy.

Looking around the yard, I tried to get some sense of the neighborhood but there wasn't much to see—dark yards, dim houses, black trees, and faint yellow light in a few windows. Down the hill Franklin was dark and quiet. Becky and I had not wanted a house in town. We had talked about a farmhouse out and away from everything. Someplace I could walk, hunt squirrels and deer. With the right kind of luck, there would be a brook with native trout. Becky wanted the isolation of a mountain farm, the time and quiet to keep her own thoughts, someplace to watch dusk settle into a piece of woods outside the kitchen window. But we thought living out of town would be hard on Chris and Shelly. They would want friends and social events—football games, parties, dances, a pizza place. We saw this house as a compromise; we would bring our kids back to Appalachia but not stick them out in the woods like hoot owls.

That night I remember thinking—or maybe hoping—that town life might not be so bad. I could hear sheep bleating faintly in the distance, and when the breeze shifted, the perfume of honeysuckle was heavy on the air. But my mind kept circling back to Chris. Coming in, we had driven past Franklin High, a red-brick building near the Southern States Feed Store on the east side of town. I liked the school, or at least the look of it. It made me think of Becky's high school in Green Bank. There were large maple trees growing on the lawn and a white sign by a lilac bush told the world that the mighty Franklin Panthers had taken the AAA baseball championship in 1983. It was charming, like something from that Andy Griffith TV show, *Mayberry RFD*.

But the building was old and very small. The high school back in Oswego was brand-new and easily five times as large. Oswego High was also well funded, which meant a wide range of courses and activities. Franklin would offer far less if only because of its size. Christopher had just started to play tennis and—if you can forgive a father's vanity—I thought he had talent. Unless Franklin was very different from other small Appalachian towns, tennis partners would be hard to come by. I knew that things like this mattered, but not how much.

As if to complicate matters, I had agreed to write a book about

Appalachia. Some of the articles I had published about West Virginia had caught the attention of a few editors and an agent, who wanted to sell a book about "this magic place." Foolishly I told him that I would send part of a manuscript within months, and this brought a lifetime of simmering confusion to a boil. At the time I still did not know where Appalachia was or, for that matter, what it meant to be an Appalachian. As I said earlier, I first heard the word in a college class-room. The professor, who was from out of state, told the class that all of West Virginia was Appalachia and that we—his students—were Appalachians. A few months after that, I went to visit my Grand-mother O'Brien in Piedmont and ended up in a bizarre conversation. We were watching a bowling-for-dollars show on television. I don't think she cared for the bowling itself, but at the end of each show the announcer gave the winner a check for several thousand dollars. The idea of someone earning more money in one day than she made at the mill in a year—just for knocking things over—seemed miracu-lous to my grandmother. She advised me to "study on" bowling in col-lege and told me that if she ever came into money she would keep part of it for herself and send the rest to the poor people in Appala-chia. We did not talk about this, but my confusion deepened.

At that time I thought Appalachia was somewhere along the Kentucky–West Virginia border. I had seen something on TV about high unemployment and poverty down there—pictures of black-faced miners and hollow-eyed children—but I became friendly with students from the coalfields who insisted that Appalachia was some-where else. One of my best friends told me that his father sometimes said that Appalachia had wheels on it. It rolled around the mountains and, like a traveling circus of hillbillies, stopped wherever the politi-cians wanted it to stop.

After leaving Morgantown, as Becky and I traveled around the country, we sometimes found ourselves in odd conversations about where we were from. More often than not, people knew nothing about West Virginia and at times even thought we were talking about west-ern Virginia. But they knew all about Appalachia—strange, backward people struggling with grinding poverty in a devastated landscape; feral hillbillies; Hatfields and McCoys, black-bearded moonshiners murdering one another. That or quaint folk in strap overalls and granny dresses playing fiddles while they clogged around. Occasionally there was just enough truth to some of these misconceptions to make them understandable. I knew about hard times in the coalfields but thought all of that had to do with American industry and exploitation rather than with "hillbillies." I had at least heard about the Hatfield and McCoy "blood feud," and while mindless violence had nothing to do with any West Virginian I had ever met, I assumed there was some truth to the story. But it was as if Becky and I had said we were from Texas and then people began to talk about gunfighters, cattle drives, "Injun trouble," and ruthless oil barons. At times trying to explain was pointless. People had read things about Appalachia or seen things on television and they knew. I should say that Becky and I never felt like poor mountain waifs lost in cold America. Most of the people we met were kind, despite their misconceptions, and the topic did not come up every day. It was just this odd confusion in the background of our life.

Promising to write about Appalachia changed that, of course. Some of the editors and especially the agent wanted a book about strange hillbillies in an exotic location. I never mentioned my confusion in letters or over the phone. It hardly seemed strategic to tell people that I really did not know the place they wanted me to write about.

4. The Heart of Appalachia

O N MAPS of the eastern United States the Appalachian mountain chain resembles a band of wrinkles running from southern Maine to northern Georgia. The region of Appalachia, pronounced Apple-*at*-cha by most residents, is at the southern end of the chain. One writer, William Goodell Frost, described the region in 1898 as "the mountainous back yards of nine states." Americans could imagine an oval with Charleston, West Virginia, at the center. Everything within the oval is, at least in Frost's view, part of Appalachia. Of the nine states he included—West Virginia, Maryland, Virginia, Pennsylvania, North Carolina, Georgia, Kentucky, Alabama, and Tennessee—only West Virginia lies entirely within the oval and is therefore called "the heart of Appalachia." This means that Piedmont, Morgantown, and Pendleton County—our new home—are Appalachian communities. But Frost aside, you could start a serious argument with any county resident about this. Like most West Virginians, no one in Pendleton County wants to be labeled Appalachian.

On maps, Pendleton County resembles a rough parallelogram in eastern West Virginia. It is on the Virginia line, three hours southwest of Washington, D.C. To describe the county as mountainous would be misleading; you stand on one mountain looking out on mountains all around. Everything is up or down. There are three narrow valleys here that resemble ax bites in the mountains and a shallow, rocky river flows north at the bottom of each one. The valleys are known as the North Fork Valley, the South Fork Valley, and the South Branch Valley. They take their names from the rivers that flow through them. Officially, the rivers have long, awkward names—the

North Fork of the South Branch of the Potomac River, the South Branch of the Potomac River, and the South Fork of the South Branch of the Potomac River—but residents quite sensibly shorten the names to the North Fork, the South Branch, and the South Fork. The three rivers come together just beyond the county's northern border. Then, as the South Branch of the Potomac, the water continues to flow north and merges later with the North Branch of the Potomac, which has flowed past my father's home in Piedmont. As the Potomac River, all of this water eventually flows through the nation's capital. I live in the South Branch, or middle valley, where Franklin, the county seat, is located.

Two roads pass through the parallelogram—Route 220 North/South and 33 East/West—and drivers on either one constantly roll up or down as they weave back and forth around snakelike turns. Traffic on these steep, winding roads offers an introduction to county life. There are probably more trucks than cars back here. You pass new pickups polished to a dazzle with enormous tires and a row of floodlights above the cab. As a rule, young men drive these. After dark, a sidekick or a young woman often sits beside them. Other pickups are old, dented, manure- or mud-splattered, and filled with nervous sheep or cattle. Middle-aged or older men—rarely women—drive these. In passing, drivers lift a finger from the steering wheel, Pendleton County's abbreviated high sign. There are larger trucks as well, some of them piled high with logs or teetering bales of hay. Semis, which resemble traveling zoos, are stacked with cages filled with snow-white turkeys.

This is farm country, then—pastures filled with mixed-breed cattle or black-faced Suffolk sheep, hay fields dotted with those huge round bales, barns off in the distance, tractors chugging through the fields, and small white farmhouses at the ends of dirt "get in" roads. With seven hundred square miles and nine thousand people, Pendleton County is the least populated community for its geographic size east of the Mississippi River. I have spent uncounted hours driving small dirt roads back through the mountains without seeing another human being.

Fifty-one percent of Pendleton County's land is national forest. This consists of mixed hardwoods for the most part—oak, maple, poplar, hickory, ash. Occasional stands of pine, spruce, and hemlock add to the mix. In summer the county's overall appearance is lush green. In fall the hills and ridges blaze with color. Winter is a somber study in black, faded brown, and gray. This is stunning country in any season.

The forests teem with wildlife: turkeys, grouse, squirrels, foxes, raccoons, rabbits, beavers, minks, black bears, bobcats, groundhogs, and deer. In Pendleton County white-tailed deer outnumber people two to one. Bald and golden eagles soar above the mountains, and each spring farmers hunt down sheep-killing bears with packs of bugling hounds. Occasionally, farmwives start for the barn to find rat-tlesnakes "six feet long and stout as a grown man's arm" blocking the way. As the proverbial crow flies, Pendleton County is 120 miles from Washington, D.C. It's a quick two-hour drive from there through the broad and lovely Shenandoah Valley to Harrisonburg, Virginia. You

Pendleton County, West Virginia (Photograph by Shelly Turner)

turn west on Route 33, leave the Wal-Mart, McDonald's, Burger King, Taco Bell, Holiday Inn—the sprawl that America has become—twist and turn up Shenandoah Mountain, then descend into another world in less than an hour. There is a clear sense of place here. Pendleton County has a memory of itself and a decided point of view. Residents have not become homogenized Americans as yet, and this has a lot to do with why I am here.

Franklin is the largest town by far. Nine hundred people live here—10 percent of the county total. Brandywine has perhaps four hundred; Circleville in the North Fork Valley comes in at about two hundred. Then there's Upper Tract, Smoke Hole, Sugar Grove, Onego—all with sixty or seventy—and on down to tiny villages like Moyers, Dahmer, and Egypt that you can drive through and not know it—two or three houses and a small white church half-hidden in the trees.

Like most of Appalachia, Pendleton County was settled in the 1750s by German, English, and Scotch-Irish families. Why those people came here and how they fared is a story about oppression, greed, ruthless ambition, corruption, determination, and blind co-incidence—that is to say, part of American history.

Until the early eighteenth century the southern Appalachians were unexplored and feared. The virgin forest was dark, gloomy, and, as far as anyone knew, endless. Along with fears about hostile Indians, bears, cougars, rattlesnakes, and unknown diseases, some people believed that dragons and monsters lived in the mountains. The first American settlers did not share our Sierra Club love of wilderness. Early writers often described mountains as "warts" or "wens" on the land and places to be shunned. Expressions like "the dire forests" appear often in letters. An immense stand of thorny locust not far from Pendleton County was so dense and impassable early mapmakers labeled it "Shades of Death."

But as available land to the east of the Appalachians became scarce, greed overcame dread. The Crown granted vast tracts of mountainous land west of the Piedmont to well-connected specula-tors, and they in turn found thousands of families desperate to escape the British Isles who were willing to buy land in America sight unseen. Many people, though, had heard or read disturbing stories about the Appalachian Mountains. So more than anything else, the land speculators needed a promotional device to reduce fears and advertise their venture. They needed an American connection.

Alexander Spotswood, Virginia's governor from 1710 to 1722, was well known and admired on both sides of the Atlantic. A dashing fellow fond of "the hunt," Spotswood was also a gentleman of intelligence and culture. Letters crisscrossed the Atlantic and arrangements were made. Accordingly, on August 20, 1716, Spotswood assembled a party of perhaps a dozen "gay gentlemen" in Williamsburg, Virginia, who would—for God, King, and Country—explore the southern Appalachians. There was nothing second-rate about the expedition; the gentlemen wore elaborate riding clothes and large plumed hats. The governor delivered a stirring speech, then commanded his party to mount up. The "gay gentlemen" started west for the Blue Ridge, followed by scores of slaves and indentured servants lugging the "equipage."

It was a remarkable journey. Apparently the "equipage" included a great quantity of "spirits." According to John Fontain, who later wrote about the adventure, "We had several sorts of liquors, viz., Virginia red wine and white wine, Irish usquebaugh, brandy, shrub, rum, champagne, canary, cherry, punch, cider, etc." When the party reached a summit or forded a river, the accomplishment called for some libation. The gentlemen toasted the king, fired their pistols into the air, toasted every member of the king's family by name, firing volley after volley, then toasted their noble endeavor. Each night ended with a raucous drinking party around a great bonfire. Surprisingly, the expedition covered a lot of ground—440 miles in eight weeks— reaching a point perhaps an hour away from present-day Pendleton County.

Upon his return to Williamsburg, the governor hosted a lavish banquet and created "the Knights of the Golden Horseshoe." After yet another stirring speech, he handed out gold, gem-studded horseshoe brooches to the gentlemen who had made the trip with him. Inscribed on each brooch was *Sic jurat transcendere montes* ("So let it be a joy to traverse the mountains"). As it turns out, traversing mountains was profitable as well as a joy. The venture netted Spotswood eighty-five thousand acres, and the other Knights also became wealthy.

Soon after this, Spotswood wrote an account of the adventure and sent it to his backers in London. The Appalachian Mountains were not at all to be dreaded, he proclaimed. Why, he had discovered not a dire wilderness but a "garden paradise," where gentle beasts cavorted at play beneath the trees. The governor also noted the splendid view of "our great inland sea" (Lake Erie) to be had—perhaps after imbibing just enough Irish usquebaugh—from atop the Blue Ridge Mountains. With this, the southern Appalachians had officially opened.

In Ulster at the time, British treatment of the Scotch-Irish was brutal. The Scotch-Irish were so called because in the seventeenth century the Crown had offered Lowland Scots free land and passage to Ulster, hoping to weaken the power of the Scottish clans. The Scottish families that took advantage of the offer did well. In fact, these Ulstermen did so well, their wool and linen exports threatened British trade in those commodities. Wealthy British merchants approached the king, who then enacted laws and tariffs that crippled the Scotch-Irish. Thousands of families lost farms they had developed for thirty years. The Crown simply gave the land to Englishmen or sometimes to Crown-aligned Irishmen. Homeless people were starving on the streets of Ulster. Conditions became so nightmarish that Jonathan Swift wrote *A Modest Proposal,* suggesting that it might be kinder to butcher and eat Scotch-Irish infants than to slowly starve them.

Living conditions in Germany—loosely aligned Germanic states at the time—were not much better. After the Reformation, the Christian church kept dividing and redividing into splinter sects. If a family belonged to the same sect as the ruler of a Germanic state, life went on well enough. Unfortunately, if families did not profess the "official" religion, they had no recourse to law. Anyone who cared to steal their land or stock, swindle, cheat, abuse, or even kill them could do so without fear of retribution. French marauders frequently crossed the border to plunder unprotected families.

The winter of 1708/09, then the worst on record in Europe, became a triggering event. Herds of cattle and flocks of sheep froze to death. Fruit trees exploded like cannon-shot, and birds fell frozen from the sky. Amish, Dunkers, Moravians, Mennonites, and other sects boarded sailing ships for Tidewater, Virginia, or Philadelphia.

Virtually all of these people—my ancestors as well as Becky's—were subsistence farmers. They wanted land to farm and freedom from persecution. The Appalachian Mountains offered both.

There is an official *History of Pendleton County* that was written in 1910 by Oren F. Morton. According to Morton, the first Caucasian to enter this area was an adventuresome Dutchman from New York named John Vanmeter. For obscure reasons, Vanmeter traveled through the Shenandoah Valley with a band of Delaware Indians and entered what is now Pendleton County "prior to 1730." His party encountered a band of Catawba Indians near the mouth of Thorn Creek, ten miles south of present-day Franklin. Vanmeter and his cohorts, in Morton's apt phrase, "got whipped" and quickly departed.

The Dutchman must have liked what he saw, however, because a few years later, two of his sons returned to build cabins. Then in 1747 the Dyer party, a group of five Scotch-Irish families, built permanent cabins in the South Fork Valley. Thirty-one years after Governor Spotswood espied Lake Erie from atop the Blue Ridge, Pendleton County had been officially settled.

Pioneers cut down massive trees with crude hatchets and turned steep, rocky soil into cropland and pasture. Struggles with the Shawnee resulted in two massacres of white settlers. The cultures that emerged in the mountains, like frontier cultures anywhere, were flint-hard and crude. These people developed an almost religious belief in hard physical labor, a passion for hunting and fishing, fundamental religious convictions, and a deep commitment to extended family—if only because you could not survive without your relatives.

If Virginia laws through the eighteenth century are any indication, and there is evidence that these laws were enforced in Pendleton County, early life was puritanical and harsh. There were stocks and a pillory in the courthouse square. An existing court document orders the construction of a "dunking stool" in Franklin. Essentially, these were rather long logs turned into a fulcrum that was set up on the banks of a pond or river. A crude chair was fixed to one end. Women deemed "scolds" or "shrews" were tied to the chair, swung out over the water, and repeatedly "dunked" in hopes of cooling their temperaments and tongues.

One Sunday law from that period reads, "No journeys be made except in case of urgent necessitie, no goods be laden in boates, no shooteing in guns." For stealing a pig, a man could lose an ear or be branded with a red-hot "R" on the palm. The felon was required to say, with conviction, "God save the Commonwealth!" as the brand was applied. A common punishment was "thirty-nine lashes, well laid-on." It was thirty-nine rather than forty because the Romans lashed Christ forty times, and authorities did not want criminals confusing themselves with Jesus—an unlikely confusion, it seems to me.

County men became accomplished forest fighters, learning everything the Shawnee had to teach them. In 1776, George Washington, who had surveyed in the South Fork Valley as a young man, said that should his revolution falter, rather than surrender he would retire to Pendleton County and surround himself with an army of Scotch-Irish forest fighters. Washington could not imagine British regulars dislodging flint-hard men from the mountains they knew so well.

The Civil War created West, by God, Virginia. There had been cultural differences between residents of the Tidewater—descendants of tradesmen who fancied themselves aristocrats—and the farmers in Virginia's mountainous western counties from the start of settlement in the 1750s. Over a hundred years of trade with Wheeling and Pittsburgh—livestock for manufactured goods—rather than trade with Richmond made those differences more striking. Virginians in the western counties "felt" northern. Unfair tax laws favoring the Tidewater added to the strain. In 1861, representatives from Virginia's western counties met to declare their allegiance to the Union, and in 1863, President Lincoln signed the bill that officially recognized the separate state of West Virginia.

The southern Appalachians are a mountainous seam between the North and South. Throughout the war, opposing armies constantly crossed back and forth, often encountering one another as they did. Many small communities were devastated not once but again and again. The town of Philippi, two hours west of Franklin, was taken and retaken many times. Franklin was occupied by twelve thousand Union troops for two weeks, and the soldiers stripped the countryside like a biblical plague of locusts, devouring every last cow, pig, sheep, goat, goose, turkey, duck, and chicken, and every grain of wheat or kernel of corn.

Mountain communities recovered quickly in the decades after the war. In fact, between 1865 and 1885, the region prospered and became one of the most progressive and productive farming areas in the country. Appalachian farm communities literally fed cities like Richmond, Baltimore, and Washington. Each fall, farmers drove astonishing numbers of cows, sheep, pigs, and turkeys out of the mountains to railheads in nearby towns. If commerce and agriculture had continued in this fashion into the twentieth century, this part of America would be remarkably different now. But between 1880 and 1920, life in the southern mountains changed with an explosiveness that would make the effects of the Civil War seem insignificant, at least for the people living in this region.

The southern Appalachians constituted one of the richest regions in the world. The mountains were covered with the largest and oldest hardwood forest known to man, and Appalachian coal deposits were common knowledge. Even Washington, after surveying in the mountains, talked enthusiastically about the region's "mineral wealth." Getting the coal and timber out had always been the problem. Roads into the mountains were poor or nonexistent, and there were no rail lines. But the Civil War, like most American wars, threw the economy into overdrive and accelerated technological progress. By the late 1860s, it was possible, and cost-effective, to build rail lines into the southern mountains.

Within months of Lee's surrender, financiers from East Coast cities were sending agents, often retired Civil War officers, into the Appalachian Mountains, and the reports they sent back quickened the pulse of men like J. P. Morgan. There were massive oaks, walnuts, maples, and chestnuts in uncounted millions. Stands of top-grade, arrow-straight poplar six feet in diameter—"twenty feet off the ground!"—covered mountain after mountain. Until the 1880s, the largest known seam of high-grade coal, a fabled deposit, was six feet wide. An agent discovered seams over thirteen feet wide in southern West Virginia.

In the 1870s, a serious recession dried up venture capital in America, but when the recession ended within the decade, it was as if a dam had burst. Thousands of ruthless, thoroughly dishonest agents swarmed into the mountains, achieving new levels of chicanery by the hour. Appalachian families were cheated, threatened, bullied, and swindled out of ancestral land. Coal and timber boomtowns exploded into existence. By all accounts these were open sewers where brutal beatings, murder, drug addiction, alcoholism, disease, malnutrition, medieval living conditions, insanely unsafe working conditions, and environmental rape were everyday occurrences. In the Appalachian Mountains, the golden age of laissez-faire capitalism was one of America's great nightmares. Within forty years, timber companies had clear-cut the oldest and largest hardwood forest that human beings would ever see. In that time, thirty billion board feet of quality lumber and an equal amount of pulpwood left the state, along with 98 percent of the profit. This was enough wood to build a thirteen-foot-wide, two-inch-thick walkway to the moon. The figures from Virginia, North Carolina, and Tennessee are comparable. Both coal and timber operations ravaged enormous portions of the mountain landscape as well as subsistence cultures that had survived peacefully for more than a hundred years. All of this transpired while county officials and local newspaper editors—who often became coal or timber executives—looked the other way.

By the 1930s, 75 percent of West Virginia's landmass and between 85 and 95 percent of the state's natural resources "legally" belonged to outside interests. This led to political corruption and to economic stasis that West Virginia would never escape. Coal and timber companies own most of the state's politicians, who pass tax and environmental laws to benefit their sponsors.

Ironically, Appalachia did not exist through most of the industrial war. In time American industry, American missionaries—members of the American Missionary Association who inundated the Appalachians to "uplift" mountain people—and the media would all play a part in the invention. By the turn of the century, industry had done most of its share, and the missionary effort had started by the 1880s, but it can be argued that William Goodell Frost conjured Appalachia into existence with a flourish of his pen in 1897.

Pendleton County escaped the outright devastation of those forty years. Limestone, rather than coal, lies below the ground here. While the industrial war raged in the southern end of the state, Franklin prospered as a picture-perfect farm community. By the end of the nineteenth century three county families—the McClures, the Boggses, and the Andersons—had become millionaires in the cattle business. There were two respectable hotels downtown and a finishing school for young ladies. Franklin reached its social and economic high point in the 1920s. As Mrs. Dorothy Wilkins, a prominent Franklin woman in her seventies, told me, "Franklin was a superior town. Superior."

Of all the things that I learned about Pendleton County, what strikes me as most remarkable is the stability of its population. In his history, Morton lists the names of the pioneer families and in part they read "Adams, Alt, Anderson, Bowers, Calhoun, Conrad, Dice, Dyer . . . Mallow, McCoy, Nelson, Pitsenbarger, Propst, Simmons." Pick up the Pendleton County phone book—all of twenty-eight notebook-size pages—and you read "Adams, Alt, Anderson, Bowers, Calhoun, Conrad, Dice, Dyer . . . Mallow, McCoy . . ." After 280 years, the descendants of the county's Scotch-Irish, German, and English settlers are still here.

This is an old community with a clear identity. At least, as I would learn, the county's identity was clear until the early 1970s. For reasons ranging from inflation to agribusiness, small farms began to fail in the mid-1950s and families were forced to sell ancestral land or lose it at public auction. Looking for work, men took their families to nearby cities just as my father had done, for rather different reasons, in 1940. By the middle of the 1970s, Pendleton County had lost 13 percent of its population. This time professionals living in Washington, D.C., and Baltimore "discovered" the county.

The cost of land, compared to city prices, was astonishingly low. So were taxes and the general cost of living. Cool summers, mild, picturesque winters, and postcard scenery added immeasurably to the appeal, and so, after two hundred years of relative stability, the county's population began to change. Sophisticated city folk with new ideas and new ways of doing things began to move in, and predictably enough, social tensions rose. Up to a point, Pendleton County is no different from other rural American communities "discovered" by urban professionals in the seventies. But once again, this is Appalachia, and some of the newcomers—"come-heres" in local speech—arrived with unfortunate opinions about hillbillies. Needless to say, this struck a local nerve.

To this tangled social mix, one must add Woodlands Institute. The institute, a small nonprofit organization with two bright Ivy League Ph.D.'s at its core and a membership that fluctuated from six to sometimes twenty, appeared on a North Fork mountaintop during the summer of 1973. Since that time, the organization has been the center of endless controversy, dark suspicion, and no small amount of hatred in all three Pendleton County valleys. In fact, by the time Becky and I arrived in August 1984, the county had become preoccupied with Woodlands, and this would lead to one of the worst community conflicts since the Civil War. Ironically, Appalachia, that place I was looking for, would be at the center of the turmoil. I can still remember the first time I heard about Woodlands. Sometime during that first year, I met a teacher friend of Becky's on Main Street. She had just left the school board office after trying to get the superintendent's approval for one of her students to be involved with a Woodlands program. After saying hello, she said, in pure exasperation, "Why, *why* does Pendleton County *hate* Woodlands Institute?" At the time I had no answer, but would later understand. That first fall Becky and I were pleased to find what we had wanted—beautiful mountains and a handsome town filled with people whom we liked and thought we understood.

IT'S A hot August day. The sky is cloudless and powder-blue and there is no breeze to speak of. We have been home five days now. Becky is hanging curtains and washing clothes. Shelly is playing with dolls in her room with two girls from the house behind us, and Christopher is in his basement room listening to *Purple Rain* and writing another letter to Angel. The music is so loud, I imagine the entire house pulsing like a heart. I keep thinking about demanding a lower volume but cannot bring myself to do that. Chris and I have not been speaking, at least not the way we used to, and I do not want to make things worse.

We have already been to the various places downtown to arrange electricity, water, phone, trash pickup, a post office box, and a new checking account. Today I need to subscribe to the *Pendleton Times*, get groceries, and cook my first real meal since moving in.

Franklin is a pretty town. Two hundred fifty homes clustered on a mountainside. Unlike Piedmont and Morgantown, Franklin is not industrial. The narrow streets are clean and the houses, mostly modest wood-frame structures, are in good repair. People keep their lawns trimmed, and in many yards a well-stacked pile of firewood sits

Franklin, West Virginia (Photograph by Shelly Turner)

near a vegetable garden. Impatiens, snapdragons, and cosmos line the borders. A few large old homes, painted pristine white, with gables, wraparound porches, and gingerbread woodwork, give Franklin a Victorian air. The town seems to be nestled in the mountains.

Franklin's main street is no wider than a mountain stream. There are fifteen small stores, four restaurants—diners really—and twelve small churches, all of them, as far as I can tell, well attended. If you add the county library—two overstuffed rooms in a house built before the Civil War—the Pendleton County Bank, the county court-house, and the office of the *Pendleton Times*, that's about it. There are no stoplights, bars, or fast-food restaurants in town. A white metal sign on the courthouse lawn tells of Francis Evick, who founded Franklin in 1746 and gave it a variation of his name.

Despite its lilliputian size, Franklin can be surprisingly busy, especially on Saturday morning. People from all three valleys come in to stop at the bank, shop for groceries, pick up items from the hardware store, get a haircut, and see a dentist or doctor. The vet's office is on

Main Street, and some Saturday mornings the sidewalk outside his door resembles a scene from a Dr. Doolittle movie. Children carry kittens or puppies, hunters lug sad-eyed coon dogs, and worried farmers wait beside trucks with a lamb or a calf that's "look'n poorly." One morning I stopped to look at two llamas that a woman brought in for a checkup.

On these same mornings, when the weather is decent, church groups or 4-H kids set up tables to sell baked goods or barbecued chicken. Public auctions are often held on Saturdays. An auctioneer rattles off like a machine gun to a crowd of twenty or thirty on the sidewalk at the bottom of the courthouse steps—sunburned farmers in coveralls, land speculators in business suits, come-heres in casual dress. Little kids sometimes sit on cars or wrestle on the courthouse lawn. Some of these mornings feel like carnivals.

But this August day is slow and quiet. A blond woman in a long blue dress walks into the post office. The county jailer, an Irishman with a ruddy complexion and prominent orange ears, passes by trailing cigarette smoke and Mennen aftershave. In his tweed coat and porkpie hat, William McCoy, owner and editor of the *Pendleton Times*, talks with my landlord, Tom Firor, on the sidewalk. McCoy is quite short and my landlord is tall and thin. A pickup with half a dozen sheep passes them. That's all. Walking down Main Street, I can feel the sun on my shoulders like a heavy hand.

The *Pendleton Times* office is in an old brick building squeezed between B & H Hardware and the Pillbox Pharmacy, and the paper's name appears in antiquated scroll on a small, dusty window. Behind the glass a quartet of stuffed birds—three owls and a golden eagle— sit side by side under decades of dust. It's like looking into a Cornell box.

Opening the door, I half expect to meet a man with a walrus mustache and arm garters, but a tall, slender young man stands behind the messy counter. The old black presses are running—ka-chunk, ka-chunk, ka-chunk. The bloodlike smell of ink hangs in the back of my throat. The young man behind the counter fixes me with an icy glare—not unlike that of the stuffed eagle in the window—and I can't think of a thing to say except: Boy it sure is hot today. Some swell town you've got here. I'm new and what I need . . . The great stone face does not blink or say a word.

I have encountered cool receptions in Appalachian towns any number of times. I'm bearded and I speak with a Philadelphia accent. Some people in this part of the country have become weary of outsiders with superior attitudes about "hillbillies," and they will hold newcomers at arm's length until they get some sense of their opinions. But this reaction is frigid rather than chilly and it confuses me. I have stepped into the wake of very hard feelings. Something is going on in this small town.

THAT DAY I carried several back copies of the paper to the Korner Shop across Main Street and paged through them while I sipped iced tea. The *Times* is a weekly paper of eight to fourteen pages that comes out on Wednesday afternoons. Some hard news appears in each issue: election results, reprints of state news from the *Charleston Gazette*, school board decisions, accidents, and sometimes accounts of local crime. (The most common offenses are DWI and "jacklighting" deer at night, the perpetrators usually being men in their late teens or early twenties.) But most of the paper is taken up with the daily events of county life: announcements of church suppers, visiting evangelists, 4-H meetings, and impending marriages; "New Arrivals from the Stork"; obituaries; heavily rhymed and metered poems about departed loved ones; birthday greetings ("Lordy, Lordy, look who's 40!"); high school sports stories; and pictures of trophy trout, buck deer, and garden vegetables shaped like famous people living and dead. A full page of personal ads offers firewood, used cars and trucks, babysitting services, livestock, hunting dogs, guns, farm equipment, and stud service. Also: "I will no longer be responsible for debts incurred by . . ." "There will be no hunting on my property on Snowy Mountain off 28 past Circleville. Trespassers will be . . ." Reports sent in from the county's outlying villages like Sugar Grove, Seneca Rocks, and Smoke Hole describe weather, lightning strikes, sheep-killing bears, coyote sightings, who came to visit who, and sometimes what they had for supper.

County life, as seen through the window of the *Pendleton Times,* is sane and measured. Becky grew up this way. But as I thought of it, county life also seemed provincial, a myopic view of the world with not much going on, sameness year after year. This was fine with me; county life made as much, or as little, sense as life did anywhere else, as far as I could see. Actually, I found the idea of sameness comforting. Writing, reading, cooking, time with Becky and the children, and time in the woods and on the streams was all I wanted. I needed less distraction rather than more, and Becky felt the same. But I wondered what Chris and Shelly would make of county life or, more to the point, what county life would make of them.

I may or may not have read about Woodlands Institute that day. By then I knew that Woodlands existed in Pendleton County if only because I had seen institute members—men and women in their late twenties or early thirties—on Main Street. Dressed in chinos, open sandals, and shirts or jackets that suggested L.L. Bean or Patagonia, "Woodies"—as some locals called them—stood out. I can remember walking past two or sometimes three institute members at tables in one of Franklin's diners and thinking they projected an insider aura like fraternity brothers on a college campus.

One "Woody" always caught my eye. With a bristling black beard to the center of his chest—like one of the Smith Brothers from the box of cough drops—and a large, oddly shaped cowboy hat, he had me doing double takes despite myself. He seemed intensely self-conscious; small gestures like looking up or down the street seemed oddly dramatic, as if he were an actor in a play. One afternoon I watched him stop suddenly in a parking lot to extract a small notebook from his hip pocket. Struck with an idea—a cartoon figure with a light-bulb above his head came to mind—he jotted something down, returned the notebook to his hip pocket, and went on. I have always been drawn to people who create their own style, and this fellow held my full attention. It would be several weeks before someone introduced us.

I did meet one Franklin personality that day. Walking out of the IGA market, hugging bags of groceries, I caught sight of a short man with close-cropped hair staring through binoculars. He was not holding the binoculars across his face eye to eye but up and down, like a U-boat commander squinting through a periscope. I was walking toward my car when the man ran past me in an odd, stiff-gaited way. Stopping directly behind my car, he bent down to scan the one lens of his binoculars back and forth over the license plate. As I approached, he straightened up and said, "Mister, you're from the Syracuse, New York, area." "That's right," I said, "I just left Oswego. That's not far from Syracuse."

The man, George Dice, had one eye that was clouded and an empty socket where the other eye should have been. I was having a hard time looking at his face; the empty socket was as red and inflamed as a fresh wound.

George abruptly asked, "When's your birthday, mister?"

"My birthday?"

"When were you born?"

"July 18, 1943. But I don't see why . . ."

George tipped his head back like a man going into a trance. Moments later, he said, "It was a full moon that night."

Later I discovered that this was true. George, a savant who specializes in license plates and phases of the moon, is the most noticeable character in Franklin. According to George, when he was born in a nearby hospital, the nurse mixed up bottles of solution and burned his eyes with something caustic. As a result, he has made his way about town with binoculars for about forty years.

George asked for a ride downtown and I said yes. That was the start of an odd friendship. I became part of George Dice's taxi service. We would bump into each other at the post office or the IGA and I would drive him wherever he needed to go. It was always interesting; George invariably had a lot on his mind and was always ready to speak his thoughts. Among other things, he told me that he could identify certain people by their scent and that his greatest frustrations were his inability to drive a car or to attract women. ("Now you take these women, I mean can you understand them? I just don't have any luck with women. I do about as well with them as I would drive'n this here car down the street.") I don't think George felt sorry for himself, but he could become quite angry with people who did not appreciate how difficult his life was. Town residents occasionally saw him at the cemetery berating the tombstone of a former employer who had had no empathy.

That morning I dropped George off at the post office and found a letter in my box from the agent who was interested in my Appalachia book. "I cannot wait to read some pages!" he wrote. I had deliberately stopped thinking about "Appalachia" and now would have to think of it again.

In fact, I thought about little else for several days and became confused and frustrated with the matter. Then one evening I had to wash blankets in a Laundromat downtown. The place was empty except for an older couple and a chubby toddler in a plastic diaper. The overweight woman, in aqua sweatpants and a man's flannel shirt, smiled at me when I walked in. I smiled back. There was a three- or four-day growth of stubble on the man's face. He was feeding the baby—a pear-shaped little Buddha on the folding table—pieces of a Little Debby cupcake. The baby's face was smeared in chocolate.

Looking in my direction the man said, "This one's an eater, I tell you now."

"I can see that," I said and smiled.

Thrown together, we began to talk. These people were open and unguarded. There was no guile about them. As it turns out, the baby was their grandson. Their youngest daughter had run off for parts unknown, leaving her child with them.

I said, "Bet that made you mad."

"Not no more," the man said. "There at first it did. He's ours now."

Pulling clothing from the dryer, the woman turned to smile in agreement. They loved the baby; that was obvious. As we talked, it came to me that perhaps George Dice and these people were the Appalachians that the agent had in mind.

The encounter led to a restless night. I sat at the kitchen table writing and rewriting sketches of George and the people I had just met. I did not know what to make of my own thoughts. In some revisions, I caught myself pretending to a compassion that was clearly patronizing. In others, George and the people in the Laundromat veered toward caricature. When I tried to correct this, my tone became suspiciously defensive. Even the revisions that seemed balanced worried me. I could easily imagine someone outside the Appalachian Mountains reading the sketches and having all of their hillbilly stereotypes confirmed.

That night I spent an hour or so paging through a battered copy of *Let Us Now Praise Famous Men.* A writer friend had advised me several times not to "rewrite Agee's book." But why did my friend think of Appalachia in terms of impoverished sharecroppers during the Depression? Once again, I found myself lost between the woebegone place outsiders talk about and the Appalachia that I knew.

It came to me that writers from other American minorities—blacks, Native Americans, Latinos, women—almost certainly confront the same problem. You spend your life rejecting stereotypes, then sit down to write and confront them once again. It comes down to this: If you go to a Laundromat after dark anywhere in America, you're likely to meet people on the ragged edge of a community. Every small town has an eccentric or two, and I have always been drawn to them, if only because I feel eccentric myself. While living in West Virginia, I had met more average, middle-class Americans than anyone else, but if I write about the ministers, storekeepers, secretaries, bankers, and about George Dice and the people in the Laundromat, who would you remember as Appalachian? As an enterprise, writing about people I have always liked began to feel more and more suspect, and I sat up most of the night struggling with this.

The next afternoon I went fishing. The South Branch River is five minutes from the house. You drive down Anderson Hill, pass through downtown, and descend another hill to the bottom of the valley. As I've said, the mountains in this part of the Appalachian range are jammed tightly together, which makes the valleys resemble ax-bite Vs. The South Branch, like the rivers in the other two valleys, flows through the very notch of the V. Leaving the car in Franklin's town park, I walked about forty yards to the river.

Like the South Fork and the North Fork, the South Branch is shallow and rocky, stretching perhaps twenty-five yards at its widest point. It's more like a mountain stream than a river, but it's the kind of water I like best. You wade right in, cross back and forth, and come to know each bend and turn like a lover's body. My father taught me how to fish small streams on Darby Creek outside of Philadelphia, and I fished just as he taught me, sloshing out to the center in old tennis shoes, flipping a tiny minnow plug into deep pockets and likely riffles. The strike of a smallmouth bass always makes my heart jump; it is the surest thing I know. I kept enough for the next day's dinner and already had the menu in mind—bass fillets in cornbread batter, applesauce made with fruit from a neighbor's tree, garlic potatoes with spuds from my father-in-law's garden, and cornbread. I had noticed blackberries along the bank and would stop to pick some before going home.

I may have waded two or three miles that night. I cannot remember that specific dusk, but I have been on the South Branch so many evenings I can fill in—cool air, the river shining black and silver, rolling ahead and disappearing into a dark green tunnel of trees; the "who cooks for you" of a barred owl from the mountainside; yellow light shines from a farmhouse kitchen across the pasture, and the fragrance from a barn is on the air. For me, this is Appalachia and I belong here.

5. Sunday

THE HOUSE is empty this Sunday morning. Becky has taken Christopher and Shelly to their grandparents' house for the day. Green Bank, where Becky grew up, is two mountains—an hour's drive—away. I have decided to stay at home to deal with writing problems. I don't have to be in Green Bank to know how the visit will go. Becky and the children will go to Sunday service with Jamie and Beaty at Liberty Presbyterian, a small white church in a grove of oak trees a few yards down the road from the house. Back home after church, Beaty flies around the kitchen preparing the main meal of the day while Jamie dozes in his recliner. This is a new pattern. When his mother, Nettie—called Gran by Becky and the other grandchildren—was alive, Jamie would drive up the road to get her. Gran attended the Methodist church. She did not drive a car and never considered learning. For Appalachian women of her generation, driving a team of horses, or any "vehicle," was man's work. Jamie would pull up as Gran locked her front door and carried loaves of homemade bread to the car. Until 1977, Beaty's dad, Grandpa Farmer, would also have joined the family for dinner. He lived next door and would walk slowly across the lawn aided by his hickory cane each Sunday. Farmer suffered terribly with arthritis, but his mind was clear and he never lost his faith or his optimism. He took great delight in his great-grandchildren, and I can remember him gently using his cane to play tug-of-war with Shelly when she was a toddler. But now both are gone, and the round oak table in the kitchen is, sadly, less crowded.

The food remains country elegant. It's pork tenderloin or fried chicken, mashed potatoes and rich gravy, pole beans, coleslaw,

Becky's parents, Jamie and Beaty Blackhurst Sheets

homemade applesauce, corn on the cob, rolls or biscuits instead of Gran's bread, and slices of a beefsteak tomato from the garden. Because the grandchildren are there, she serves pumpkin pie— Christopher's favorite—and one of Shelly's favorites, a dish of peanut butter fudge, each piece as heavy as a brick.

After dinner, Beaty washes the dishes and sings "Shall We Gather at the River" just under her breath, and Jamie, who is rarely still during six days of the week, sits in his recliner watching football, occasionally taking catnaps. In Appalachia, Sunday is a day of rest—for men at least.

Chris and his cousin Troy, who is one year younger, play basketball in the gravel drive by the old shed. The hoop above the door is bent and wobbly and it's hard to dribble in the gravel, but they play with all their hearts. These cousins are best friends until one of them picks up a basketball.

Sunday afternoon settles into the house. Beaty has imposed her character on every room: warm, earth-colored carpets; furniture that is comfortable rather than showy. Sunlight streams through the windows of the back porch onto a table filled with African violets in spectacular bloom. A half-finished jigsaw puzzle lies on the dining room table. In passing, everyone stops long enough to locate a piece or two. Through the afternoon, the grand vista takes shape. The people in the faded black-and-white photographs on the walls—patriarchs in stiff black suits scowling through their beards, serious ladies in long, heavy dresses—would be astonished at the ease and comfort of this life, but would have approved of the peace and order: a spotless house with everything in its proper place; people getting along with one another. Life was meant to be this way.

If the visit goes like most others, Jamie will rouse himself later in the afternoon to offer a truck ride on some back road, maybe to the top of a mountain. Jamie and Beaty will sit in the cab and Becky and the children will ride in the back of the truck, talking and laughing. Jamie drives up the steep dirt road, through the dappled shade and sunlight beneath the trees. Occasionally a deer or wild turkey flashes across the road ahead. They stop at an abandoned family cemetery, a scant half acre under the trees on the mountainside. Some of the gravestones are impossible to read; the hand-chiseled names and dates are almost completely weathered away. Sometimes all you can find are broken pieces of sandstone or a faint depression in the ground. Jamie and Beaty tidy things up by way of remembering.

Jamie often ends his truck rides on Asbury's Knob, a high knoll on the farm where his father, Becky's grandfather, grew up. The family no longer owns the farm, but the new owner allows Jamie to bring friends and family to the Knob anytime. Facing east, you can see the old family farmhouse at the bottom of the steep slope, a white two-story home with gingerbread woodwork around the porches. Becky played with cousins in the yard when she was a little girl and remembers a grape arbor, raspberry bushes, apple trees, and a well where you could draw up fresh water in a bucket attached to a rope.

Becky on Asbury's Knob

The greatest pleasure was drinking the cold water from a long-handled dipper. Looking northwest from the knob, there is a beautiful view of Green Bank in its high alpine valley surrounded by mountains. It's comforting for Jamie and Beaty to stand here with grandchildren, our children. To a large extent, this is why we have returned to Appalachia.

MONTHS BEFORE leaving Oswego, I started a memoir about my father and wanted to go on with it. The empty house that Sunday let me do that. Looking back, I'm tempted to think that the memoir, like coming back to West Virginia, was part of the attempt to reconcile, but I'm not certain. I have been writing about him, off and on, since I was in graduate school in Morgantown. My first two childish poems were about rabbit hunting with him. In fact, I always seem to be writing about my father, even when I think I'm writing about something else. In some stories and poems, he appears as a cameo character not unlike Alfred Hitchcock in one of his own movies. The odd thing is, I sometimes do not recognize my dad until a second or third revision. I will read a page of manuscript to find him sitting across the aisle on a bus or appearing as a bartender.

That Sunday morning, I read through half a dozen legal pads, hated every word, and littered the kitchen floor with balled-up pages. Several cups of strong coffee and a mile or two of pacing did not help. I remember thinking that it was like groping around for a gear in the rental truck that I had driven from Oswego.

By early afternoon I gave up and decided to set my bird feeder on the lawn. This was a simple job; I pounded an upside-down "L" of two-by-fours into the ground and hung my blizzard-battered feeder from an eyehook. I had bought seed and suet from the feed store the day before.

That small job finished, I walked around the yard to feel the hot September afternoon. The early fall sky was almost colorless and a warm stop/start breeze smelled like horses and carried the sound of bleating sheep from a farm on the next ridge. It came to me, I think for the first time, that my hilltop neighborhood had been a farm not long before. The Andersons, one of the Franklin families that became wealthy near the turn of the century, once owned this mountain and considerably more.

The Anderson house, impeccably white and the most imposing home in Franklin, sits at the base of the hill and I pass it when I go downtown. I'm invariably struck with its loveliness. It's an example of Queen Anne architecture—gables, turrets, and gingerbread woodwork, topped by a wonderful old weathervane. It suggests another time and another Franklin. Rich families lived here once. I have seen old black-and-white photographs of the original Mr. Anderson. He was a white-haired man with a fine handlebar mustache and some merriment in his eyes, like a man well pleased with his house and farm. But Mr. Anderson's descendants sold the farm a few years before I moved into the county, and his pastures have been divided and subdivided. From the yard that day, I could see a new two-story brick apartment complex above my house, and all of the houses scattered around me were new. Other homes were under construction. I remember thinking that my hilltop neighborhood stood for all of

Pendleton County. The Anderson farm had become Anderson Hill just before I moved in and it was fast becoming Anderson Heights, a conventional suburban neighborhood—albeit a very hilly one. I could not decide whether this was progress or decline.

When the soft breeze died, I was struck with the absolute stillness of the afternoon. I had been on the hill long enough to know the sounds. On most days, children's voices rose up from behind several houses. A basketball thumped with that odd ringing sound from a driveway just out of sight. Loud music grew louder or faded as pickup trucks went up or down the hill. On Saturdays, the neighborhood buzzed with lawn mowers and weed whackers. But as I walked around, the Sunday quiet had weight. A line from Stevens's "Sunday Morning" came to mind: "The day is like wide water without sound."

Back inside, I put on a Bach tape and watched the feeder. I know very little about serious music. Like everything else in my life, this interest has developed haphazardly. Hank Williams, George Jones, Billie Holiday, Miles Davis, Bach, Mozart, Mahler, James Brown, and the Flying Burrito Brothers—I have either wildly eclectic taste or no taste at all. That aside, I can be passionate about Bach. Beyond the beautiful sounds, I am drawn to his precision. It's the very opposite of my life, and on some level, I want great Bach to put all things into graceful order. I often play his music on Sunday as a substitute for Catholic mass. That Sunday, with Bach swelling the house into a cathedral, the first sparrows and finches came into my feeder. Seeing the birds brought my father back.

IT's SATURDAY in the house on Francis Street. My father is down on his hands and knees scrubbing the kitchen floor, work pants rolled up because "pants wear out, and knees don't." He takes a smoke break at the kitchen window: store-boughts now, Lucky Strikes or Camels. His homemade feeder sits in a slender maple at the end of the alley near Lady's dog box. Starlings are out there jabbing their picklike beaks into the suet ball he has made. He wants cardinals, tanagers—the very bird of paradise—to appear at his feeder, but mostly he gets dingy sparrows, nondescript finches, and much-hated starlings. He never gives up. For my dad, feeding birds is like saying prayers.

I am serving 5 a.m. mass on the small side-altar at St. Clement's. It's Sunday. After mass, I meet my father outside the rectory door. Sometime before, a young priest told him to wait inside out of the cold, but he will not do this. He is neither priest nor altar boy, and it does not seem right.

In the old station wagon, we drive toward Tinacum Wildlife Refuge, but first we stop at a makeshift bakery. It's on an alley-wide side street that feels dank and cavelike because it's in the shadow of the GE plant. Small, skinny rowhouses line both sides of the street, but toward one end, two houses are gone, like missing teeth, and a low garage is there. At least it used to be a garage. A German man and woman have turned it into a bakery. These are people from some fairy tale. The large German woman with her gray hair in a bun, rosy cheeks half-covered with flour, sprinkles powdered sugar on trays of doughnuts behind the counter. Her husband, who tends the giant mixer at the far end of the room, has lost one arm and one leg on opposite sides of his body. He creates a syncopated rhythm as he hops around on his peg and makes perfect quarter-sized circles on the flour-covered floor.

My father puts a nickel on the counter for a bag of "day-olds." The German woman smiles and barks something out in German. Her husband looks our way and hops over to a wooden barrel. The German man has a chrome hook where his missing hand should be. Watching him reach into the barrel to pinch the doughnuts holds me spellbound. He pauses with a filled doughnut in his hook and squeezes until red jelly squirts out. Just the hint of a smile flickers across his face. He knows *everything* about me, and I flush hot and red.

Pulling away from the bakery, the two of us eating doughnuts, my father says, as he always does, "Sometime I'm gonna ask that jaybird how long he thinks a day is."

Down Island Avenue into a neighborhood called the Meadows. The marshy land is crisscrossed by ditches filled with stagnant water. They say the people here have webbed feet. We pass the city dump and drive out along a dirt road into the swamp that surrounds the international airport. The metal sign on the concrete observation tower tells about the wildlife refuge and my father reads it out loud each time we come here.

We climb to the top with our bag of day-olds. My father scans the swamp with his black binoculars. Waterbirds are everywhere—rafts of green-head mallards and smaller black ducks glide about; inky coots scoot around like windup toys; great blue herons stand still as statues; ducks glide down to the water with their wings beautifully set, while other flocks lift off flapping madly. My father gets excited about uncommon birds like cattle egrets, arctic terns, and ospreys. He loves wood ducks; like paintings, he says. I am only mildly interested, but happy to be there making myself queasy on stale doughnuts.

The airport is only a few miles away. The stupendous jets come in low over our heads or seem to rise up out of the swamp. When they throttle up, we become a pantomime of father and son. I remember this moment: A jet thunders over as my dad points out into the swamp. I watch his mouth move but hear nothing. He takes my head in both hands and turns it toward whatever is out there. I see only the usual ducks, but fake wild excitement, so afraid to let him down.

I BEGAN to miss him that Sunday afternoon and considered calling home. I remember staring at the phone and imagining a silly conversation: *Hey, it's me, your prodigal black-sheep son. I've come back to West—by God—Virginia. I just set up a bird feeder. I got great birds already. Come down here for deer season.*

It would never work. Sooner or later our stifled talk would come around to what I was doing in West Virginia, and unless I lied, I would have to say I was writing. My parents had made their feelings clear about this: Writing stories was not work. You could never argue with either of my parents. At best my mother humored disagreement and at worst she battered your personality into submission. My dad never argued. He knew what he knew, and disagreement only reaffirmed his sense of hopelessness. His son John had missed the essential point in life, and that confirmed his despair. I knew nothing except that I missed my dad. My mother had written perhaps half a dozen times in as many years, but my father never wrote or called. My mother's letters were strange in that she claimed to be completely ignorant about the break. In each letter, she asked the same question: Why have you done this to us out of the blue? We have done nothing, absolutely nothing, to you. Each letter made me remorseful, guilty. Why couldn't I rise above all of this and do the right thing? I cannot explain this, but somehow making the call meant accepting his despair. I could not do it.

Becky came home early that evening. Chris and Shelly had decided to spend the night in Green Bank, which pleased their grandparents. I took this as a hopeful sign; Chris had his cousin Troy in Green Bank.

Over the years I have become the family tea maker, despite the fact that I rarely drink it. I made a cup for Becky and talked her into sitting on the back steps. I sat on the grass a few yards away. It was one of those sweet evenings in late summer. The air was cooling down and the Anderson Hill neighborhood had come back to quiet life. I could hear small children behind the next house and the basketball was bouncing in the driveway once again. There were no lawn mowers or weed whackers.

Sipping tea, Becky told me about her day in Green Bank. "Everything's good over there. I stopped down at Jake and Esther's. Jake asked about you. 'When's that John comin' over to go a-fishin'?' You know the way Jake talks. They both seem good but older. Everybody's older. Sometimes I look at my mom and dad and I just get scared. My second-grade teacher died."

After staring off, Becky picked up again. "Some trees on top of Elk Mountain are taking color already. It's always faster up on top."

Becky has always given me the reports from her visits, but I have begun to notice a sad undertone. Everything was changing much too fast at home. Sitting on the steps, she began to type against her thigh, then caught me noticing, and curled her fingers into a fist.

I stretched out in the grass. A mourning dove was cooing from a walnut tree in the next yard and the sky above the house, colorless through the afternoon, had turned deep blue. It was crisscrossed with contrails as it often is—jets gliding into Dulles or Washington National. The old hazy trails, like skim milk, were as fat as thumbs, but the new ones were hard chalk lines. A jet was making a new trail as I watched—a silver glint dragging a pure white razor cut across the blue. It reminded me that Washington was only minutes away by jet. I was struck, as I often am, by how close Pendleton County and Washington, D.C., are. All that imitation Greek architecture, congestion, and street crime a stone's throw away from black bears and unspoiled mountains. It requires a small adjustment in my mental picture of America, one I'm happy to make, I should say.

Becky said, "People around here will think you're a crazy man."

"For lying down in my yard?"

"I don't see other men doing that. Kids do that sometimes. Not grown men."

"They don't know what they're missing."

"Why are you doing it? Or do you know?"

"I'm letting mountain energy come up through me."

"Really."

"I'm soaking up Appalachian earth knowledge so I can write about this place. It's research. I can feel it surging into my back."

"Maybe you're lying on some ants."

"Nah. It's Appalachian energy. Mountain wisdom. You should come lie here with me."

"I'm doing fine here on the steps."

In time that spot would become my moon-watching post. On pleasant nights I sit there to watch the moon rise over the ridge, white, yellow, orange, or silver; enormous, filling the valley with pearly light. I don't think I saw it that Sunday. I spent a little time looking toward Piedmont and told myself I would go there when things settled.

6. Franklin High

I T I S the first day of school and I am standing at the stove stirring Cream of Wheat for Becky's breakfast. I can feel Prince singing "Purple Rain" in the soles of my stocking feet, booming up from Christopher's basement room. I have grown to hate that song, but find myself singing along under my breath. It's like being in purgatory. More music comes from Shelly's room down the hall. The *Today* show is on the TV set, which is on the living room floor between several unpacked boxes. In the bathroom doorway, Becky is blow-drying her hair with a ray gun contraption right out of *Star Wars*.

Shelly rushes into the kitchen, an excited fourth-grader ready for anything. She wolfs down a bowl of Froot Loops—the "good" breakfast battle having been lost some time ago—and runs out the back door to hook up with the neighbor girls. Franklin Elementary School is a five-minute walk down Anderson Hill. I do not have to worry about Shelly walking anywhere in Franklin. Chalk one up for an Appalachian small town.

Prince stops singing mid-song, and Christopher thumps up the basement steps. We have been getting along, but not much more than that. Today in the kitchen he appears as "cool Chris": jeans, striped button-down shirt, the latest in Nike footwear. His downy mustache is darkened—I believe—with a pencil. The pose is less convincing than usual. He is extremely nervous, almost frightened.

I say, "Morning, glory."

He mumbles.

I say, "Kickoff day. New worlds to conquer," in my W. C. Fields voice.

He grimaces.

The night before, he had talked about the best way to get to school. Franklin High is less than a mile from our house. A school bus stops behind the elementary school to unload smaller kids and pick up high school students, but I don't think he liked the idea. The new guy on a school bus could be in for a very hard time. Then again, the new guy walking all alone and being seen *from* the school bus is bad style too.

Stirring the Cream of Wheat, I say, "Want a hop to school?"

Christopher glares at me fiercely, and I realize immediately that this is a very stupid idea.

After breakfast, Becky calls from the front door, "Bye-bye, wish me luck."

"Luck," I say.

Christopher stares out the living room window while I wash dishes. Taking a chance, I say, "It'll work out. You make friends quick."

But when I turn around, he is gone. I hurry to the window and watch him walking down Anderson Hill like a man headed for the gallows. My son disappears around a turn in the narrow road.

THE NEXT ten or fifteen days blur together—weekday mornings like fire drills, cleaning house, and struggling with the memoir about my father through the day. I put dinner on the table at five, much too early for me, but everyone is home and hungry then. I have never thought of myself as a "househusband." With ten children in his family and a wife who worked, my father did his share of cooking and housecleaning. He never saw it as "woman's work" and he liked to cook—especially wild foods like eels or fish. When Becky and I married, we fell into a pattern of sharing the housework without discussion or argument. I cook and more or less run the house day by day because I'm home to do it. I was right about one thing: I was having a hard time trying to cook interesting food in this small Appalachian town. I told myself that things would improve once I got a deer.

One day does stand out from that September. We would heat the house with wood, and I called someone who had put an announcement about wood for sale on the bulletin board at the IGA store. A few days later, late in the afternoon, I was rolling out pastry for quiche when someone thumped on the door like a lumberjack.

The man on the front steps was in his late twenties or early thirties. He had an unkempt beard, soiled jeans, scuffed high-top boots, and the yeasty smell of beer. As I remember, he was wearing one of those caps with a manufactured joke on it—"Professional West Virginia Beer Drinker" or "Born to Raise Hell."

He said, "You the one called about firewood?"

I said, "Yes, sir," and walked out onto the steps.

He said, "We don't do the stacking. We'll pitch it wherever you want, but if you want it stacked, that's your job. You know what they say about firewood."

"I'm not sure."

"It warms three times—cut'n, stack'n, and burn'n."

"Sounds like a good deal," I said. I pointed the rolling pin to the other side of the driveway and said, "Pitch it over there."

When I turned back, he was staring at me openly, looking me up and down. I was covered with flour.

"Making quiche," I said. When he squinted in confusion, I said, "It's like pie."

He looked back down at his friend behind the wheel of the truck. They exchanged wide-eyed looks, and then he turned on his heels and hurried off. I went back inside.

They backed up in the driveway and began tossing wood into the yard. As I went on with the pastry, I could hear them through the screen door. The man who had come to the door would say something like, "Oh, sugar babe, are you a-baking me pie?" His friend would answer, "Yes, dear," in a falsetto. When I looked out the bedroom window to check on their progress, I occasionally saw one of them stop to wipe sweat away and then perform a little drag queen bit, an extended limp wrist, the other hand on his hip. This made his partner laugh out loud. They were entertaining themselves at my expense.

I was more amused than offended, at least at first. For one thing they were talented cutups and made me think of Heckle and Jeckle—those cartoon wise-guy crows. I also knew men like them: knockabouts who lived the way I did as an undergraduate, drifting from one minimum-wage job to another. The marginal business of cutting and selling firewood would appeal to them because they could work as hard as they wanted to, when they wanted to, with no boss to push them around. They probably ate more deer and trout than store-bought meat.

If the biography I imagined was off, I don't think it was off by much. They came closer to resembling "hillbillies" than anyone I had met since arriving in August. But I have met men like this every-where—deckhands from crab or salmon boats in Kodiak, ranch hands drinking beer in cowboy bars in Montana, oil-rig roughnecks in Louisiana, lumberjacks in Maine. If I had met the two of them along a trout stream, we might well have become friends. Now, of course, they had the wrong idea.

After they left, I found the encounter less amusing. It highlighted the downside of Appalachian culture, a provincial intolerance that runs like a current through mountain communities. The fact that the same current exists in most of rural America was of little consolation; I had brought my family here.

I don't think Christopher said anything about school through September. This was not unusual; Chris had always taken school seriously but never cared to talk about it at home. The problem was he was not talking about much of anything. On most days he was preoccupied and clearly unhappy. I remember a lot of tense, quiet evening meals. On the weekends he went over to Green Bank to spend time with cousin Troy and other friends. The distance between us might not have been growing, but it wasn't shrinking either. When I talked to Becky about this, she said, "Quit worrying so much. Chris will do just fine. Let him get settled in."

Franklin High is not far from the IGA grocery store where I shopped every other day. From a road above the market, I could look down on the back of the school and the athletic field. I would some-times park there for five or ten minutes and wonder where Chris was right then. Most of the time I wouldn't see anyone there—only a few crows on the grass. But occasionally, it was a madhouse. The football team, the marching band, and squads of cheerleaders would all be out practicing. In their scrub uniforms, the boys would do jumping jacks and wind sprints or slam into one another while the coach, a man called Big Smith, barked at them. On the sidelines, ranks of girls would shake pom-poms and chant while the band marched through intricate patterns to the clicking of drumsticks. There was something lovely about all of this. Excited kids getting ready for the football season. High school football and basketball are Appalachian passions. Parents, grandparents, aunts, uncles, older brothers and sisters pack the sidelines of the fields they played on in earlier years. Family, community, and local history all come together across the generations—small towns, bright fall days, the excitement of rooting for the home team.

But there is also something worrisome about Appalachian preoccupation with high school sports. Adolescents in towns like Franklin can be so consumed by football and basketball there is no room for other interests in their lives. Boys want to be rugged footballers and girls want to jump around in short skirts to cheer them on. Up to a point, as I have said, I have nothing against this. Becky was a cheerleader and her brother Bob played football as well as basketball. Jamie and Beaty had done the same a generation before. Like many of the successful, interesting adults in Pendleton County, they all had survived the experience with pleasant memories. But at nine years old, Shelly was a passionate reader and had started to write poems. How would these interests compete with the flash and dazzle of high school cheerleading?

Christopher had already made it clear that he did not want to be tested for Franklin High's "gifted" program. Most of the "regular guys" thought of gifted students as geeks and he was not about to label himself that way. This did not trouble Becky and me too much. Gifted programs, in our opinion, were good ideas that too often went astray. They ended up reinforcing notions of hillbillies and class in mountain communities where those imaginary distinctions already caused trouble. Still, Christopher's decision left me uneasy.

One evening near the end of the month, Chris came home outraged. Slamming the door, he yelled, "This place sucks!" and launched into a tirade about "rednecks" pushing him around in the hall between classes. He was so upset his account of what happened was incoherent. When I asked him to slow down and back up, he glared at me, then stormed down the basement steps. Prince rattled the windows once again.

Later that evening I knocked on Christopher's door. The music was so loud he may not have heard me. When I opened the door, he was sitting on the bed bouncing a tennis ball on his new graphite racket. I turned the volume down and made a lame joke about my eardrums, but he did not look away from the bouncing ball.

I said, "You wanna play some tennis?"

"Yeah, right," he said, losing his concentration. The ball bounced off to the other side of the room.

"Like with who?" he said.

"Me?"

He looked at me and said, "This is a joke, right?"

I shrugged.

We pulled into the small park below Franklin filled with kiddy swings, seesaws, a roundabout, and monkey bars. You can pitch horseshoes or play softball in a wide field that still looks like a pasture. There are two tennis courts behind a Cyclone fence next to a small basketball court. No one was playing tennis, but half a dozen boys were playing basketball, shirts against skins. Seeing them, Christopher stiffened and an odd expression took his face. We watched them run up and down the court for a few minutes without talking.

I am overweight, disheveled, and cannot play tennis. Chris was not about to walk onto the tennis court with me while those boys were there. Sparing my feelings, he said something about homework and playing some other night. I suggested another tennis court over in the South Fork Valley twenty minutes away. It was off in the woods above a farm, and rarely used. I knew about it because a friend lived nearby and years ago we had gone walking there.

As I expected, the rustic court was deserted. It was this strange small place in the oak woods. The Cyclone fence around it sagged, and the asphalt surface was cracked and weedy, but the net was in decent shape. For our purposes, the court would do just fine.

"There goes a lizard!" Chris shouted.

He dropped his tennis bag and ran down along the fence. A gray swift, as long as my index finger, was skittering along between the fence loops like quicksilver. I darted into the court to chase it from that side and we ran back and forth trying to outmaneuver it. At the end of the fence, I made a wild dive and ended up on the ground as the lizard disappeared into the grass.

Chris said, "You're slowing down," and laughed out loud for the first time since leaving Oswego.

Playing sets was impossible. I could not return Christopher's blistering serve. Given that, we decided to forgo games and work on his serve. On the far end of the court, Christopher moved from one side to the other slamming balls over the net while I called out "short," "long," "wide," or "on the money!" Moving in counterpoint, we fell into a kind of rhythm that felt good to me. Locked in, we lost sight of ourselves and became the activity itself, the "pock" of tennis balls rising through green shadowy trees on a September evening.

But at some point I realized that Christopher was trying to hit me. He would loft the ball gently above his head, twist his body into a corkscrew, then fire with a tortured expression on his face. I skipped left or right half a dozen times, then just stood still. After three or four balls whizzed past, Chris stopped and said, "Now what?"

I said, "It's Freudian."

"What is?"

"You trying to hit me."

"I'm not."

"Yes, you are, but you don't know it. You know what Siggy vould zay?"

"Not that guy again."

Chris, Becky, and I sometimes talked about Freud. Becky dismissed it all—especially penis envy—as "foolishness some man made up." Chris wasn't quite sure. He gave me a look and broke into a broad southern accent, saying, "You know what your trouble is, O'Brien?"

He didn't have to say any more. I knew he was going to quote Tom Andrews, my fishing partner from Virginia. He was Christopher's adopted crazy uncle. Tom was always taking the time to straighten me out, and among other things he had once said, "You know what your trouble is, O'Brien? You do all that damned deep thinking and it never gets you anywhere. You're spinning your wheels, boy."

I said, "Too much deep thinking?"

We both laughed.

Driving back we talked about Tom, the crazy things he had done and said when Chris and I went down to fish his pond over the years. Things were right between us again. I had my best friend back. Whatever lay ahead, we would deal with it together. That's all that mattered.

I rarely remember entire dreams but sometimes flickering images stay in my mind: That night I was between my father and my son, playing tennis with them. Shadowy figures stood lined up behind Chris and my grandfather stood behind my dad. We were all trying to hit one another with the ball.

ON SEPTEMBER 12, the *Pendleton Times* ran a front-page picture
of the bearded man I had been noticing on Main Street. There he was,
beaming through his black whiskers, handing a rocking chair to Jennings Randolph, a retired U.S. senator. According to the caption, the
donor's name was Jim Underwood, and as I had guessed, he was part
of Woodlands Institute. The rocking chair represented a Woodlands
award for distinguished service. Senator Randolph, a man of considerable influence in West Virginia, seemed understandably pleased.

The photograph meant little to me, but county people thought a
great deal about it. By then, Woodlands had been in the county for
about twelve years and its relations with the community were poor.
Simply put, most residents did not understand or trust Woodlands
Institute. Each time McCoy published a front-page article about the
organization—and he had done so many times over the years—the
county gossip network switched on. For weeks after September 12,
when people spoke in post office lobbies, country stores, diners, or
church parking lots, or on kitchen phones, the talk included Underwood and Woodlands: What were "those people" up to this time, and
where was this business headed?

The difficulty began when Woodlands arrived in the summer of
1972. Five come-heres—two men, two women, and an adolescent
boy—just seemed to materialize on a mountaintop in the North Fork
Valley one August morning. Within days people began to notice the
new arrivals on the streets of Franklin and Circleville. The woman
was blond and attractive. One of the men, named King, wore bamboo
sandals without socks and sported a red cowboy bandanna around his
neck. The other, Dan'l—as in Dan'l Boone—was bearded and wore
an Australian Digger hat with one side pinned up. He kept a long
sheath knife hanging from his belt as he walked in or out of country
stores. In provincial Pendleton County, the men's appearance struck
people as strange.

Small things created still more apprehension. The gates on the
entry roads to the institute's mountaintop property were locked, but
when Dan'l was asked why, he insisted the gates were never locked.
Deer hunters were run off the land. A reporter from the *Highland
Gazette,* in neighboring Highland County, Virginia, drove up to the
Woodlands property but was sent back home without an interview. In

time, county farmers learned that the institute had paid $250,000 for the forty acres on the mountaintop—twice the amount that steep, high land normally sold for. Families struggling to make ends meet, and losing ground, wondered where "that kind of money came from." Then county people learned that the newcomers were sleeping on the floor of an abandoned farmhouse that sheep had used as a storm shelter. If they had $250,000 to buy the land, why were those people sleeping on the floor of an abandoned house? For that matter, what was Woodlands Institute and why had it landed in Pendleton County?

All of these questions had straightforward answers. Woodlands Institute, at least at the start, was a wilderness school that in some ways resembled Outward Bound. Dan'l Taylor-Ide (Dan'l Taylor and Jennifer Ide married in the seventies and, like many young professionals at the time, joined last names) hoped to attract students from private schools in Washington, D.C., and Baltimore. Pendleton County provided wilderness and proximity to both cities. Dan affected the Digger hat and sheath knife hoping to look the part of a wilderness school director. There is nothing wrong with locking gates on your own property. Many come-heres do not approve of deer hunting and in fact often run hunters off their land. Refusing an interview with a small weekly paper may not have been the wisest public relations move, but there is nothing sinister about it. The $250,000 came from the Nature Conservancy. Dan'l had little ready cash in the seventies and had started his wilderness school with little more than his wits and determination. But county people did not understand Woodlands, and in Appalachia what is not understood presents a threat.

As time passed, encounters strained relations further. Dan'l, the obvious leader, had dark eyes that seemed quite large—"Napoleon eyes," one South Fork Valley man observed. He was extremely bright and intense. After what should have been casual meetings with him, people spoke of feeling "used" or "manipulated." One man describes his first chance meeting with Dan'l as ". . . an interrogation. He bore into me, firing question after question for over an hour. It was like being verbally machine-gunned. He was going to rip out of me every last fact I knew about Pendleton County."

A Franklin woman described an evening with Jennifer Taylor-Ide: "We were supposed to go to the PTO meeting together in her car. I put on makeup. It's what we do when we go out around here. Well, she just thought I was funny-looking and said, 'Well I guess I'll just have to get all dressed up next time I go to a meeting.' It was the way she said it, snickering and making fun."

I should say that reactions like this—and unfortunately there were far too many of them—have as much to do with Appalachian sensibilities as anything else. Like black people or Native Americans, Appalachians struggle with stereotypes. They are often inclined to take offense when none is offered or perhaps to make too much of something that should be ignored. Still, brief encounters reinforced the community's bad opinion of Woodlands.

Oddly, the *Pendleton Times* added to the institute's problems. There are no reporters for the county paper. People submit "articles," and if McCoy deems them accurate and newsworthy, he prints them. As editor, he had never advanced an opinion about Woodlands, but seemed eager to publish anything the institute submitted, often on the front page. About a year after the institute moved in, he printed a long and detailed "Statement of Purpose" submitted by Woodlands. According to the statement, the institute was "a school for schools" organized on a complicated two-tier system. On one tier, Woodlands offered psychological counseling for troubled individuals or families. On the other, they offered programs for "all schools—elementary, high school and college . . ." Courses were arranged around "backpacking expeditions, white-water rafting, rock climbing, cave exploring, trout fishing, topography, falconry, nature photography, survival skills, and wildflower collecting. . . . At present we run survey courses in literature, history, biology, geology, philosophy, physical education, and ecology. Schools and colleges are coming and from as far away as New York City."

Reading the statement, one might have concluded that Woodlands was an extremely busy small college on the mountaintop. But people in the North Fork Valley had noticed no busloads of people passing their farms on the way to the Woodlands facility. In fact, when they drove past the mountaintop property, nothing seemed to be going on. One Franklin man took a group of thirty 4-H children on a tour of the Woodlands campus. The institute was to provide lunch. Watching Dan'l Taylor-Ide make grilled cheese sandwiches two at a time on a small hot plate, the Franklin man wondered how all of the things mentioned in the paper could possibly be taking place when there was almost nothing on the mountaintop.

Then in 1978, a very strange incident involving the Pendleton County School Board made relations much worse. Taylor-Ide wanted the state of West Virginia to officially recognize Woodlands as a private school, and this required the county board's approval as a first step. The board insisted on an inspection of the institute's mountaintop facility. A date and time were set. Taylor-Ide called the superintendent a day and a half before the tour and confirmed arrangements.

The day in question, a December Sunday in 1975, was cold and miserable. An icy rain fell through most of the morning. The board members met at the superintendent's office, then drove into the North Fork Valley and up the dirt road only to find the Woodlands gate locked. The men waited for an hour, but no one came to let them in.

Taylor-Ide's account sometime later strained credibility. As Dan'l explained things, he had come down with excruciating back pain the day of the tour. He called the superintendent and canceled, but by the time he offered the explanation—months later—that superintendent had left the county "under a cloud" and no one knew where he was. At that time calls from the North Fork Valley to Franklin were long distance and Dan'l should have had a record of his phone call. Unfortunately, as Dan'l explained things, the office phone was out that day, and he made the call from a pay phone in Circleville. An assistant flew Dan'l to a New England hospital for medical treatment in a very small plane. There, from his sickbed, he wrote a letter of apology to the board, but the letter was lost in the mail. The copy from the Woodlands file also mysteriously disappeared. Given the fact that Dan'l needed the board's approval, it made no sense to "slap the board in the face." On the other hand, Dan'l's explanation just seemed too bizarre. The community was caught between two interpretations and could not quite believe either one.

The institute's reputation took a surreal turn in December 1983—eight months before Becky and I moved to Franklin. On the front page of the December 8 issue of the *Pendleton Times*, beside a large picture of a bear skull, half-inch headlines proclaimed: "Pendleton Expedition Discovers New Mammal Species in Nepal." The article went on to say that on a Woodlands expedition to Nepal, Dr. Taylor-Ide explained that "he . . . had discovered substantial evidence of a new species of small bear that lives in treetop nests high in the Himalayan Mountains." According to the article, Taylor-Ide added, "Although the evidence discovered up to now does not firmly prove the existence of the new species, it is substantial enough to warrant announcement to the scientific world. . . ."

But in a bizarre coincidence, the King of Nepal was the guest speaker at a National Press Club luncheon in Washington, D.C., on the very day the discovery was announced in the county paper. After King Birendra's brief speech, a reporter asked him about the discovery of the new bear. The king replied, "As far as I know on this, it is not a *new* bear. It is a new bear in the scientific term because it has not been recorded in the books. But for Nepalese, we have known about it. . . . And we have them in the *zoo*."

A county woman named Ingrid Hailer was listening to the Press Club luncheon on the radio that day. She wrote a letter to the *Pendleton Times* congratulating "the scientists of Woodlands Institute on discovering a rare new bear in Nepal," but added, "Why didn't they visit the zoo in Katmandu, where one of these exotic bears has been living?"

Dan'l's response, printed a few weeks later, was virtually impossible to understand. He seemed to be saying that the bear was common in zoos but unknown as well. Once again, county people were perplexed. Making unfounded claims about discovering "the first new mammal in one hundred years" would be a wildly dangerous thing to do if your organization depended upon grants. It was extremely difficult to believe that Dan'l would do something that reckless. But his letter of explanation made no sense. How could he have discovered a bear in the zoo? The Woodlands mystery deepened.

By the time the Underwoods—Jim, Janet, and their son, Yar—moved into the North Fork Valley community of Riverton, the community's opinion of Woodlands, or of anyone involved with Woodlands, was extremely negative. Jim, naturally gregarious, is not shy about introducing himself and starting friendly conversation. But residents of Riverton—population eighty—resented the Underwoods from the start and responded to Jim's open smile and extended hand with icy glares and stony silence. He was part of Woodlands and that was all they needed to know.

Those two years in the North Fork Valley were hardest on Yar, who was ten years old when the Underwoods moved in. With an IQ in the Mensa range, Yar stood out. He had no interest in football, basketball, hunting, or fishing, and while not a show-off, he did nothing to disguise his remarkable intelligence. Being a smart newcomer in a rural school is trouble enough, but county boys thought of Yar as part of Woodlands and this made things considerably worse. For Yar, the bus rides to and from Seneca Rocks School were pure horror; catcalls, hoots of derision, and broad imitations were followed by rounds of cruel laughter. Some mornings, he simply refused to go to school. In Riverton, he would not step off the front porch without one or both parents. In fact, Yar was living the nightmare I sometimes had about Christopher.

Jim moved to Franklin in 1983, and here too some of his neighbors resented his presence at once. Some people were more concerned about his picture with Senator Randolph than with the other articles about the institute in the *Pendleton Times*. Most West Virginians feel uneasy about their politicians in Charleston. State politics has been, and still is, notoriously corrupt, and people around the state are not convinced that Charleston has their community's best interests at heart. As John Sites, a Franklin man, observed, "These people think we're a bunch of ignorant hillbillies. They talk to us like we're morons. You get that bunch cozying up with the crooks in Charleston, and it can't be good for us. You watch." Sites did not know how prophetic he was.

I don't know how aware Jim was of his neighbors' resentment in September 1984, but I do know he was happy. After Riverton, Franklin with its nine hundred inhabitants felt virtually cosmopolitan. In Jim's opinion, there were interesting people to talk with and things to do. Come-heres in and around the county seat have a lively social year, and they invited the Underwoods to most events. Jim joined the choir of a downtown church and became a member of Franklin's Rescue Squad. The Taylor-Ides had also moved from the North Fork Valley into Franklin and now lived five minutes away. Yar could walk rather than ride the bus to school and had come to better terms with his situation.

AS SEPTEMBER fades in the southern Appalachians, the light gets thinner, and something stirs the air. When the wind moves through the trees on the mountains, I find myself staring at the treetops, expecting something to announce itself. "Surely some revelation is at hand," as Yeats wrote. The season has not changed, but you sense that it's about to. A spicy smell laces the air, something vaguely like ginger and oregano. The birds get restless. Robins, solitary through summer, start to appear on lawns in flocks of forty or fifty. The turkey vultures begin to spiral east to their wintering grounds in the Shenandoah Valley. The first thing to take color is Virginia creeper, a lovely vine that threads up and around tree trunks and branches. One September evening fishing the South Branch, I stopped to look at a scarlet ribbon threading the green wall on the bank. The slanting light making magic with the red and green took my breath.

On the third weekend of September, county churches and civic organizations sponsor Treasure Mountain Festival. The event is billed as a celebration of Pendleton County's history—complete with a myth about Shawnee treasure in the mountains—but the two days are really an opportunity for local groups to make some money. And why not? An hour away, just over Shenandoah Mountain, the Wal-Marts and the malls put more Franklin businesses under every year.

On that third weekend, booths pop up like mushrooms after a downpour. You can buy local crafts, raffle tickets on trucks or hunting rifles, cornbread and beans, country ham sandwiches, hot dogs, hamburgers, pork BBQ, apple cider, and buckwheat pancakes. For a few dollars, you can ride a horse through the mountains or tour Franklin's historic homes. Bluegrass bands pick out tunes like "Keep on the Sunny Side" in parking lots while Hank Williams Jr. or ZZ Top blares from passing trucks. There is a parade, of course; antique cars and fire trucks from Pendleton and nearby counties cruise down Main Street with their lights flashing. Pretty girls wave self-consciously from crepe-paper floats and high school marching bands accompany squads of Twirlette girls in outfits that sparkle in the fall sunlight. It's small-town Appalachia strutting its stuff. Wonderful Americana, if you like that sort of thing.

The weekend does involve some county history. Each year descendants of the original settlers reenact the Fort Seybert massacre of 1758 in the South Fork Valley. County men and women dress as Killbuck, his braves, and their own ancestors who took shelter in the fort.

Sly speeches in pidgin English are countered by noble speeches in English without contractions. Earsplitting reports from black-powder rifles and war whoops echo down the valley as people tumble to the pasture grass. In two hundred years, our descendants could make a play about us watching this play.

Out Smith Creek Road in the South Branch Valley, the county theater group has transformed an old church into the Smith Creek Playhouse. Each year they present a play. One year it was *Torn Valleys*, a Civil War drama about a North Fork woman who walks to the South Branch Valley on a winter night to warn relatives of an impending raid. The ride out Smith Creek Road is as good as the play. The town of Franklin gives way to farms and farms to deep woods in quick time. Then you come to a church deep in the woods. One night on the way back a great horned owl swooped through my headlights with a writhing skunk in its talons.

After dark on Friday and Saturday night, downtown looks like a carnival—lights, music, milling crowds, and the buzz of many voices, all punctuated by the delighted squeals of small children. As I started home one night, a short man with a head that seemed much too large and round stepped right in front of me, blocking my path. When I tried to step around him, he said, "Hold on here just a minute. I got something for ya." I said, "What's that?" He held out a raffle ticket for a pickup truck and said, "This here's a brand-new truck for ten dollars. You can't beat that now, can ya?" "How do I know I'll win?" "Well now, you look lucky to me." I said, "I don't have that kind of money," and started to walk away, but he quickly stepped sideways and blocked my path, saying, "Hold on just a minute now. I need to show you something."

Reaching into his back pocket, he pulled out an old postcard picture and said, "Just look here at this." Despite myself, I looked. It was a photograph of a man dressed in a loincloth who weighed more than six hundred pounds. He was "Happy Jack," the biggest Ruritan in the world. I said, "My God!" and could not take my eyes from the picture. Before I knew it, I had bought a raffle ticket, and the man was off stalking his next victim.

The salesman's name was Everett Mitchell, of whom a Franklin man once said, "Everett ought to just go out and get himself a gun and a mask. It'd make things easier on everybody."

As I started up Anderson Hill, I saw George Dice looking at the scene downtown through his binoculars. It must have looked like Borges's Aleph through one lens, this bright sphere of color and motion containing the entire world. A festival in town and an orange moon above the valley means the end of summer in Pendleton County. I was pleased to be here.

7. Fall in the Mountains

IN OCTOBER the haze of late summer gives way to diamond light. The smell of wood smoke and apples laces the air like perfume. Chain saws snarl from the hills and ridges as men top off their winter woodpiles. Temperatures get a little crazy this time of year. The midday sun can strike like a hammer and feel hotter than it does in August, but step into the shade of a mountain, and you shiver. In the evenings, shadows stretch longer and seem darker and more mysterious. The narrowness of the valleys limits the amount of sunlight the county gets all through the year, but by October, the days grow perceptibly shorter, and when the sun drops behind the western ridge, the night air has the ashy taste of winter.

Everyone has a theory about what brings on the best fall color: little rain and mild frost, no frost or rain at all, hot afternoons and cold nights, how serious the end-of-summer drought has been. So far I have no theory, but when fall is at its best—pure light and blazing color on every ridge—it's my favorite season in the Appalachian Mountains. At least it is until spring arrives.

October is a busy, anxious month on county farms. Families have kept their cattle and sheep in mountaintop pastures during the summer and must move stock down into valley bottoms before the weather turns. The timing of this operation can be tricky. Farmers want to keep stock in high pastures "as long as the grass holds on top." Bringing stock down means the start of winter feeding, tossing out hay every day. Cows gain weight on good grass, but at best only maintain weight on hay. If you bring them down early, they lose weight and you lose money. But winter feeding is the dreariest job on a mountain farm—frigid mornings when the truck won't start, wind-driven sleet or snow—and once started, it seems to go on forever.

On the other hand, getting caught by an early storm can mean serious trouble. When heavy rain turns unexpectedly to snow on the mountaintops, farmers must drive up steep dirt roads with wagonloads of hay, and sometimes even the largest tractors cannot plow through. Faced with starving stock, men become reckless and suicidal. Slamming tractors into wall-high drifts again and again, they sometimes end up pinned beneath upturned tractors, bleeding or freezing to death in the snow.

In October, families sell some of their summer-fattened cattle, the largest source of farm income. An operation can earn or lose a little on lambs throughout the year, but farmers "make it or break it" when they sell cattle each fall. In September men begin to call buyers. Buyers are often local men who gave up farming to go into the cattle business, and this makes relations somewhat tenuous. Buyers are still neighbors, but in a sense, they've "gone to the other side" and are therefore almost traitors. These phone conversations are often meandering—how's the family, crazy weather lately, local gossip, a joke if you're that kind of fellow. Eventually the talk drifts toward prices and numbers, though farmers avoid commitments for as long as possible. After talking to other buyers, and a few trusted neighbors, a man often calls the first buyer again. In the end, both parties agree to dates, times, locations, and numbers.

As sale day approaches, farmers become hard to live with. They have sleepless nights filled with doubt. Perhaps they should hold more cattle back until spring, hoping for better prices. Then again, feed prices are rising and they're calling for a bad winter. Maybe that buyer up in Pennsylvania a neighbor mentioned . . . Generally all of the second-guessing is pointless. The regional market sets prices that are announced on the radio several times each day. Buyers never offer less and very rarely offer more. The truth is, most men know how well or badly they have done before they agree to the sale, but refuse to accept facts until the check is signed. It's gambler's logic.

Sale days vary depending upon the number of cows involved, but most start at dawn. Farmer and buyer meet at a designated pasture and, after a transparent attempt at friendly talk, perform a small ritual. Both men have brought a hundred-pound sack of feed with them. They check the scale with both sacks and then begin a long, crazy day. Shouting farmhands push, kick, and prod bawling cows up a wooden incline to the scale. Men yell numbers out while top hands, or sometimes wives in nearby trucks, write them down. They beat and kick the terrified animals into the buyer's semi all day long, and then, depending upon the size of an operation, farmers drive home with checks in their coverall pockets written for amounts like $16,000, $45,000, or $280,000. This can be considerably more or substantially less than the year's operating expenses and loan payments, but for most Octobers since the 1970s, the latter has been true.

As anywhere, the cattle business in Pendleton County has always been chancy. Disease, drought, erratic market prices, and plain hard luck create bad years. But in the past a smart farmer with an eye for "growthy" cows, and just enough luck, made good years more than pay for bad. This changed in the seventies. The federal government began to sell grain to the Soviet Union, which made cattle feed expensive. Dairy subsidies fluctuated wildly. The American Medical Association's pronouncements about beef and cholesterol added to problems. More than anything else, it was agribusiness. Sitting in some Manhattan skyscraper, a man who may never have been within ten miles of a live cow could tap a computer key and flood the American market with half a million head from Argentina. Since the early seventies, the real question in Pendleton County has been not whether October would be good or bad, but rather just how bad it was going to be.

Also in the mid-seventies, something baffling began to happen to Pendleton County sheep. Although farmers do not sell lambs in large numbers in the fall, sheep, like cattle, must be rounded up and driven into the valley bottoms before winter. In most cases, this gives families the first opportunity since spring to take an accurate count. With flocks summering on isolated mountaintops, people expect losses in October. Farm dogs, responding to what remains of wolf genes, occasionally form packs on moonlit nights and go on murderous sprees, returning at daybreak as the same loyal, albeit blood-soaked, pets. Marauding black bears can devastate flocks. Bald and golden eagles occasionally kill new lambs.

But in the seventies losses to predation rose dramatically and county families were mystified. Predators leave calling cards: Dogs tear sheep into pieces and leave pastures littered with bloody carnage. Bears rip the milk-filled udders from lactating ewes. Eagles leave talon marks and eat the eyes from lambs. This new predator—

whatever it was—left two vampirish punctures on the dead lamb's throat, but rarely blood or any other sign of struggle. At times, the predator opened the body cavity to devour internal organs and intestines, but it even did this with surgical precision, as if a deer hunter had field-dressed the carcass. County farmers had never seen anything like this, and nothing in the stories and lore of 250 years explained it either. (One October morning, I drove into a high pasture with a North Fork man named Raymond Phares. Standing above two dead lambs, Phares stared off at the surrounding trees and sky, trying to read the world's intention. Out rabbit hunting, I have watched my father do the same thing—as if the world was a book written in cryptic text.)

Then, reports of coyote sightings began to appear in the *Pendleton Times,* and as the sightings became more common, losses to predation spiraled higher. Finally, on a rainy day in 1978, a South Fork Valley man shot one of the animals. As news spread, neighbors stopped at his farm "just to get a look-see." Well, yes, it did look like a dog—sort of. But that thick, foxlike tail did not belong on a dog, and when men lifted the dead animal's upper lip, they found enormous eye-teeth, real fangs. Those strange puncture marks on a dead lamb's throat—right there it was.

Within a short time, turkey hunters shot several other coyotes. For a time, county men thought they could simply kill coyotes off. The animals were incredibly elusive, however. When losses reached double figures in several North Fork Valley flocks, two young men drew a line in the sand. Outstanding hunters, they would camp out for an entire summer back in the mountains and learn to hunt coyotes. They shot a dozen, but found signs of fifty or sixty and gave up. Not only were coyotes "damn near impossible to hunt," they were breeding faster than rabbits. Gradually, it became clear that all three valleys would be overrun and that sheep farming in Pendleton County would end.

In many ways this was harder on families than the decline in cattle. There had never been much money in sheep—far less since the advent of vast sheep corporations in Australia and New Zealand—but for many people, raising sheep felt more like subsistence farming than raising cattle. Families held on to flocks long after shrinking profits justified the time and work because it was something

Appalachian farmers had always done. But even the most determined families could not raise sheep just to provide food for coyotes. Still, selling off the family sheep was wrenching. After selling the last of his flock, Raymond Phares—the man who took me into his high pasture—said, "Some evenings I go by that pasture and can't believe it's empty. It's the quiet that gets to me. You stand there and just hear nothing. I'm the first Phares without sheep in two hundred years. It don't seem right."

But where had the coyotes come from and why had they suddenly appeared in Pendleton County? County farmers came up with an Appalachian answer: "They turned them loose on us. Maybe just a dozen one night and a few dozen some other time. Now they're breeding." In this case, "they" means the politicians in Charleston, more specifically the Department of Natural Resources. Ask why the DNR would release coyotes in sheep country, and farmers say, "To make the tourists and come-heres happy. All those people have this idea about wilderness and wild animals." It is pointless to suggest that coyotes have been expanding their range eastward from the Midwest for several decades; that's "their" cover story.

Like other American minorities, Appalachians—or many of them, in any case—believe that some mysterious "they" is always behind the scenes exploiting them. If a chain of unfortunate events lacks an obvious explanation, certain people conclude that somewhere in the foggy distance "they" are up to no good again. It might be the politicians in Charleston or those vegetarian, animal-rights, New Age, gay, lesbian, politically correct, drug-crazed hippies from the strange world beyond the mountains. In fact, sometimes these people and "the crooks in Charleston" conspire.

This explanation of events, at least in part, amounts to a counter-reality held by an American minority that has always felt maligned. Listen long enough and it begins to sound like paranoia, but before dismissing the view altogether one might consider a number of things. The same agribusiness that has devastated the cattle business in Pendleton County manifests itself in flocks of New Zealand sheep running into the millions. "Shepherds" in helicopters talk to computers. As agribusiness puts small Midwestern farms under, the abandoned land—especially when it stretches into miles—offers perfect breeding grounds for coyotes, and the animals expand their range east. As Pendleton County farms fail, come-heres buy up three or four adjacent properties to create what amounts to private parks that provide ideal habitat for coyotes. More coyotes kill more sheep and this speeds the rate of failure, which provides more coyote habitat. This may not be a conspiracy in any strict sense, but the idea that people, money, and power can dovetail to exploit minorities isn't altogether wrong either.

And so in October 1984 this is what county residents saw—disastrous cattle sales, a plague of coyotes, failing farms, deep anxiety over where the community was headed, and mounting fears about Woodlands Institute. When I look back on that October, I can see these elements coming together in an explosive way, but this is only hindsight. That first fall I was, as they say, blissfully ignorant. The farms I drove past looked like Appalachian postcards. The fences were up and tight. The barns looked good. The cattle and sheep in pastures, at least to my unpracticed eye, looked fat and healthy. Smoke curling from farmhouse chimneys suggested warm family life inside. Franklin was a toy town set below a Christmas tree. With the cool, bright weather, my neighbors stepped faster on Main Street and they seemed to smile more quickly and more often. On bright October mornings, surrounded by diamond light and blazing color, it is hard to worry about anything for very long. Like most county people, I felt lucky just to be alive and in the mountains.

A BLACK walnut tree stands in the corner of my yard on Anderson Hill. For the past week, sitting on the front steps on restless nights, I have heard the nuts hit the ground with a decided thunk. October is the time to harvest them, so on this brisk morning I cross the yard with my stew pot. As large and round as billiard balls, the nuts are encased in a thick green husk that brings rhino skin to mind. In all of nature, there is no smell like fresh black walnuts—astringent, biting, spicy. That too brings my father back.

We are in the kitchen in the old place on Greenway Avenue. He has spread the *Evening Bulletin* across the table and we are cracking walnuts with a brick and a ball-peen hammer. That unforgettable smell fills the kitchen and my memory now. Smashing off the husks, my fingers stain nicotine yellow, like the world's heaviest chain smoker. The Indians used walnut husks to dye things, my father tells me.

He always put the shucked nuts on the roof of the back shed to "ripen up." Having no back shed in Franklin, I arrange mine along a board against the east side of the house, then step back to admire my accomplishment. I sometimes make an apple pound cake with black walnuts and brandy. I will make one on some cold November night, when the nuts are ripe. Sitting here, I can almost taste it. After I've washed my hands three times, the stain and smell, though diminished, lingers.

Pacing between fits and starts of writing, I look out the kitchen window to see a red squirrel running across the lawn with one of my walnuts in its mouth. Red squirrels—"fairy" squirrels, old-timers call them—are quite small, perhaps twice the size of a chipmunk. This makes the walnut seem as large as a baseball in its mouth. I laugh out loud.

The phone rings. I think it's going to be Tom Andrews calling from Virginia. I called Tom a few days after Chris and I played tennis in the South Fork Valley, and since then he has called back several times just to annoy me. He begins each conversation with a rank hillbilly joke. "A West Virginia virgin? An ugly first-grade girl who can run faster than her father." "How many West Virginians does it take to eat an opossum? Three, one to eat it and two to watch both ways for traffic on the road." "The state bird of West Virginia? The housefly." Walking toward the phone, I brace myself for another onslaught.

It was the agent. We had a conversation not unlike a farmer and a cattle buyer.

"I'm just fine, and you?"

"Marvelous. These fall days in Manhattan!"

"Beautiful down here, too."

"All moved in?"

"Pretty much. Got a few more boxes and . . ."

As always, the talk meandered to "How's the writing going, by the by?" I had been sliding artfully around the truth for some time but worried about losing an opportunity, I lied outright. "Going great! I've got eighty or a hundred pages of terrific stuff."

I went on to tell him about George Dice, the people in the Laundromat, and the two men who brought the firewood while I was making quiche. He said, "Wonderful! Wonderful!" and asked when the pages would be on his desk. I told him before Thanksgiving, and he said "Perfect" and told me for the second or third time that he admired me for actually moving into Appalachia to do this project. We said good-bye.

Hanging up, I thought, Now you've done it. I paced around awhile wondering about the mess I had created for myself and then about where the agent imagined I had moved. Why did he admire me for moving to West Virginia? As he sat in his Manhattan office talking on the phone to me, what image filled his mind? I should say that this man, who died several years after that call, was bright, genteel, and empathetic. He wanted a compassionate book about the Appalachia he had in mind. But what place was that?

Pacing around, I also began to wonder about Tom's jokes. Beyond getting on my nerves, Tom meant no harm and I had done my best to turn the jokes back on Virginia. But I have heard jokes like this all my life. In fact, a radio station in Washington, D.C., had a West Virginia joke last night. Listeners called in to tell Appalachian jokes as rank as Tom's. Could there be a night for black or Jewish jokes? Why was it acceptable to ridicule Appalachians but not other minorities? In any event, I did not want to lose an opportunity, so I decided to tour Pendleton County "looking for Appalachia."

As I pass the Anderson House at the bottom of the hill, the twin maples on the lawn are in full color, making the house appear luminescent white. Downtown is almost deserted. A woman walks into the B & H Hardware Store. The black-and-white Border collie that I sometimes see crossing my yard trots across Main Street with a stick in its mouth. George Dice stands at the post office door, binoculars hanging from a strap over his shoulder. His head is tilted up as if listening, or perhaps smelling, something on the wind. Perfect, I think. I will start with George. I pull up at the curb, and his face brightens. He calls out, "Hello there!," as he often does.

"It's me, George—O'Brien," I shout. "You want'n a lift somewhere?"

" 'Deed I do," he says, hurrying toward the car.

As always, George speaks his mind immediately: "I surely do appreciate this. It's a daggone pain, have'n to walk everywhere. Some don't mind giv'n a ride. But I tell you there's people in this town that just get mad because I ask."

"Hell with them, George."

"Well now, I don't know I'd say that."

"It's just an expression, George."

"You've got to be careful about what you say. Do you believe in Hell? I mean, do you think there's a place like that somewhere or other?"

"I don't know. It's not something I know about."

"I'm sure there's Hell. I've done a lot of thinking about it."

"Really."

"What do you think?" he says. "Do you believe God would put a person in the Lake of Fire for doing away with himself? What I mean is, I've burned myself bad a few times. That's just awful pain. Awful. The idea of feeling that kind of pain all over my body forever just makes me shake. You think God would do that to someone whose life got so bad they gave up? I mean, they've got these people in the nursing home in terrible pain every day. More dead than alive. Those doctors 'n' scientists keep them hooked to those machines. How about someone like that? Do you think God would send someone like that to Hell for ending it all?"

"George, I really don't know about this kind of stuff."

George tells me to pull over at a small white house with a lilac bush by the door.

"Lemme see now," he says. "Your wife's named Becky and you got two kids. Shelly's nine and your boy is at the high school."

"That's right," I say, impressed once again with his memory.

George bolts out of the car but turns to stand at the lilac bush.

"I surely do thank you for the ride," he says. "There's some that won't give me a ride. Some people get mad just because I ask . . ." He is still talking as he walks off.

Pulling away, I realize George has interviewed me, rather than the other way around.

Half an hour later, I'm walking parallel to a long cement channel of water at the state fish hatchery with one of the attendants. Spring water runs through five channels like this and each one boils with trout. Huge rainbows, browns, or brooks fill several—fish with shoulders and jaws. Smaller fish fill the others. The hatchery worker carries a long aluminum pole with a wire net on one end and from time to time stops to scoop out a dead fish, or clean fall leaves from screens at the ends of the channels.

"What a great job," I say.

"About like raising chickens," he says and forces a pained smile. Here is a man who has spoken with too many excited fishermen.

"Anybody ever sneak in here to go fishing?"

Another pained smile as he walks along.

"Not really," he says. "Well, sometimes boys drink a little too much beer and get to fooling around."

He stops to scoop out oak leaves and says, "This one time a boy cut a hole in his pocket and ran some fish line down his leg. His buddies stood all around, covering up you know. You think about that—pulling a live fish up to your privates."

He grimaces and shudders.

"Birds are more trouble than people," he says.

"Birds?"

"Kingfishers. Ospreys. Them big old blue herons. Some people call them cranes. Well, the ospreys don't get the fish. I've never seen one anyway. They hover over the trout like they're maybe thinking about it, but I've never seen one dive down. I guess something don't look right down here. The big herons eat a lot of small trout. Just walk along and snap them up like popcorn. They think this place is a cafeteria."

"What do you do?"

He stops and says, "Tell 'um to leave."

So much for my second interview.

I stop at Kile's Grocery Store in Upper Tract. This is a real country store, not a tourist stop. Kile's offers canned goods, clothing, and household items; bullets, hunting rifles, and shotguns that you can buy, sell, or trade; fishing rods, hooks, flies, plugs, spinners, night-crawlers, mealworms, and minnows out back in a tank with a garden hose stuck in it; beer, pop, and lots of junk food; tools, three kinds of snuff, a bewildering number of pocketknives, and gas and oil for your car. The hardwood floor has been worn smooth over the years, and the store smells of fishing waders, scalded coffee, hot dogs, winter-green snuff, and just a trace of WD-40—a spray lubricant for rusted nuts and bolts.

Two men in coveralls talk to the woman behind the counter. I discover that I—as an intruder—control the volume of their conversation. When I'm way back by the frozen food, they talk loud. As I approach, the voices get lower and lower, then stop altogether. I experiment a few times just to be sure. There's no doubt about it; I have become a kind of rheostat. In the county's gossip network, stores like this are central station, second only in importance to kitchen phones. I love these little stores, close to the heart and soul of West Virginia.

A little later in the North Fork Valley, I walk into a diner and it's like an old cowboy movie. I can hear people talking and laughing through the screen door as I walk across the parking lot, but *the tinkling piano music dies away and the laughter fades to silence when the mysterious stranger pushes through the swinging doors.* Two workingmen at the counter stop flirting with the champagne-blond waitress to glare at me. After staring for thirty seconds, the waitress says, "Can I help you?" Again, I have the sense that I have walked into the wake of hard feelings. I drink my Diet Sprite, mount up, and ride away.

Weaving along, going up and down the mountains, I sometimes cross into Virginia and back again. These twisting, narrow roads were dirt rather than blacktop until the 1950s. Those old dirt roads were simply improvements on the farm lanes county people made in the early 1800s, which most often followed the Shawnee hunting trails. The Indians, of course, took the trails created by the animals they hunted. Driving along I am part of something ancient and this feels almost like religion. I pass place names like Snowy Mountain, Trout Rock, Roaring Creek, Reddish Knob, Crab Bottom, Sugar Grove, and Smoke Hole. The original Appalachians had a literal frame of mind and named things what they were. It is American poetry. My father would love this. I imagine him in the passenger seat saying the names out loud.

Off onto the dirt roads, the incredibly low population numbers seem more real. I drive for miles and miles through gorgeous mountain landscape without seeing another human being. When a rare pickup truck passes, the driver lifts one finger from the steering wheel, and returning the gesture makes me feel less a stranger.

Over a rise, I hit the brakes to avoid a large doe that flashes out of the woods onto the road. Two stutter steps and she is up and over a split-rail fence with that exquisite pause at the top of her perfect arch. Two yearlings immediately follow her, each making the same flawless leap in turn. I watch them zigzag through a weedy field, white tails up and swaying back and forth like warning flags. My father always told me to look back into the woods after a doe comes out. Wise old bucks often send them into the open first. I see nothing except more woods.

After passing the same woman in her garden for the second time, I stop to get my bearings. There are few signs on these back roads and I cannot remember what the last one said. Left, right, up, down—it's all beautiful mountains in fall color and all pretty much the same. I conclude that I am lost and a memory of my dad comes back. Driving home from fishing or hunting trips, he often took "shortcuts." After meandering around on back roads for an hour, he would stop to ask directions in some town with an improbable name like Moosick or Muldoon, then end up talking about fishing in "this here burg." Even as a boy I suspected that my father did this deliberately, that he liked getting lost. It may have been the closest thing to adventure in his life. There on the dirt road I decide I like being lost as well. Driving along, that odd thing happens: I see myself as if from some great height, this tiny figure in an old blue car weaving along the dirt road dragging a small cloud of lilac-colored dust behind. It's sweet delirium on an October day and I find myself smiling.

I blunder back onto the paved road near a road sign that says Moyers, a name I recognize from the *Pendleton Times;* it's one of the county's villages. Except for the sign, I see nothing but pastures, mountains, and trees. A little farther down the road, there is a white store no bigger than a garage. One old gas pump sits in front. Inside is the proprietor, a man named Eugene—that's *U*-gene in the Appalachian Mountains. In his forties, Eugene is trim, wears wire-rimmed glasses, crisp, clean clothes, and has every hair in place. He is also quick-witted. "You ever get bored out here?" I ask.

"Don't have time for it," he says.

"What goes on in Moyers?"

"Way too much if you ask me."

Seeing a sign on the wall, I order a sandwich. Eugene says, "We got bologna, yellow cheese, and bologna with yellow cheese."

I order bologna with yellow cheese and watch Eugene expertly slice a thick slab of bologna with an old black butcher knife.

I eat the sandwich in front of Eugene's store. The bologna is very good, the store bread fair, and this evens out to good. There is no breeze. Nothing moves. The silence is punctuated only by the faint scree of a red-tailed hawk from high above the ridge. I stand immersed in the exquisite stillness of Moyers.

Sandwich in hand, I cross the narrow road to a clear brook that flows under a small bridge. A spring burbles to the surface on the bank. Kneeling down, I scoop up handfuls of sweet, cold water. I notice watercress in the spring water, pull a handful, shake the water off, and put some on my sandwich. A bit too peppery this time of year, but pleasant all the same.

There are native trout under the bridge. Brook trout spawn in the fall, and the males are in full color, iridescent pink spots along the sides, orange fins tipped with creamy white. My mind seems to shift gears, and for a moment, I feel giddy.

Later, in the North Fork Valley, I stop for gas. The man filling my tank is in his seventies, and with the pump running on its own, he comes up to wash my windshield. He wears his billed cap so low over his eyes he must tilt his head to look at me.

"New York," he says, obviously having seen my license plate.

"Left there in August."

Pausing at my window he says, "Must be something—all them buildings and mugger people and taxicabs and so on."

"I wasn't living in New York City."

He looks at me, tilting his head farther back.

"What's that?"

I have bumped into this before. Rural Americans sometimes think New York State and New York City are one and the same. I explain that I have come from a small town surrounded by farms in central New York State, which apparently makes no sense to him. It crosses my mind to mention that New York City is considerably more complicated than tall buildings and street crime, but I decide against it. He is confused enough as it is and I am tired. It's a waste of time really. It occurs to me that some Appalachians are as confused about New York as some New Yorkers are about Appalachia.

THAT DAY I ended my quixotic tour in the North Fork Valley at Big Run, a spring-fed brook that holds native trout. I fished for half an hour—research, you understand—but the water was clotted with fallen leaves, and I gave up.

A little later I parked beside a tiny community called Big Run to write things down. To me, the people I had met that day were hardly Appalachian hillbillies. George, the hatchery worker, the people at Kile's Grocery, Eugene the sandwich maker, the diner cowboys, and the gas station attendant stubbornly refused to be anything but distinct individuals in my mind. I can remember staring out the window at houses and trailers across the road and thinking that the agent imagined me in a place like this as he spoke on the phone. Big Run is a tiny, worn-looking community—a few well-kept, tidy little homes, but also many battered trailers and some shacklike houses with plastic instead of glass in some windows. In one yard an old school bus sat up on blocks and some chickens pecked around beneath it. A nondescript dog slept on the wooden step that led into one of the houses. Presently a teenage boy came down the road and stopped a few yards from the car window to stare at me without a trace of self-consciousness. When I waved, he did not respond or even blink but stared a moment longer and went on. For a moment, I thought, This is Appalachia, this is what I'm supposed to write about.

But Big Run is just a poor county neighborhood and the people who live here are no more distinctly "Appalachian" than the doctors, lawyers, ministers, bankers, teachers, and farmers I saw on the streets of Franklin every day. The people in Big Run represent 3 to 4 percent of the county's population. I think it is fair to call these people poor, but what community does not have poor folk? Beyond that, I have hunted and fished with people from small communities like this and have learned not to make quick judgments. Some of them have bad character and appalling habits—just like some Harvard professors, though their lifestyles are somewhat different. But in my experience, other families were decent people living exactly the way they wanted to and they seemed to be as happy as most other Americans.

Thinking of the agent, I imagined myself moving in with one of the more colorful families across the road, and perhaps writing about a year in their life. I did not know it that day, but this kind of thing has been done countless times since the 1880s. Gothic Appalachian stories constitute an American genre. Reporters and writers come here expecting hillbilly squalor and they find it at the exclusion of everything else. Even writers from the region, almost always middle-class, have done this. There is an established audience for Appalachian

Gothic fiction beyond the mountains, and some middle-class writers from the region write stories with that in mind. I have nothing against this. Fiction writers should be free, or perhaps must be free, to write whatever they want to write. The trouble is, outside readers consider the stories realistic rather than Gothic and middle-class writers from the region do nothing to disabuse them because it's their bread and butter. There in the car I wondered if I had not started down the same road that morning on the phone. I knew what the agent wanted to hear and did not disappoint him. "Writers are always selling someone out," Joan Didion said, and she would know. I did not trust myself.

Oddly, I knew this part of Pendleton County well. My Grandfather Bell told wonderful stories about coming here to fish in the early 1900s. From Piedmont it took him a full day in his Model T to get to where I was parked that afternoon. Dirt roads led to logging trails and the logging trails turned into paths that disappeared into virgin timber. The people he described in his fishing stories "didn't often see outsiders. Wild as deer, some of those kids. About as fast too, by jacks. See you comin' and take off through the woods like a shot." But my grandfather spoke of these people with envy rather than scorn; he worked at the paper mill and they had a better life in the wilderness.

In fact, a lot of people came here to fish in the early 1900s. A sparse population, bad dirt roads, and the highest land in West Virginia kept this part of the state isolated, which resulted in the best native trout fishing in the mid-Atlantic region. The fishing even attracted a few American luminaries. In 1918 Henry Ford, Thomas Edison, Harvey Firestone, and John Burroughs fished on Cheat Mountain a few miles from Big Run. The four men, who often traveled together and called themselves "the Vagabonds," began their junket in Pittsburgh, fished in West Virginia, and then traveled down to the Vanderbilt mansion in North Carolina. I have seen black-and-white photographs of them standing side by side along a West Virginia trout stream like school chums. Looking at the photograph invariably made me wonder what they thought of the people here.

When I was in college, I fished Big Run with a roommate one spring. His father and grandfather also fished here in the early 1900s; it was a family tradition. We camped in a mountaintop pasture that belonged to a friend of the family. Across the pasture, the man's unpainted house sagged slightly to one side. He parked his old truck on a steep hill so he could jump-start it. Two little girls in print dresses danced around the yard without music. I can still see them in my mind.

The man operated a sawmill with his son for cash money but closed down for all of deer season. When the greens and "haystack mushrooms" (morels) came up in the spring, he closed down again. He kept a milk cow, butchered pigs each fall, and raised chickens for eggs and meat. Any deer foolish enough to wander into his wife's garden ended up on the table. When we approached the house, the little girls ran squealing inside and hid behind their father, who sat at the kitchen table with both hands wrapped around a white, rock-heavy coffee mug. Winking at us, he would reach around to tickle his daughters and say, "Come on out here now. These boys don't bite. I believe they like little girls." The girls giggled and squeezed in tighter behind the chair and would not come out.

In the evening, he would come down to our campfire. I can still see him, lean, angular, walking into the circle of light, saying, "Eve-nen', eve-nen'." He would hunker down on his haunches for as long as an hour—try that if you think it's easy—tossing small sticks into the fire, and talking about his frustration with "these daggone VISTA [Volunteers in Service to America] people. Who is it sends them? Where is this Appalachia place and why do they think I live there?" After so many years, it seemed strange to be asking the very same question.

It was almost dusk by then. I decided to drive to the top of Spruce Knob, the highest point in West Virginia and only a few miles from Big Run; it seemed the perfect way to end the day. Up on top, the spruce trees were stunted and twisted into strange shapes by the constant wind. It already felt like winter up there, and the low, melancholy sound of the wind moaning through spruce branches added to the chill. Looking out into endless mountains all in color, it came to me that I was the highest person in West Virginia at that moment, and for some reason, this delighted me. I declared myself the Emperor of Appalachia. Now that I had a kingdom, all I had to do was find the damn place.

8. Into the Heart
of the Heart of Appalachia

"**Y**OU BE extra careful," Becky says. "It's another country down there."

My wife is standing at the front door holding on to my wrist to keep me from running off too fast.

"Sure, sure," I say. We embrace. At the bottom of the cement steps, I turn to say, "Off like a . . ." Becky grimaces and waves me off.

I am on my way to Charleston, the state capital, five hours south through the mountains. I am going to an art exhibit at Sunrise Gallery and will come back in two days through the southern coalfields. The Emperor of Appalachia is still searching for his kingdom.

I go up North Mountain, down through Judy Gap, and across the North Fork River. I am traveling north in the valley bottom, following the course of the river. In a pasture on the right, a man in high rubber boots walks behind a massive black bull, whacking it with a slender stick from time to time. Brueghel.

At the top of the mountain, high pasture opens on both sides. I have come this way in late spring, when the lilacs were blooming in the valley bottom, to find new lambs standing in snow. As county farmers sometimes say, "It's all different on top."

I leave Pendleton County and enter Randolph, named after an ancestor of Jennings Randolph, the grateful recipient of the Woodlands Institute rocking chair. The land continues as deep forest, occasionally broken by a farm. Each small dirt road that disappears into the trees is an invitation. What's back there? Maybe there's a trout stream or a valley I've never seen.

A dreadful statue of Pocahontas that I sometimes think of blowing up announces Elkins. Entering this town brings stories back. Becky grew up in Green Bank, an hour south over Cheat Mountain, and the family came to shop in Elkins once a month. Saturday morning departures were exciting with everyone dressing up for town. Gran made most of Becky's dresses. Becky would look through a Sears catalog—"the wishbook"—and point out dresses that pleased her. Gran "studied on" the pictures and then made the dresses. Despite Gran's considerable gifts as a seamstress, the dresses always had the look of homespun. Each time I drive through Elkins, I see Becky in my mind on a shopping trip in one of Gran's dresses; country mouse has come to the city.

On the other side of Elkins, I pass a life-sized bronze statue of a man on a horse. It's an unusual monument. The man has removed his very round hat to hold it against the bronze flank of the horse and has lowered his head and closed his eyes as if grieving. This is Henry Gassaway Davis, partner of Stephen Benten Elkins, two of the so-called robber barons who came into Appalachia in the late 1800s. Like all of these men, Davis ran roughshod over the laws, institutions, and people of the region, then died and left his name on buildings and towns. In fact, his statue stands in front of Davis & Elkins College, an extremely small Presbyterian school that once described itself as "the Harvard of Appalachia." The statue brings Tom Andrews to mind. During the two years Becky and I lived in the farmhouse in Green Bank, Tom drove up to go fishing several times. On one trip we went to Elkins for a night of beer and pool and ended up at the statue before starting back. I was talking about the things Davis had done and about how ferocious the man had been while Tom walked around the monument knocking on the bronze horse with his knuckles. At one point he stopped and actually seemed to be listening. He said, "Damn! Some old boy jacklights a deer and they throw him in jail. Jacklight half the state and they name shit after you." This may not be the only accurate view of Appalachian history, but it's one of them.

As Henry Davis recedes in the rearview mirror, I leave Elkins behind and will not pass through another town until I reach Charleston three hours from now. Interstate 79 South passes high along the ridges, offering wonderful views of forested mountains and small farms. Cobalt sky, brilliant fall leaves, tiny houses tucked into shady hollows, a surprising number of them painted lavender for mysterious reasons. In a steep yard beside one of the lavender houses, a woman hangs wash on a line, each shirt or blouse a bright new flag. Are the owners of these Easter-egg homes expressing solidarity, or has there been a stupendous sale on lavender paint? I fall in love with West Virginia again.

The state capital comes on abruptly. I come around a turn and there it is in the valley bottom. Rusted bridges arching across the foul Kanawha River are fixed upon a grid of power lines and angled streets. From this height and distance it's Léger again, but after three hours of unspoiled mountain scenery, his painting seems dingy and soiled. Becky's right: It's another country.

WITH fifty-seven thousand people, Charleston, the largest city in West Virginia, is little more than a good-sized town. Most of it is down in the valley bottom by the Kanawha River. Kanawha, pronounced Ku-*naw*-wa, is the name of an Indian tribe that once lived in this part of the state. Like so many of the eastern tribes, the Kanawhas have perished. The river's pollution is not as bad as it once was, but it still smells disagreeable in summer.

Sixty-five percent of West Virginia is forested land, but Charleston, its capital, is industrial. The chemical plants along the river—among them DuPont, Nitro, and Union Carbide—dwarf the city itself. At present West Virginia's annual per capita income is $19,362—forty-ninth out of the fifty states. But a number of years ago, Charleston ranked second in millionaires per capita. Every city has rich and poor, but in Charleston the distance between haves and have-nots can be measured in light-years rather than miles.

The distance is made more glaring by the proximity of the extremes. South Hills, a few blocks above downtown, is a neighborhood of expensive homes and mansions—a few qualifying as castles—and residents park their BMWs in driveways that curve through sculpted lawns. But drive off the mountainside, and within minutes you pass through neighborhoods of run-down houses, vacant lots, and boarded-up stores. Driving into the communities around the chemical companies is like entering a Third World country. Long rows of tiny boxlike homes are surrounded by weedy, junk-filled lawns. There is mud, grime, and debris everywhere. Everything is smeared, soiled, and foul-smelling. I remember a kitchen chair sticking out of the broken window of a house and Christmas decorations still up in August. The beer joints here are often makeshift, transitory places. Someone will throw up a ragged sign in front of a bankrupt burger joint with shaky letters announcing "Teana's Place—Beer." Bars like this don't last long; they are torn apart during Saturday night brawls or the police shut them down. Another sign goes up blocks or miles away. On one trip through the chemical communities, I drove past a cinder-block cube fronted by a hand-lettered sign that read "Brothers of the Wheel." By pure coincidence I had been thinking of Charleston as medieval; its politicians and business leaders held the absolute power to create and then ignore this kind of squalor. An image of a medieval punishment came to mind—to be broken by the wheel. The king's henchmen would stake a man to the ground, then roll an immensely heavy wheel back and forth across his body, breaking every bone. Doubling back to the cube building, I pulled in to discover a bikers' bar with doors and windows barred like a jail cell. The land around the building was muddy and littered, but a cardinal was singing his spring song from a nearby tree despite the fact that it was early winter.

The gold-domed Capitol building reflects imagined glory and phony elegance. There are heroic statues, noble paintings, grand pronouncements, and marble floors, but the building is surrounded by one of the worst neighborhoods in the city. The most notorious street for drugs, Washington Street, is only two blocks away and it is possible to watch drug deals go down from the Capitol building itself.

Then again, downtown Charleston, three miles upriver from the Capitol complex, has a decided charm. There are perhaps two dozen office buildings twenty stories high, some of them new and glass-sided. Others are old but well kept and have character. A few fancy restaurants charge too much, and several stores sell overpriced clothing or expensive furniture. The streets are clean and during weekdays busy but not congested; car horns create a tiny canyon echo at rush hour. The well-dressed professional men and women would not look out of place on Park Avenue.

But minutes from downtown, traveling west on Route 60 toward St. Albans, you drive through the Badlands, an area of seedy beer

joints, live sex acts, massage parlors, adult bookstores, more beer
joints, and private "clubs." The clubs are simply bars where patrons
sign a membership card and pay too much for drinks. All of these
establishments, in Charleston and across the state, have one or more
video poker games on the premises. In fact many "clubs" have dozens
of them lined up against the walls. Essentially, these are slot
machines. Signs on the wall state "For Amusement Only," but in
the Alice-in-Wonderland world of Appalachia, signs often mean the
opposite of what they say.

Strange things happen in Charleston's Badlands. People routinely
lose entire paychecks and go into debt. One man lost an $85,000
inheritance in about two weeks, though not all the money went into
video poker: he was paying $1,500 a bottle for domestic champagne
to keep an "exotic dancer" happy. A bank teller convicted of embez-
zling $150,000 lost half the amount to poker machines.

Video poker is against the law in West Virginia, but sheriffs and
state police ignore this and everyone knows it. Since the games are
illegal, no one regulates the machines. When distributors set them up
in joints or clubs, they tinker with the mechanism to set the odds
remarkably low. Patrons win easily and often for several weeks, which
creates gambling fever by word of mouth. Then distributors reset the
odds impossibly high. Corruption is so blatant and tawdry one thinks
of Chicago and the Roaring Twenties. Distributors carry twenty-
gallon buckets of uncounted, untaxed money out of beer joints, staggering under the weight. Their wives and girlfriends drive Lincoln
Town Cars and vacation in the Caribbean. Precise figures are of
course impossible to obtain, but it has been reasonably estimated that
West Virginians lose up to $1 billion to video poker games each
year—this in a state with an annual per capita income of $19,362.

Until 1995, Earl Ray Tomblin, the Democratic president of West
Virginia's senate, owned Southern Amusement Company, one of the
largest distributors of video poker machines in the state. In 1995,
Tomblin sold Southern Amusement to former state delegate Joe C.
Ferrell. Ferrell, who resigned his delegate's seat in 1992 because of a
campaign contribution scandal, was elected to the same seat in 1998
and once again in 2000. Both men, in one way or another, have been
part of the coal industry, and this is in keeping with an historic state
pattern. Sooner or later in West Virginia, most political roads lead

back to coal. This is not to say that the coal industry creates all of the state's corruption, but since the 1880s, coal companies have been financing political campaigns and then rewarding elected officials after their terms. This has created an atmosphere in which corruption flourishes. Coal company executives, their sons, grandsons, associates, or puppets, serve as senators, delegates, and governors. All too often, West Virginia politics resembles a game of musical chairs; the same players circle around the offices until the coal company stops the music. Occasionally someone drops out of the game to plea-bargain but returns to play again. Arch Moore, governor for three scandal-ridden terms, finally went to prison in 1990, but remained on the coal company payroll while incarcerated.

For me this will always be the quintessential Charleston story: In 1952 the people of West Virginia elected Democrat William C. Marland as governor. As a rule, coal companies vet political candidates before or at least during the primaries and effectively stifle anyone with wild ideas about changing the status quo. Insiders considered Marland the political machine's candidate. As my dad would say, the man knew what was what, or was supposed to. But three days after taking office, Marland "dropped a bombshell in the laps of the startled legislature," as one newspaper story put it, by proposing an excise tax of 10 percent on each ton of coal. Inexplicably, Marland seemed to think that the coal beneath West Virginia ought to benefit the people of West Virginia, especially given the fact that once it was gone, it would be gone for good. Further, Marland planned to use the tax money to improve West Virginia schools and highways. No state governor had ever seen things this way.

Marland's announcement infuriated the coal owners and everyone aligned with them, which included every Republican legislator, the editor of the *Charleston Gazette*—a newspaper with a coal executive on its board—and virtually all of the state's wealthy families. Marland had either deceived them, betrayed them, or perhaps gone mad after winning the election. This was extremely inconvenient for the coal companies, but there was never any real danger since they controlled all of the key senators and delegates. Marland's plan for an excise tax was effectively dead the day he made the announcement, as were most of his proposals and nominations in the next four years.

After his term, Marland returned to law practice and then filled a

U.S. Senate seat left vacant by the death of a Democratic friend. After that, he seemed to vanish. Then in 1965 the manager of a national firm informed a Chicago executive that he was being transferred to the West Virginia office, which did not please the man. After leaving the office, the executive got into a cab and grumbled to the driver, "I've just been sent to West Virginia." The driver casually responded, "You know I used to be governor of West Virginia." Assuming the driver was deranged, the disgruntled executive said nothing.

But later that evening, he had second thoughts and called the *Chicago Daily News*. After a reporter named Jack Lavin made several phone calls of his own, he located former Governor Marland eating a $1.25 chicken dinner in the basement of a Chicago YMCA. A few days later at an impromptu news conference in the cab company office, a reporter asked, "Governor Marland, why did you go to work as a cabdriver?" Marland said, "Well, at that particular time, it seemed to me I needed a vehicle to help me compose my character, which had fallen apart."

"What happened to your character, Governor?"

"It got drunk."

As it turns out, Marland, who was perfectly sane, had had serious trouble with alcohol for a few years, then joined AA and sobered up. A few months after he was discovered driving the cab, Marland died of pancreatic cancer.

WHEN I'M in Charleston, I stay at the cheapest place available, which means a motel near one of the chemical plants on the Kanawha River. One night I opened a drawer in the bedside table in such a place to discover a message in black Magic Marker: "For a good time, call Wanda." The phone number was there as well. This struck me as ingenious advertising, and for about an hour, off and on, I considered calling Wanda. I had no interest in an intimate encounter but was intrigued with the idea of Appalachian prostitutes. What would Wanda sound like? Would she have a farm girl accent or sound like a hard-boiled city gal? I could ask, "What's a nice girl like you doing in a drawer like this?" and then interview Wanda on the phone. I decided against this but still could not sleep, so opted for another kind of research. I decided to get up and drive around.

Fifteen minutes later I found myself in an empty parking lot beside the Capitol building staring at the gold dome, which at 4 a.m. looks like a mirage. For no reason I started down a side street past boarded-up stores and forlorn houses. Several cars passed me, but the only person I saw was a black man in a rust-colored sweatshirt. He had pulled the hood so tight around his face all I could see was a small circle of eyes, nose, and mouth. Hands jammed hard into the pockets, he paced around in a small tight circle on the street corner, arguing with someone who was not there. He shouted, "That's what you think it is? *That's* what you think? If that's what you *think*, it's only something in your head." I thought of him as a voice crying in the wilderness.

A few miles on an interstate and I was out by the chemical communities again. Pulling off on a high road above one plant, I got out to look down. The complex seemed to go on forever, silver storage tanks and silver-white buildings tangled in a maze of pipes that went up, down, and sideways. Some of the pipes looked large enough for a man to crawl through. Others appeared, at least from that distance and height, like yarn. Pipes of all sizes intersected at certain points, creating intricate knots that looked like gigantic computer chips. Twists of steam, plumes of steam, and small, pale clouds rose up here and there, and everything was lit by an unnatural white light that made me think of burning phosphorous. It was like a set from *Blade Runner* and in my mind I could see a small antigravity ship rising like a cloud of steam in eerie silence.

Down in the valley bottom I drove along a dark, empty street. A high Cyclone fence rose up on my left and both the street and the fence seemed endless. I was passing Union Carbide, the largest chemical company in the state. Outside the car nothing moved—no cars, trucks, people, dogs, breeze—nothing. I might have been the last living thing on earth. I began to notice an oily taste in my mouth again. This always happens when I'm near the chemical companies. It tastes like oil, or at least a petroleum product, and makes me extremely anxious. What the hell am I breathing in? The death rates for certain rare cancers are enormously higher in the chemical communities than anywhere else in America. Company doctors and scientists explain this in terms of coincidence or "mitigating factors" and the state backs them up. This does nothing for my anxiety. Driving along I kept clearing my throat. One chemical community, Institute, has been called the Bhopal of America. MIC, the chemical that killed fifteen hundred people in Bhopal, India, is produced at the Institute plant. I spoke with a Union Carbide worker some time ago and asked him if he ever worried about MIC. He said, "Hell no. Carbide's making shit that would eat MIC for breakfast."

That night I stopped at Union Carbide's main gate to read a sign that caught my attention. On the sign a goofy cartoon turtle in red tennis shoes named Wally Wise advises, "In an Emergency, (1) Go Inside (2) Turn on the TV (3) Stay off the Phone. BE WALLY WISE!"

I drove back to my motel, went inside, turned on the TV, stayed off the phone, and waited for dawn to break.

THE STRAND is a big, funky diner downtown. You walk past a few modern glass-sided buildings, a fancy store or two, turn down a side street, and there it is. The chalkboard menu on the sidewalk announces food like pork chops, mashed potatoes, homemade vegetable soup, white beans, cornbread, and greens. When I'm in Charleston, this is where I eat.

Inside on the left, a long counter runs front to back, but booths take up most of the room. What you notice first is the mix of high and low; at the counter a young man in a blue pinstripe suit and wing tips, Rolex flashing on his wrist, might be talking to an emaciated older man in coveralls with bloodshot eyes and uncut, oily hair. In one booth or another, impeccably dressed lawyers often discuss court cases over beans and cornbread while construction workers sitting behind them exchange blue jokes over the same meal. The strain of social class—"hillbillies" and Appalachian elite—is more felt in Charleston. The vast distance between top and bottom and the geographic proximity of communities like South Hills and Institute explains this, I think. But for some reason, the Strand is wonderfully free of that tension. People check their social pretensions or feelings of inferiority at the door.

The Strand opened its doors in 1926 and has not changed much in sixty years. A Charleston landmark, it has always been a free-fire zone. You come here to buy cigars from the Strand's cigar menu—50 cents to $8 a smoke. (A sign on the cork bulletin board, surrounded by postcards of bathing beauties with helium-filled breasts, reads,

"Life's too short to smoke bad cigars.") You can bet on college football, get tips on a horse or directions to a poker game. In the back room, four good pool tables provide serious play for serious money. Late one afternoon, I watched two young men with custom-made pool cues begin a series of nine-ball games. The older man who racked the balls—portly, cigar down to a button in the corner of his mouth—was wearing an old cardigan. Each time he bent over the rack, I could see the outline of a pistol in the small of his back. It's that kind of place.

In keeping with the Strand's funky ambiance, the walls are hung with dubious photographs and bad art. On one wall of the poolroom, there is a huge blown-up photo of four people standing at urinals with their backs to viewers. Three of the four are men, the fourth a shapely young woman in short-shorts. One large painting that depicts Babe Ruth hitting his sixtieth home run looks old enough to have been painted the day the Bambino hit it. Another is of a bullfight. There is also a dreadful portrait of John Kennedy.

Kennedy has been called the patron saint of West Virginia but, like everything else in state politics, not for reasons that make real sense. At the start of his presidential campaign, Kennedy needed to establish himself as a man of great compassion and to demonstrate that his Catholic faith would not be a serious impediment to his candidacy. Since West Virginia was, as my father's Piedmont relatives knew, suspicious of Catholics, he set his sights on the state as a proving ground. West Virginians have always felt that their state has been treated like America's unwanted stepchild, alternately abused and ignored, and no other presidential candidate had ever campaigned here. Kennedy capitalized on this. When he came into the coalfields in 1960, with national TV cameras trailing behind him, West Virginians loved the attention and rewarded him with a victory. (There have also been rumors ever since about votes being bought.) Rumors aside, you can still find pictures of "St. Jack" on the walls of many homes here, and some residents still hoard Kennedy half-dollars.

People talk a lot of politics at the Strand. One day I was sitting in a booth opposite a conceptual artist from the coalfields named Lynn Wyatt. Lynn is a broad-shouldered man with large square hands and the thick wrists of a sculptor. He has worked with Rosenquist—a pop-art star—on a few of his billboard-size paintings. Balding, with wire-rimmed glasses, Lynn wore a tweed workingman's cap and had an easygoing presence. A bearded friend sat beside him, strung out on something.

Jay Rockefeller's second term as governor was winding down and Arch Moore was running for his third term—and was on his way to prison. Beyond a hazy mistrust of politics, I rarely have strong feelings about any one politician, but I had heard Rockefeller described as a "carpetbagger" a number of times. In that cynical view, Rockefeller had come into the state to buy a ticket into national politics (which never transpired). He had chosen West Virginia because here the ticket would cost his family perhaps $2 million as opposed to $30 or $40 million in New York. Standard Oil is also one of the corporations that own a good part of West Virginia and so Rockefeller was, in a sense, one of the state's many landlords. For what it's worth, I thought he was rich enough to refuse coal company bribes, and in West Virginia that's hopeful.

Lynn's view was close to mine, but at some distance from his companion's. The bearded man said nothing as we talked, but at a pause in the conversation he blurted out, "There oughta be a season on Rockefellers in West Virginia."

"A what?" Lynn said, eyeing him.

"A season," his friend repeated. "It could come in right after deer season."

Lynn looked hard at his friend, who retorted, "We wouldn't have to eat them, for Christ's sake!"

This is an Appalachian view of the power and money that control West Virginia.

IN 1892, the people of West Virginia elected William Alexander MacCorkle as governor. Governor MacCorkle, who bore an astonishing resemblance to Colonel Sanders of Kentucky Fried Chicken, was a tireless promoter of the state's coal and timber. He was known as a "silver-tongued orator," and the very mention of West Virginia was enough to send him into flights of poetry about ". . . dark wilderness, the beetling Craig . . . smiling valleys . . . Our mountains filled with coal and clothed with timber rich enough for a king's heritage . . ." MacCorkle made many trips outside the mountains to meet with financiers and industrialists, who then swarmed in to clear-cut forests, mine coal, and make fortunes. The governor's plan to develop West Virginia's fabulous resources was clearly a success. How good all of this was for the state and its people is another question.

After his term, MacCorkle became a lawyer, land speculator, millionaire, bank founder, and then a millionaire several times over. The heart of his fortune was the rich coal-bearing land that he sold to outside interests. He was an anomaly only in that he expressed concern that people outside West Virginia were "purchasing the immense acres of the most valuable lands in the state. In a few years, at the present rate of progress, we will occupy the same position of vassalage to the north and east that Ireland does to England. . . ." This puts MacCorkle well above the average laissez-faire industrialists whose business ethics were perhaps best summed up in 1897 by railroad executive Milton H. Smith, who observed, "Society is created for the purpose of one man's getting what the other has, if he can, and keeping out of prison."

In the early 1900s, MacCorkle built two great houses in South Hills overlooking Charleston. Both were built of huge sandstone blocks and in an architectural style that brings the word "baronial" to mind. MacCorkle lived in the larger edifice, which featured three enormous floors and cathedral-high ceilings. His grandson Torquil lived in the slightly smaller house eighty yards away. The governor named his estate Sunrise. In time, both mansions passed into other hands, and then in the 1960s the Charleston Art Association bought them and turned Torquil's home into the Sunrise Art Gallery.

Sunrise was lit up beautifully on the lovely October evening I visited. There was a little chill to the air, but it was still warm enough to go without a topcoat. Well-dressed people strolled from expensive cars toward the front door or stood in the curving drive to chat with friends. You know this scene: Women with their hair done up telling stories with their fingertips pressed against their chests; bemused, silent men beside them. Inside the mansion, the buzz of voices—like a very small orchestra tuning up—filled every room. Wine was served in plastic glasses. There were hors d'oeuvres on one linen-covered table and small, delicate pastries on another. People stood, drinks in hand, in front of the paintings, saying, "Oh, I like that!" and "Look what he's done here." I could have been at an art exhibit anywhere in the world.

It was a pleasant evening. I met any number of interesting people, was taken with a few of the paintings, and was more or less pleased to be there. But I began to feel anxious and oddly out of place. In time my unease got the best of me and I slipped out a door to walk around the grounds. I could see Charleston down in the valley glinting through the trees; the lights of town and the moving lights of cars on streets created a spectacular effect. Even the poisonous Kanawha River looked good from that high on the mountainside. I tried to locate the chemical company communities, but the dark hid them. Those communities and the Sunrise Art Gallery should have been on different planets. For some reason, I thought the heart of the heart of Appalachia here in Charleston should have been something else but had no idea what that might be. Standing there, I thought of *The Great Gatsby*. It came to me that Governor MacCorkle's mansion and the others in South Hills were being built as Fitzgerald wrote that book. MacCorkle had come from impoverished circumstances and his determination to succeed was something that he shared with Jay Gatsby. And here I was standing with Torquil MacCorkle's mansion at my back looking not toward the green light at the end of Daisy Buchanan's dock, but at the lights of Charleston, reaching for Appalachia.

LEAVING CHARLESTON, you can take Route 119, which meanders southwest past time-forgotten towns like Ruth, Sod, MacCorkle, and Julian, then cut east on Route 85 into the land of coal. Or you can follow Route 77 southeast out of the capital past Marmet, Chesapeake, Chelyan, Cabin Creek (the home of basketball star Jerry West), and on to Beckley, where you take Route 16 southwest into Sophia, where Senator Robert Byrd grew up. After Sophia, the landscape changes. Entering the coalfields, you seem to spiral down lower and lower. If the valleys in Pendleton County are ax-bite Vs, then these southern valleys are knife cuts in the land. You wind along through one dim alley that leads into another alley and then into another like a maze. At times, the valley walls appear to go straight up and almost close over at the top. The air is damp and cool on the hottest days. They say some hollows are so tight, sunlight must be piped in.

These coalfield valleys often have less than a hundred yards of bottomland. The inevitable stream takes up part of each bottom, and as often as not, so does a railroad line. Coal and land companies own 98 percent of the acreage, which leaves little room for houses or private businesses. Towns on scarce available land have a tight, squeezed-in appearance, or sometimes look like stacked blocks going straight up steep mountainsides. And there are company towns, which are narrow lines of matchbox homes side by side along the road, each house a perfect clone of the other. Many village-sized company towns appear to be laid out on a grid—uniform houses in perfectly straight lines at exactly the same distance from one another, each postage-stamp lawn square and uniform as well. You almost expect to see people in livery. The overall feeling is otherworldly and claustrophobic.

Everything here has become darkened by coal. The road shoulders are black. Small white churches are tinted charcoal. Yellow dogs look brindled. Some streams appear as thick as glue, others as black as tar. In fact, there is a tarlike smell to the air you breathe. Run your finger down an oak leaf and it comes away blackened. King Coal, as the nuns of St. Clement's Grade School said of God, is omnipresent.

Oceana, Pineville, Tams, Helen, Wolf Pen, Man, Red Jacket, War, Mullens, Matewan—coal towns follow one another through the labyrinth of knife-cut valleys. A few towns seem to be doing quite well. As I drive through, the oversize coal trucks bull down the narrow roads forcing me to ride with two wheels on the shoulder. The trains loaded down with coal creep along the spur lines behind the trees and make me wait at crossings. People hurry in and out of stores, and diners are full.

I pulled into one town just as its Homecoming Day parade was starting. An excited crowd stood on both sidewalks cheering as the marching band high-stepped down the street. Pom-pom girls jumped and cheered, and uniformed football players struck muscleman poses as they rode past in the backs of pickup trucks. This coal town is alive.

Others have clearly seen better days—storefronts are boarded up, few people walk the streets, and the company houses look empty. Like Piedmont, these towns are dying.

And some towns have died and been abandoned. Driving through large sections of McDowell County along the Kentucky–West Virginia border made me think of old World War II movies, the Allies marching through bombed-out villages in Germany or France. Windows in most homes had been smashed and doors stood open. Burnt-out shells of buildings were commonplace and broken furniture littered the streets. The only thing moving in the wreckage was the occasional dog rummaging through a trash pile. In McDowell County the mines have been closing because inexpensive Australian and western American coal, as well as environmental restrictions, have driven the profit margins down. In the coalfields, there is no work except mining and so thousands of families have piled into clunker cars packed with children and scant possessions and driven into North Carolina. There they live in "hillbilly ghettos," find day-work well below minimum wage, sell their blood, go into prostitution or petty crime, drink, and take drugs. Many families come back, preferring to struggle in the Appalachian Mountains rather than struggle outside. American industry is responsible for all of this, and has been since the 1880s.

WHEN THE recession of the 1870s ended and the army of agents swarmed into the mountains, the region suffered mass hysteria. Land that you could not sell for $1.25 an acre one day had buyers frantically offering $15 the next, based upon rumors of a railroad passing nearby. Communities that might have seen three outsiders in a given year were suddenly besieged with wagonloads of strangers every day. Everyone wanted to buy or sell something. In subsistence cultures where cash money had been virtually nonexistent, people were suddenly talking about staggering wealth.

In their log cabins, most people were caught completely off-guard. To them coal was just something lying on the ground, or perhaps just under it. The agents who materialized in cabin doorways, hat in hand, were thoroughly dishonest as a matter of policy. They mesmerized people with sugary compliments and the jingle of coins. Families sold ancestral land for pocket change before they realized what they were doing. (One man traded an entire mountain of timber and coal for a Singer sewing machine.)

As people began to understand what was happening, they refused to sell their land, but the agents found ways around this. At the time, many extended families owned vast tracts of mountain land jointly. Two hundred people might share a deed for several thousand acres, and according to state law, any one owner could request a legal ruling from the county court: In the court's opinion, was it better *for all concerned* to sell the jointly held property piece by piece or all at once at public auction? Rather quietly, an agent would find a disgruntled family member willing to sell his parcel of land. The same agent then made arrangements with a county official or two and perhaps with the local newspaper editor. If state laws had to be addressed, the agent made a quiet trip to Charleston to "grease the tracks." Once all the sly talk was over, things moved fast. The agent, and now part-owner, petitioned the county magistrate, who quickly ruled that it was best *for all concerned* to sell the entire property at public auction. The magistrate set the auction date for as soon as law permitted and the newspaper editor posted the notice in small print on a back page or ignored the matter entirely. On the day of the auction, when the bid went over a hundred dollars, the subsistence families living on the land could no longer bid. By the time people realized what was happening, it was too late. In this way coal companies bought up entire mountains of timber and coal for pennies an acre and turned thousands of families into refugees in the process. In one transaction a company "bought" sixty-four million tons of coal for $200. State and local politicians stayed out of these controversies, insisting that they would let the system work and that everything was "legal." Beyond that, coal and timber companies represented "progress," and these local people had to be taught about that.

The agents, politicians, and local elites employed other methods as well, such as crooked surveys and phony papers. An infamous "short form deed" left an owner's land in his name but gave all the minerals and timber away, leaving the family with the obligation to pay taxes and repair coal company roads. By the 1920s, Governor MacCorkle's fears had been realized. West Virginia was in a state of "vassalage" to outside interests, and the creation of mythic Appalachia was well on its way.

As I would learn, the infamous Hatfield-McCoy "feud" had a great deal to do with the formation of the myth. In brief, the Hatfields and McCoys were families in the Tug River Valley on the border between West Virginia and Kentucky. In the 1870s, an older man named Ranel McCoy, known locally as a crank, had become jealous of Anse Hatfield, a Civil War hero. On Election Day in 1882, a few young men got drunk—a common occurrence on Election Day across America at the time—and a fight broke out. Two young hotheads murdered Anse's brother Ellison. And one of them was related to Ranel McCoy.

The authorities arrested the men and set the trial in a Kentucky county seat at some distance from the Tug Valley. At the time coal and timber companies controlled county courts, and Anse, like most residents, did not trust them. He petitioned to have the men tried locally, explaining politely that people in the Tug Valley had seen what happened and that it only made sense to try the men locally. When the authorities twice refused, Anse executed the men. Tug Valley residents were shocked both by Ellison's death and by the executions. With the exception of the violence created by the Civil War, the Tug Valley, like virtually all mountain communities, had been remarkably free of violent crime.

Five years passed without incident. Ranel never stopped carping about Anse, but the community, including his own family, ignored him. There were many eyewitnesses to Ellison's murder, and the men responsible never denied killing him. Beyond this the fight had been outrageously unfair. Two men armed with knives had attacked and killed Ellison, who was unarmed. During the Civil War Anse had led a band of paramilitary rangers and often had to administer rough justice. As dreadful as all three killings were, people from both families, with the single exception of Ranel, thought rough justice had been served.

Then in 1886 a Tug Valley sheriff shot a McCoy man trying to escape arrest. The shooting was unrelated to anything that had happened earlier, but a Hatfield happened to be a deputy on the scene. He had nothing to do with the shooting, but his mere presence was enough to make Ranel approach a county-seat lawyer who had lost valuable land to Anse in a lawsuit years before. The lawyer then conferred with Kentucky governor Simon Buckner behind closed doors.

Like all of the region's governors, Buckner, who later became a wealthy coal executive, was frantically trying to attract industrialists into his state. When they came, levels of violence rose dramatically. As companies cheated more and more people out of land, men who had no recourse to law began to shoot at railroad crews and crooked survey teams from the tall timber. When the social order collapsed, families pulled apart and neighbors, now suspicious of one another, began to quarrel. Bitter after losing everything they had, men drank too much and turned on one another. All of this was the inevitable consequence of the industrial onslaught, but the coal and timber barons blamed the people, as did state and local politicians, county-seat lawyers, and newspaper editors who would benefit from industrial development. The myth of blood feuds began with this dynamic and these self-serving delusions.

The industrialists were pouring into the region. They could choose to set up shop in Virginia, West Virginia, Kentucky, Tennessee, or North Carolina. The best way for a governor to encourage more industrialists into *his* state was to strike a strong antiviolence or "antifeud" stance. This in mind, Governor Buckner of Kentucky declared everyone named Hatfield in West Virginia an outlaw and placed a bounty on their heads.

Buckner's decree had the immediate effect of sending scores of armed vigilantes into the mountains hunting anyone named Hatfield. Anse, having no police protection and no recourse to law, armed himself and his family. In the next ten years, twelve people died in this wildly charged environment, but the deaths had nothing to do with anything that resembled a blood feud. The men involved did not align themselves along family lines. Hatfields fought on the "McCoy side" and vice versa. In fact, two-thirds of the men on the McCoy side were unrelated to either family but hoped to gain financially by siding with Governor Buckner and the industrialists. In effect, the governor of Kentucky invented a feud in order to become wealthy by pretending to suppress it.

When reporters from Pittsburgh, Baltimore, and other cities covered the story, they accepted without question everything county-seat politicians and local newspaper editors told them. The Hatfields and McCoys, along with everyone else in the Tug Valley, denied the existence of a feud. The money and corrupt politics involved were blatantly obvious at every turn. (Ranel's lawyer even boasted to reporters about finally getting even with Anse for winning the court case about the land years earlier.) But the reporters wrote accounts of "white savages," "a war of extermination," "West Virginia barbarians," "vendettas," and of course "blood feuds." The editors of major American newspapers like the *New York Times* followed suit and even wrote editorials suggesting that all of "these strange people" be forcibly removed from the mountains and the path of progress.

The so-called Hatfield-McCoy feud captured the attention of the American public. Reporters went on to write fanciful books in which "Appalachians" appeared as feral throwbacks filled with a blood lust that other Americans—that is, white Americans—had evolved beyond eons before. Cartoons and stories appeared endlessly in magazines. Jokes and references about "Appalachian hillbillies" became part of the country's cultural vocabulary. And so the region in a state of vassalage was now seen to be populated by a violent subspecies.

Coalfield boomtowns added to the myth. Simply put, the average coal town was hell on earth. The bosses employed by the owners had work crews throw up rows of shacks. Uninsulated, they were impossible to keep warm through mountain winters despite an endless supply of free coal. Several families shared privies behind the shacks, and the owners made no provision for waste removal. Rotting garbage piled up behind the shacks and in the streets. Pigs, cows, and chickens wandered freely through the towns. Raw sewage from overfilled privies ran in the gutters. Mountain streams that had held native trout a year or two before ran rust-red, sulfur-yellow, or sometimes clear but deadly with mine acid. Stream banks were often littered with the skeletons or the rotting carcasses of dogs, cats, rats, raccoons, and opossums that died shortly after drinking the water. Malnutrition, tuberculosis, influenza, impetigo, ringworm, rickets, and intestinal disorders were commonplace. Men earned $2 for a ten-hour day underground. Boys of ten or twelve earned less for eight hours. The owners deducted rent from the miners' pay. Miners had to buy their own picks and shovels, at inflated prices, from the company store. Families had to buy all clothing, furniture, and food—mealy flour, beans, and rancid fatback—at inflated prices from the company store as well. The owners hired certain people as spies. If a miner or his wife was seen purchasing something out of the coal camp in a noncompany store, the man was fired and mine guards evicted his family, often brutally, from the shack and the coal camp. Appalachian coal mining had the highest profit margin in the history of American industry.

Between 1906 and 1935, forty-eight thousand men died in the mines. Sixteen percent died as the result of explosions and 71 percent because of roof collapse, which clearly indicates shoddy, unsafe construction. West Virginia courts ruled every death an "act of God" and absolved the owners of responsibility, pointing out that the miners had more than once been given pamphlets that advised them to "be careful." As one West Virginia governor, who eventually became a coal company executive, observed, "Why, it's only natural for miners to die underground."

It was not at all uncommon for an Appalachian man to work three or four months in a mine, then abruptly quit and return to his farm— if he had a farm to return to. A growing number of other men, after listening to neighbors describe life in the coal towns, never applied for jobs. The idea that able-bodied men would refuse "honest work" to live an indolent subsistence life of hunting and fishing outraged the coal owners. The editors of local and state newspapers, now part of the coal industry, shared their outrage and wrote scathing editorials chastising their shiftless neighbors. They begged the industrialists not to become impatient with the backward culture, which they had managed to escape, and not to withdraw the gift of progress from their sad little communities. Above all else, their backward neighbors needed to learn that work in the mines was a "blessing rather than a curse."

As operations expanded in the early 1900s, the mine owners needed more men. The coal barons sent recruiters to Europe and the Deep South with pamphlets promising the American Dream. Roughneck Appalachian men who had been swindled out of their land, black men from southern jails, and Europeans who spoke no English created an extremely volatile mix. To this, add the absence of police and an endless supply of rotgut whiskey at ten cents a bottle, and the savagery of the coal camps seems inevitable. The mine owners, absolute monarchs in their respective towns, did nothing about health, nutrition, sanitation, or the daily brutality. In fact, company spies and agents actively promoted racism, mistrust, and hatred among the groups. Men who hated one another were less likely to form unions.

But the unions did come, and, as impossible as it might seem, the almost twenty years between 1912 and 1930 made the previous two decades in the Appalachian coalfields seem pastoral in comparison. The owners hired armies of thugs, many of them with criminal records, and turned them loose on the miners. Both sides took part in vicious beatings and murders daily. The governor and legislature of

West Virginia "officially" stayed out of the controversy. American workers and American owners, they said, should be left to sort out their problems as they always had. This was absurd, and everyone knew it. As a condition of employment, the coal companies forced miners to vote for handpicked politicians. The governors and legislators were former company executives or would become executives after a few years in office. Then as now, there was little difference between the state government and the coal industry. The moment it looked as though the struggle had shifted in the miners' favor, the governor ordered the militia and state police to help the owners.

The brutality escalated into what historians have called the "Mine Wars." The first war, from 1913 to 1917, ended when Senator Martine of New Jersey learned that a mine owner, in the middle of the night and without provocation, had strafed a tent camp of striking miners and their families with a fifty-caliber machine gun. The machine gun was on a train, and after passing through once, the mine owner said, "Let's back up and give the sons-a-bitches another round." Upon hearing this, Senator Martine, a member of the Borah committee appointed to look into the violence, asked, "This man, who in the name of heaven can he be? Who would propose to go back and kill more? Is he an ordinary citizen?" The coal company lawyer replied, "He will be before you, Senator." Martine exclaimed, "Well, God help us all then." This kind of attention temporarily reined the coal owners in and the first mine war sputtered to an end.

The second war, from 1920 to 1922, ended with more than five thousand armed miners marching toward Charleston. With the exception of the Civil War, this was the largest armed insurrection in American history. The battle line was drawn on Blair Mountain, fifty miles southwest of Charleston, when three thousand mine guards and state police, armed with fifty-caliber machine guns and gas grenades, dug in on the mountaintop. In keeping with established patterns, Governor E. F. Morgan stayed out of the controversy and refused to speak with union representatives. Ten thousand miners armed with deer rifles began to maneuver at the base of the mountain. This was not an unruly mob—the men had organized themselves into highly disciplined squads and units. They had a strategy and were determined to dislodge the mine guards and march into the state capital. The mine owners hired a small fleet of biplanes that began to drop bombs on the miners, which only made the miners more determined. It was going to be bloody.

When it became clear that the miners would prevail and march on Charleston, Governor Morgan appealed directly to President Warren G. Harding, who decreed martial law and sent federal troops to support the mine guards. When the miners understood that they were about to fight the United States Army, they laid down their deer rifles and walked out of the woods. The miners were not frightened, but many of them were loyal Americans who had fought in World War I.

The government took no action against the owners, but scores of union representatives were tried and some went to prison. The owners summarily fired fifty thousand miners and threw them out of their shacks in the coal camps, forcing the men and their families to spend the winter in caves or tents. No one knows how many men, women, and children starved or froze to death, but by spring the miners had caved in and begun to work in nonunion mines again.

By the late thirties, the union had prevailed and the worst was over. Living conditions and safety conditions improved. Miners' pay rose substantially. But fifty years of savagery had devastated the coalfield landscape as well as the subsistence cultures in that part of the region. Thousands of families that had been swindled out of their land became refugees entirely dependent on the boom-and-bust cycle of coal. In the early sixties, automation in the mines created widespread unemployment and families migrated out of the coalfields into Midwestern cities. Now, as I have said, many families traveled into North Carolina. As always, the erroneous assumption of outside observers is that these backward people created their own nightmare.

THIS WRENCHING history resolves itself in images: driving along, I keep noticing streams littered with plastic bags, paper, shopping carts, aluminum cans, rags, broken furniture, household appliances, car parts, a baby carriage, and at least one dead dog. No one cares about this land. The people have been living in company homes on company property for more than a hundred years. Everything belongs to King Coal, so why should they care? The owners—a few up on Squirrel Hill, but most outside the state—don't care either. This is their factory, their slaughterhouse floor.

In diners, at least one table always seems filled with unemployed miners, rough men who surround their coffee cups with both hands and reek of aftershave. They are like a Greek chorus commenting on the coal-town play. Invariably, one man looks up and holds my eyes for several seconds. I can almost hear him think, You ain't from here. You've come down to do some kind of survey, write something up for a newspaper, screw us one more time.

In a Burger King, one man tells his companions, "Well now, buddy, they said they moved the bodies, but what they done was move the headstones. That's all they done. Somewheres, they're burning my grandpa." He laughs and his friends laugh with him. It's dead-end cynicism that makes me think of Indian reservations I've been on out west where lives seem forever on hold.

At a long ramshackle bar that might have been a train depot, the bartender says to me, "Come on in. Yes, sir, come right on in. It's a little early; the girls aren't here just yet." Moments later, as I walk out, a long white Pontiac pulls up against the curb. A blond woman wearing a snow-white dress with her hair up in a huge beehive struts toward the front door. Another car pulls up behind her and two young women, coal miner's daughters, get out and smooth down tight, short skirts.

In Man, there is an XXX drive-in movie. Up against the sooty coal-town sky, a gigantic woman fakes sex with four men. Miners pull in and leave fifteen minutes later. Something human has been reduced to less than that.

Driving into a tight hollow past tiny houses jammed side by side, I am delighted. The miners are apparently working in this small town, and individual families have been fixing up the company houses to their own idiosyncratic tastes. Houses covered in aluminum siding stand beside houses painted wild purple. Others are covered with fake brick or green stucco. The lawns are filled with what my father called "do-hickies"—wooden ducks and woodpeckers that flap their wings when the wind blows; wooden cutouts of Granny bending over in her flowerbed exposing her polka-dot bloomers; entire families of plaster-of-paris deer, ducks, chickens, and squirrels; and stupendous colored glass balls sitting on pedestals. By the sheerest coincidence, a Spike Jones song comes on the radio. Spike deconstructs "Tea for Two" with sirens, Klaxons, honking bicycle horns, someone gargling followed by someone hiccuping. It's a variation of what I'm looking at outside the window. For a moment, I am freed from the oppressive weight of middle-class taste and find myself laughing out loud.

I climb the steep hill behind the courthouse in Pineville and come upon a lovely old home hidden in the trees. A flagstone walkway bends around rhododendrons to the front door. No one answers when I knock. This is the home of Bobby Bailey. Bailey is a big name in the coalfields. When John Kennedy campaigned here in 1960, this was his first stop. I knock again, but no one answers.

As I turn to leave, a young man in topcoat and tails, black silk hat, and walking stick appears around a turn in the path. At last, I have found the magician who has conjured the extraordinary visions I have seen since leaving Becky in Pendleton County. It turns out to be R. D. "Bobby" Bailey III himself, a man in his mid-thirties who plays in a rock-and-roll band and performs magic tricks at children's parties. He has just returned from such an engagement.

Later, after Bobby has changed into jeans and a sweatshirt, I climb higher up the mountain with him, and he explains, "Dad was the one Kennedy came to see. He lives right up here." The house is quite new and has been built by an architect obviously influenced, three or four times removed, by Frank Lloyd Wright. The lines are long and clean and everything is on one floor. The interior is beautiful—elegant furniture, costly antiques, two enormous china closets filled with crystal. There are Japanese prints on the walls and cut flowers in a Steuben vase. R.D., "the old man," and Mrs. Bailey are gracious, intelligent people. Turning to Bobby, R.D. says, "Fix us something, son." Bobby hurries off and returns with a beer for me and a mint julep for his father.

As I sip my beer, Mrs. Bailey shows me her prized possession, a concert grand piano that Paderewski once played. About Kennedy, who came to call, she says, "Charming fellow on TV, but in person the coldest man I have ever met." The slightest suggestion of a smile takes R.D.'s face.

And so, there is a middle class here. Local politicians, coal managers, schoolteachers, small businessmen, doctors, dentists, ministers, librarians—and they live and aspire like middle-class people all over America. They are every bit as "Appalachian" as the coal miners or my neighbors in Pendleton County, but would be just as quick to reject the label. No one wants to be an Appalachian hillbilly, two words too often taken to be synonymous.

Coal dust is in the air as I descend into yet another coal town and I sense that I have come to Appalachia's coal-black cellar. The streets are deserted. There is a restaurant in what was once a public building, perhaps a school or bank. One gigantic room is filled with small tables, which are mostly empty. The proportions are all wrong here. The cavernous room makes the tables and the people sitting at them seem like fixtures in a doll's house.

Halfway through my meal, an older man reading something at a nearby table scoots his chair back and approaches me. He resembles the Wizard of Oz.

"Good evening," he says.

I say, "How you doin'?"

"Fine," he says.

He smiles and nods and then stutters a bit.

"Might I—might I ask about your business here? A survey, perhaps? A report for some journal?"

"Just sightseeing."

"Ah," he says, "a tourist."

"Sort of."

His smile brightens once again. I smile back. He returns to his table. On my way out, I circle past his table to see what he's reading. It's the *Wall Street Journal* opened to the stock-market pages. Here in the cellar of Appalachia, the Wizard peruses his stocks.

9. A Fifth Season

A FEW days after returning home from Charleston and the coalfields, I walked out of a store on Main Street and was struck, once again, with how pretty Franklin was, this lovely, vest-pocket town in the unspoiled mountains. I was happy to be back after my ramble through Charleston and the coalfields. It came to me that Franklin could have been like one of the bombed-out coal towns I had driven through if Appalachian geology had been slightly different. Had there been coal below my feet, the industrialists would have come for it. Half a dozen families would have become as wealthy as the MacCorkles and perhaps built mansions. Driving back up Anderson Hill, I remember thinking how lucky Pendletonians were to live above worthless limestone.

As winter approached, I went fishing on the South Branch one last time. I built the first fire in the basement stove with Heckle and Jeckle's wood. Christopher made the freshman basketball team, and one afternoon some friends came to hang out in his room for the first time. I was introduced to Jim Underwood. I drove George Dice around Franklin and heard more of his philosophy and frustrations. The leaves dropped from the trees on the mountains, slowly at first and seemingly all at once after a rainy night. And then it was deer season.

In Pendleton County, when elementary school teachers ask their students to name the seasons of the year, children sometimes offer "deer season" as one of them. For many county families, deer season is a more important holiday than Christmas and New Year's. The season opens on Monday of Thanksgiving week and lasts fourteen days, but the first week, as a hunter once told me, "is what it's all about."

Men who have left the county to find work take Thanksgiving week off and come back home.

Until the early 1960s, county schools closed only on Thanksgiving Day and the day after. But holding class on the other three days became more and more absurd. On opening day, most boys from fourth up to twelfth grade came down with mysterious illnesses, and so did many of the male teachers. The teachers who did show up had to teach combined classes of students (mostly girls) from various grade levels. For a time, the board tried closing school on opening day *and* Thanksgiving Day, and while attendance improved, it remained spotty throughout the week. Given the disruption, board members and teachers alike began to wonder how much real learning was going on during this short week. In light of a very tight budget, the board also realized that they were heating empty classrooms and keeping almost empty buses on the roads. Opting for realism, school is now closed for all of Thanksgiving week.

The advance elements of the deer-hunting army arrived on the Friday afternoon before Thanksgiving. County roads and Franklin streets became crowded with cars and camper trucks from out of state. I can remember being downtown and admiring the camper trucks decorated with decals of marlin-sized rainbow trout and buck deer that would dwarf the Hartford Insurance stag. By that evening, town diners and stores filled up with hunters in a riot of camouflage outfits and those Day-Glo orange hats that make you squint.

Near dusk, I went grocery shopping at the IGA and ended up in a checkout line behind several men in camouflage outfits buying hunting supplies—little pull-top cans of Vienna sausage, beef jerky, Campbell's pork and beans, Dinty Moore beef stew, beer, lots of beer, and "Buck Lure," a liquid that can make hunters smell like lovesick does.

That night a friend I will call Murray took me to the Moose Club as a guest. I knew about the Moose. It was on a side street downtown. An orange neon sign, the only neon sign in Franklin, spelled out "Moose" vertically and cast its glow on the dusty window of Carl's Barber Shop, which had been closed for some time. On rainy nights when the blacktop was wet, the street reflected the sign, the orange bleeding off in a lovely way. It was one of my favorite Franklin images.

As Murray led me through a small parking lot, he said, "You won't believe this place; it's a trip." At the door, he pushed a button and then smiled idiotically into a one-way mirror. I said, "My God, it's a speakeasy." "Not much different," he said and smiled into the one-way mirror again. A loud buzzer sounded as the door popped open. I followed Murray inside.

I suddenly found myself in the middle of a blue-collar festival. At the time, the Moose Club was two rooms on the bottom floor of a musty old building. The barroom, the one you entered, was the smaller of the two. In the larger room there were pool tables, several video poker machines, and a round wooden table that might have come from someone's dining room. That night both rooms were so crowded men had to hold their beers hard against their chests. A dense fog of cigarette smoke, yeasty beer, and Mennen aftershave filled the air and everyone was supremely happy. Brothers, sons, fathers, cousins, and old friends had come back home to hunt, and there was talk of impossible bucks and improbable shots. Just below the crowd noise, the same record played over and over on the jukebox. The song, a ragged polka, went, "Oh, it's the second week of deer camp and we ain't got no deer," then went on to rhyme deer and beer half a dozen times. It was the perfect song for the festival.

I lost sight of Murray and began bumping through the crowd on my own. Someone poked me in the back, and when I turned, a man that my dad would have described as three sheets in the wind said, "Here, you old sombitch," and jammed a can of Old Milwaukee beer in my hand. He apparently thought he knew me, but before I had a chance to say a word, he squeezed back into the crowd. I was inexplicably happy. I could well have been at a wedding reception with my friends and brothers. I had come home again.

I spent about three hours at the Moose that night. I remember standing near the big, round table with a crowd of other men watching a poker game. A heavyset man with his billed cap on backward shuffled cards while he delivered a verbal riff. "Now here's a little game them boys brought over from Old Ireland on a sailing ship. You know it, you love it, can't hardly get enough. It's that old crisscross."

The evening rose to this point: A man at a table across the room stood up to pantomime the motions of shooting a deer, and for a second he became my father.

On Saturday morning, I wrote about my dad. We are back in the kitchen of the house on Francis Street, and he has spread the *Evening*

Bulletin on the tabletop to clean his 30-30. There is the biting smell of solvent and the wonderfully efficient sound of oiled metal as he works the lever action. His polished gun is beautiful. He lets me hold it and work the action. It is heavy and seems more real than I am.

Now he stands at the kitchen window with the gun at his waist, a distant look in his eyes. I think he is off somewhere. In my mind, I see him in the mountains around Piedmont, in that imaginary place that has become the center of my daydreams. It's a shadowy forest; the giant trees rise up to the sky. Moss. Fallen leaves. Suddenly his expression changes, and the gun jumps to his shoulder. In my mind I see Oscar, his trophy buck, plunge to the ground in slow motion.

I decided to buy a 30-30 that day. When I left Alaska, I had given my high-powered rifle, a 7 mm Magnum, to an Athabascan friend and had planned to hunt with a shotgun, but the day I toured the county I had seen a secondhand 30-30 in a country store in Sugar Grove, a village in the South Fork Valley half an hour from Franklin, and began to think about buying it. That fall day, I had decided I could not afford the gun but, on Saturday morning—after a night at the Moose Club—I convinced myself I couldn't do without it.

I left early in the afternoon. It was a typical November day in the county. The hills were gray and black, the open fields were textured patchworks of tan and faded browns, and the sky was pewter. When I looked up along the ridge tops, the twiggy black treetops made strange calligraphy against the gray. I drove up and over South Fork Mountain, which is substantially smaller than North Fork Mountain on the western ridge, and down into the South Fork Valley. Of all things, there is a Navy base in the valley, which is involved with coordinating the defense of the mid-Atlantic coast in the event of nuclear attack. They have dug tunnels deep under the mountains for super-secret equipment, or so I'm told. Passing the base, I watched two sailors in dress blues walking by a pond—a wonderful incongruity in the mountains.

Sugar Grove is ten houses, a Methodist church, and Bowers's gas station/store/post office. Old Mr. Bowers, grandfather of the present Mr. Bowers, built the small store from river rock. On November afternoons, the slanting light does a little magic with the stones, adding blue shadow to everything.

County people sometimes describe their Sugar Grove neighbors as "pretty Dutchy." This part of the South Fork Valley was settled by religious German families that kept to themselves and dealt with people outside their sect only when necessary. In 1748, as the story goes, George Washington, a strapping young man unaware of his destiny, surveyed in the South Fork Valley. From that expedition, an entry in his diary reads, "A great company of people, men, women, and children, attended us through the woods. They seem to be as ignorant a sect of people as the Indians. They would never speak English but when spoken to they speak only Dutch. . . ." In the late 1940s, a young woman from Virginia married the present Mr. Bowers, and for a time the new Mrs. Bowers worked in the family store. When certain older farmers came in, she had to fetch her father-in-law from the back room because, after more than two hundred years in America, they spoke "only Dutch." A few Sugar Grove families still speak German in their farmhouses, but the old language is almost gone.

The present Mr. Bowers, a man in his sixties, with an impressive set of muttonchop whiskers, has arranged his small store the way some people arrange their attics—find an open space and stick something in it; there are car tires behind the stuffed fox and so on. I had planned to be a shrewd trader, but there was no hope. Bowers understood how much I wanted the gun as soon as I held it. When I suggested a lower price, he just looked toward the ceiling and pursed his lips in silence. As my dad might say, the man saw me coming. I paid too much, but it was my father's gun, an old heavy Winchester with a lever action that made a wonderful steely click.

With the *Pendleton Times* rather than the *Evening Bulletin* spread on the kitchen table, I cleaned and oiled the 30-30 late into the night. Standing at the kitchen window, throwing the gun to my shoulder, I shot imaginary bucks in the side yard.

In bed that night I kept thinking about my father, wondering whether he would be deer hunting in the morning. I thought about his Oscar story. As a boy, it had been my favorite. I would ask him to tell it and he would say, "But I already told you." I'd plead a little and he'd give in.

The story went like this: A year or two after leaving Piedmont, my father was a redheaded hillbilly working at General Electric. When the men on his shift ate lunch sitting on the floor against one wall, my father sat by himself. In October, a small group began to talk about deer hunting in the Poconos. My dad pretended to be lost in thought, "but see, I got my radar switched on. I'm hearing everything." He had not hunted deer since leaving Piedmont and desperately wanted to go, but was far too shy to ask, especially because the other men sometimes hazed him, calling him "Hillbilly" or "Li'l Abner." It was best to keep his distance. Then, just days before the hunt, one of the men got sick, and the other three needed someone to pick up expenses. They asked my dad.

Things went well enough driving to the Poconos and on the night they arrived. But the next morning, the men told my dad to hunt by the cabin. They had good stands picked out, but were not about to take my father near them. If only to spite them, my dad did hunt by the cabin. As he told it, "It's getting light and I'm standing by this tree and I see something in the laurel. I'm thinking, is that legs sticking down? Maybe my mind's playing a trick on me. Then one leg moves. I must have held my breath for twenty minutes. Then he takes a few steps and I see him in an open place. Blam!"

At that point, I always jumped and then laughed. But that wasn't the best part of the story. My dad field-dressed the buck—removing the intestines and inner organs—and hung it behind the cabin. "Me, I just go back in where it's warm, drink some coffee, you know, take a little nap. They all come back at dark time. Wore out. Never saw no deer. They start in on 'Hey Red, where's your buck?' and 'You get your trophy, Li'l Abner?' and I just say like 'Yeah, he's hanging out back.' They all laugh and say, 'That right?' 'How many points that buck have?' 'Oh about eight,' I say. Then the one goes out to the johnny house and comes running back in with his mouth open."

I knew the story had to do with deliverance long before I understood what deliverance meant. Those men at work had to respect someone who shot a deer like that. He wasn't a hillbilly. He had spent his life backing up, apologizing for being alive, but that buck was transcendence.

OPENING DAY and I wake to an ice storm. A sudden rain and plunging temperatures have encased every black branch in a sheath of ice, but the roads are clear and I leave the house well before dawn. On a steep mountainside I sit by the roots of an upturned oak—a natural blind—with the 30-30 cradled on my lap. With first light, everything turns silver-white, the sun tops the ridge, the light splinters and flashes all around me. I'm sitting inside a diamond. Two hours pass and nothing moves. As the morning warms, ice begins to crash down from the trees and I leave.

At the same spot the next day, I see broken branches and toppled trees in all directions. The beautiful ice storm has caused great damage. Within an hour, two does and two yearlings pass seventy yards away, making my heart race. Half an hour later, three shots in quick succession and two more half a minute later come from a hollow just below me. My father is with me—*Look sharp now; they could send 'um right at you.* Something crashes through the woods and another doe flashes past, white tail flying, not fifty yards away. *Hold tight now. Just wait. The old buck may have sent his ladies on out ahead.* Moments later, something crashes on the slope above me, but when I look, it has disappeared over the ridge.

I turn back to see a spike buck standing thirty yards away. He cannot see me, but has caught my scent. Doubling back into the hollow is certain death, but going farther up the mountain, given what is on the air, alarms him. An older buck would know what to do, but this small deer is perplexed. He turns to look back over his shoulder, and I raise the 30-30 and brace against a root. He fills the scope and I can see muscles twitching under his dark hide. He stomps one foot and then stomps again. I push the safety off and watch him walk into a laurel thicket. I have let the deer go and do not know why.

Driving back toward Franklin, I pass a pickup parked along the road shoulder near a spring. Two men in camouflage were staring into the back of the truck. That image *is* deer season in the Appalachian Mountains. I turn around and go back to look at their buck. Over the years, it has become difficult for me to look at dead deer, at the blood and the wound and the soft brown eyes coated with dust. I found myself staring hard at the rack, forcing my eyes there and there only. It was a fine eight-point that I found less imposing than Oscar, but my dad's trophy still grows in my mind. "Beauty," I say.

One man said, "By God, yes," and his companion, who probably shot the deer, grins. They drive off.

Back in the car, I became frustrated with myself. I had held that spike buck in my scope for a good two minutes and could not have missed at that range. Becky, Chris, and I like venison more than beef. I had bought the license, bought the gun, then let the damn deer walk off. Killing animals, even bass, has always created conflicting emotions in me. I am my father's son, and there will always be something religious about feeding my family food from the wild. But I have come to love the things I hunt and fish. The pleasure I feel in catching or shooting something has always been mixed with sadness, but as I get older, the sad part gets stronger.

That evening a couple stopped by the house. The woman was one of Becky's new friends and the fellow, a few years younger than me, was a grown-up farm boy. He was one of those West Virginians more comfortable in the woods than inside a house and, like many of these men, a little shy around people he did not know. He hung back by his truck, adjusting and readjusting his cap in a way that made me think of my father. The woman explained that he had shot a six-point buck, but, like many county hunters, wanted to keep looking for a better trophy. If we would like to have the deer, I could use my tag and make it almost legal. Becky said, "We'd love it. John hasn't even seen one."

In Alaska my Athabascan friends taught me to get the hide off an animal as fast as possible, then hang the carcass right away. So I got started by driving two nine-inch nails into a roof beam in the garage. Then I cut slits in the hide just above the deer's rear ankles and tied small loops of rope through each cut. Becky stood on a kitchen chair while I bear-hugged the deer, raising its back legs toward the nails. As always, this was somewhat difficult. At about a hundred pounds, the field-dressed carcass was not that heavy, but it's awkward weight. I huffed and puffed and stumbled around while Becky directed me left and right. With the loops over the large nails and the deer securely hung, Becky left the garage.

The deer now hangs upside down, its antlers almost touching the cement floor. Facing the deer's back, I cut a circle just above the ankle on each hind leg with my fillet knife. Then walking around to the belly side, I cut a straight line through the hide of each inner thigh from the circle in toward the deer's middle, being careful not to cut the meat. The rest of skinning is a process of tugging the hide down as you lightly cut at sticking points. Getting the hide over the front shoulders can be a little tricky but is not all that difficult. If you are good at this, you can remove the head with a pocketknife, but I must use a butcher's saw. I stand back to look at the naked carcass, glistening silver white and rose pink hanging upside down from the rafters, and feel a certain satisfaction. I have done right by this animal; its death has not been pointless.

For the next week I check on the deer two or three times each day. The red and pearly white skin becomes as dry as parchment, which is what I want. Moisture, stickiness, is my enemy in this process, for it will induce rot rather than aging. The dry, papery skin protects the meat from bacteria while it hangs. If the weather is right, below fifty-five but not freezing, a carcass should hang for at least a week. An Athabascan friend explained it this way: "Steak meat is like these long strings of paper clips all hooked together. When it hangs, the paper clips start to come apart. It's better to eat like that." Aged meat also has more flavor.

A full week has passed. Standing at the deer's back I insert the tip of my fillet knife into the flesh just below the large ham muscle on one side until it hits backbone. When the knifepoint stops, I run it easily down toward the head of the deer, feeling the backbone against the blade the entire time, then stop at the shoulder blade. Back up at the ham, I make a horizontal cut away from the backbone across the deer's back. The long cut down along the backbone and the short one across the back connect at right angles. By gently pulling down and slicing lightly against the backbone, a long beautiful strip of meat easily pulls away, almost falling into my hand. This is what Appalachian hunters call "back strap," the equivalent of "New York strip," but far more interesting as food.

Laying the back strap on a sheet of white butcher paper on the floor, I repeat the process on the other flank, and then cut the front shoulders free. Next I saw through each set of ribs and the backbone, which I save for soup. With a cleaver and a hammer I free one hindquarter from the other. The hams now swing free on their ropes. I will let them age a few more days.

This work is not as gruesome as you might think. Field-dressing an animal can be messy and unpleasant but if a hunter has done that part properly—and the man who shot the buck was an expert—the rest is clean work. There is virtually no blood and very little mess. The obvious quality of the meat would excite any cook, and being part of the process connects me to the world more directly. A man cannot be a complete loss if he can skin and butcher a deer, even if he cannot bring himself to shoot one.

The next day, I took the antlers, head, hide, bones, and scraps out into the woods. Coons, opossums, turkey vultures, or possibly a bear roused from winter sleep on a warm day would make good use of it. Field mice would even gnaw away at the antlers until they were gone.

For dinner I cut half of one back strap into butterfly steaks and marinate them in a decent burgundy, shallots, and half a teaspoon of extra virgin olive oil. I make fruit chutney with apples, dried apricots, prunes, almonds, honey, nutmeg, a little lime juice, and just a touch of hot sauce. I broil the butterfly steaks until they are just pink at the center and put a teaspoon of hot chutney on each one. I make rice pilaf and open a jar of pole beans from Beaty's garden. Salad and garlic toast completes the meal. Thinking about my father is part of this recipe.

10. Woodlands Mountain Institute

I T'S IMPOSSIBLE to say exactly how or when each rumor in the counterreality about Woodlands began, but here are the most common rumors: *Some say they're Communists.... I heard tell they got tunnels dug all under that mountaintop.... I tracked a wounded buck onto that land up there and found this small plane hidden under a brush pile. You tell me now ... They're growing marijuana.... It's all some experiment on us.... All of 'um go to different churches, spread'n out you know.... One of them cults ... I've seen the CIA set things up like it in Africa.... Oh, it's a money-making deal. These elite people with connections have found a way to get rich.... I can't rightly say what they're up to, but it's like my neighbor said just the other day, they bear watch'n.* Most of this was absurd, of course. The institute never had anything to do with the CIA, marijuana, social experiments, or cults, and there were no tunnels under the mountaintop property. The fact that Woodlands members went to different churches merely reflected a diversity of religious beliefs. Dan'l Taylor-Ide and Jim Underwood were both interested in small experimental aircraft and so they constructed one on the mountaintop. Rightly or wrongly, county people have always been willing to believe *anything* about Woodlands.

The largest part of the problem was the evolving nature of the organization and what county people saw as bizarre behavior. In 1972, as I have said, Woodlands started as a kind of wilderness school. Then in 1982 it became a "technology center for mountain people." The transformation occurred, as some people pointed out, not long after an announcement in the paper stated that "millions" would become available from state and federal grants for projects involving energy-efficient technology like earth shelter construction. At about the same time, Woodlands also became a "Scholars Program" that served as a conduit between West Virginia's brightest students and prestigious universities. Then it became a travel agency that offered tours to Nepal, a provider of hostels for the elderly, and a manager of an international park on the Chinese-Nepalese border. Dan'l Taylor-Ide had also expressed an interest in buying a regional newspaper. In short, the institute seemed to be a swirling mirage that had no boundaries or limits, nor, for that matter, a specific identity. From Pendleton County's point of view, Woodlands could evolve into anything.

Sometime after my first deer season, people added yet another rumor to the list: Woodlands had come into the county "to tell us how to live." The institute's mission statement at that time—"advancing mountain culture and preserving mountain environments"—had begun to appear in newsletters and brochures sent to foundations and potential donors. Oddly, this was not announced in the *Pendleton Times*, but somehow the information filtered back, raising levels of anxiety and anger in the county. The notion of "advancing mountain culture," in local opinion, meant that Woodlands had evolved into a missionary organization, and this was a serious problem. Social and religious missionaries have been coming into the southern Appalachians for more than a hundred years, and this has created a great deal of resentment. As a man at the Moose Club said one night, "Those people have been shooting themselves in the foot since the day they got here, but deciding to save us from ourselves, that was it. There's been too damn many missionaries in this part of the country. We've been damn near saved to death."

Like almost all of the region's problems, the difficulty with missionaries began between 1880 and 1920 during the industrial war. Viewing the region's history in the broader context of American history will make things more clear. In the decades after the Civil War, middle-class Americans were caught up in the "Christian America movement." Simply stated, the movement was a shared conviction that America was, or perhaps should be, a monolithic Protestant culture rather than a ragtag jumble of many cultures. In newspapers, articles, books, and especially in missionary literature, expressions like "one Christian nation" or "one Christian America" appeared again and again like a mantra. Given the fact that the Civil War almost destroyed America as one nation, the preoccupation is understandable.

As part of the Christian America movement, the American Missionary Association (AMA), a consortium of Protestant churches that included Methodist, Presbyterian, New Baptist, and Congregationalist, became involved with the Freedmen Schools in the South. These schools were established to educate former slaves and to make them part of one Christian America, if only as servants, cooks, and maids. Some black scholars are extremely ambivalent about the AMA's efforts during Reconstruction, but the Freedmen Schools succeeded on at least one level, in that black families flocked to them.

Unfortunately, the idea of "Yankee" missionaries teaching black people enraged Southern whites, who shouted "nigger teacher" whenever the missionaries, primarily unmarried women from the East and Northeast, appeared on the streets of Southern towns. Being persecuted, from a safe distance, excited the missionaries and stiffened their resolve, but the prevailing bitterness also created a serious dilemma. White Southerners would have nothing to do with the churches that supported Freedmen Schools. Needless to say, the AMA wanted to save white Southern souls as well as black, but in a sense the missionaries had become victims of their own success. The problem became more desperate when Mormon missionaries appeared in the South in the late 1870s. At the time Mormons considered black people a subspecies, which gave them an advantage with embittered Southern whites. The AMA was confronted not only with the loss of white Southerners but with their conversion to a "false religion," which threatened the AMA's vision of one Christian America.

The AMA believed that if it could successfully launch an extensive recruiting effort in the Appalachians, where only whites lived, their missionaries might gain new life in the South. Unfortunately, according to its own bylaws, the AMA could only send missionaries to "unchurched people" who belonged to an "exceptional population." (In the AMA's view, an "exceptional population" was a population like American blacks, Native American tribes, or immigrants from the same country who shared the same language, backward customs, and "false religion"—Judaism or Catholicism.)

There were active Christian churches all through the southern mountains and the missionaries knew this. In fact, people in the Appalachians may well have been among the most "churched" people in America at the time. The churches did not belong to the AMA, however. No one, least of all the people in the southern Appalachians, thought the residents of five different states shared a distinct culture. But thought proving father to the deed, the AMA officially declared residents of the southern Appalachians an "exceptional population of unchurched mountain whites" and with this invented a new American minority.

Between 1880 and 1920 the AMA established "Home Missions" throughout the Appalachians at an astonishing rate. Relations were difficult from the start, beginning with the assumption of religious or social backwardness; no matter how softly missionaries spoke or how good-hearted they were, their very presence suggested inferiority to local people. A striking difference in theology added to the problem. The missionaries, who had been profoundly influenced by the theology taught in New England seminaries in the early nineteenth century, saw themselves as "exponents of the purest form of Protestantism in the world." In their view, God was a logical Being and Christianity was a logical enterprise. Reason led to salvation. Good Christians *thought* their way to Heaven.

But people in the southern Appalachians had come from a different, though equally valid, religious tradition that placed emotion over reason in spiritual matters. In this view, the Holy Ghost informed the heart rather than the mind. Man's intellect was dreadfully flawed and therefore of no use in the search for salvation. People in the southern mountains valued intellect in earthly matters but they believed God was beyond human understanding.

Contrasting the services makes differences clear. Missionaries conducted quiet, dignified services in small chapels. A seminary-trained minister in clerical dress delivered a well-reasoned sermon and led the congregation through tasteful hymns. Hopefully everyone went home thinking about the sermon. Mountain ministers, "preachers," were untrained and sometimes illiterate. Appalachian communities more or less elected their preachers: The Holy Ghost would move this brother or that sister to testify, and if this touched people's hearts, the congregation asked that person to be their preacher. They held mountain services in log barns or, when the weather was pleasant, in groves of sugar trees. These were wildly emotional affairs. Touched by the spirit, a preacher paced or danced in front of the congregation shouting in a syncopated rhythm about sin, hellfire, and the fast-approaching end. People shouted, spoke in tongues, danced, wept, or occasionally passed out cold. Mountain services were cathartic, and people walked home emotionally exhausted but spiritually renewed.

At first, people in the Appalachians were extremely curious about the missionaries and their new religion, and there are many accounts of families walking great distances through the forest to attend Home Mission services. Time and again the missionaries were struck with how quiet and attentive these people were. Sitting as still as statues, probably worried about violating some commandment of the new religion, mountain families hung on every word.

Missionaries found mountain services appalling and rarely attended them. In letters and reports sent back home, they often expressed exasperation and disgust with mountain people and their "so-called religion." Mountain "ministers" were not trained or paid. They did not live in a parsonage apart from people but worked in the fields like everyone else. Some of them were even women, which was heresy. Mountain ministers "pretended" to preach and the people "pretended" to be moved. The missionaries had real "thoughts" about the world and God, while mountain people had childlike "impressions."

What most offended the missionaries was the horrifying display of emotion during mountain services. Being Victorians, they naturally imagined God as a Victorian gentleman who expected his children to be clean, well-mannered at table, properly dressed, grammatical, and above all else, restrained. Actually having emotions was shameful enough, but public displays were an abomination.

The realities of raising money added to missionary difficulties. Home Missions were funded by supporting churches, grants, and donations, and as more and more missions opened, competition for limited monies grew increasingly intense. In their determination to go on with their work, the missionaries were compelled to make the strongest case for desperate need in their own corner of the mountains. In letters, fliers, pamphlets, and speeches, they systematically emphasized aspects of mountain poverty and "otherness" at the expense of anything that might have been considered normal or even admirable.

Establishing cultural "otherness" was at least as important as establishing poverty. If one thinks about it, mainstream Protestants rarely, if ever, missionize their social or cultural equals. The people in need must not only be lost in a false religion, or savages without religion, but also childlike people lost in a strange, inferior culture. In fact, the notion of being "cultured" or "sophisticated" was far more important than faith or dogma. In their determination to create one Christian America, the missionaries saw any deviation from their own view of appropriate speech, dress, or manners as substandard. Their work would not be done until *all* Americans had become homogenized into proper Victorian ladies and gentlemen. To this end, distortion became a habit.

How aware the missionaries were of their fund-raising exaggerations, especially at the start of the missionizing effort, is an open question. They had left fine homes and a highly mannered society for an American frontier. A few miles beyond prosperous county-seat towns like Franklin, families lived in log cabins and drew water from springs. People still grew, gathered, shot, or caught almost everything they ate, and dressed in homespun. The bloodthirsty Hatfield-McCoy culture created by the industrialists, the politicians, and the media never existed, but mountain cultures were gritty and visceral. Like cowboys, loggers, deckhands, and tough immigrants in cities, Appalachian men often settled disagreements "out behind the barn" and in fact considered "a knock-down, drag-out fight" prime entertainment. Like frontier families anywhere, these people were not terribly concerned about personal hygiene or appearance and had crude table manners. Much of what the genteel Victorians witnessed no doubt shocked them, and this surely made it easier to overlook what was vibrant and admirable about mountain cultures.

In short time, distortion became a deliberate practice. In 1915 and again in 1917—as David Whisnant recounts in *Modernizing the Mountaineer: People, Power, and Planning in Appalachia*—U.S. Commissioner of Education Philander Claxton addressed the annual conference of mountain missionaries in Baltimore. Claxton had been Superintendent of Schools in Asheville, North Carolina, and knew the people in that part of the region. He admonished the assembled missionaries, saying, "There is a good deal of sentiment displayed when people talk about the mountains . . . and those living in the mountains are called 'Mountain Whites' or by some other term that sounds like a popular rose. . . . There is a general impression that these are a peculiar people, and I think that you who are engaged in mountain work are largely responsible for it." In a 1917 speech to the same group, Claxton said that there was "no such thing as a breed of 'Mountain Whites.'" In *All That Is Native and Fine,* Whisnant describes Mary Routzhan of the Russell Sage Foundation criticizing a group of mountain missionaries in 1928 who had recently sent potential donors thousands of staged photographs depicting barefoot children. Children were not shoeless in the Appalachians, and Routzhan suggested that it might be better to tell the truth. Unfortunately admonitions like this had little or no effect on missionaries convinced they were doing God's work. For people passionately committed to any vision, means and consequences seemed far less important than the ultimate end.

The inherent awkwardness between missionaries and missionized people compounded problems. Telling people they are backward and that you have come to save them from themselves only makes them angry and the work of "uplift" more difficult. Understanding this, Appalachian missionaries became circumspect about their reasons for coming into the mountains. When people asked why they had come, the missionaries said things like "to do the Lord's work" or "to help." But this constant evasiveness created deep mistrust and suspicions of rank hypocrisy. When missionaries met an "Appalachian" after a church service or along a mountain trail, they smiled and spoke softly, often complimenting the person for no apparent reason. People felt talked down to, considered the compliments false and calculated, and suspected that the kindly missionary would be entertaining friends in Washington or Baltimore with raucous hillbilly stories in the months ahead.

As it turns out, these suspicions were often true. In 1915, according to Whisnant in *Modernizing the Mountaineer,* a public health nurse from North Carolina attended an AMA conference in Baltimore and was stunned to hear groups of missionaries regaling one another with "gossip of the rankest sort" in the hotel lobby. She refused to attend another conference, saying, "There are too many preachers for a heathen of my stamp and standing."

This suspicion remains a fact of life in the southern Appalachians. Once mythic Appalachia became part of the imaginary American landscape, the region became, as a writer named John Fetterman observed, "Mecca for those driven by demons and by self-guilt to do unto somebody somehow." The parade of religious and social missionaries that began in the 1880s has never stopped. AMA missionaries, Mormons, Seventh-Day Adventists, Catholics, VISTA workers, soldiers in the War on Poverty, Appalachian Volunteers, the Appalachian Regional Commission, and freelance radicals keep coming to save us from ourselves. Generally, these are good-hearted people whose desire to be of service is genuine but, blinded to their own cultural assumptions, they end up becoming part of the problem. They love Appalachians in the same way they love their pets and see themselves as three-dimensional figures in full color moving through the black-and-white movie of Appalachia. The various missionaries have differing agendas but the assumption about the people here remains the same. These colorful Appalachians, hillbillies, Mountaineers, Highlanders, or Celts can be appalling or beguiling by turns, but essentially they are children who need the assistance of adult missionaries.

From the outset, the relentless effort to "uplift" Appalachians has been fraught with irony. The AMA created an "unchurched minority" in order to pursue its own agenda, and then, hoping to convert people to the "purest form of Protestantism," displayed what a contemporary religious scholar named Deborah Vansau McCauley described as "an astonishing theological arrogance and intolerance." Missionaries frequently expressed contempt for the people they had come to "help" and, as they raised funds and entertained their friends, created stereotypes that people in the Appalachians will never escape. One mountain "problem" that early missionaries worked hard to address was violence. They saw the brutality that resulted from corrupt politics, greed, and social turmoil as the manifestation of backward culture and were determined to lead these childlike people to the gentle ways of Christ. But as soon as the Home Missions opened, the denominations began to fight vicious turf wars. Their battles entailed rumor campaigns, bickering, name-calling, backstabbing, dirty politics, contempt, and hatred that lasted longer than any imaginary feud.

In fact, Appalachian missionaries still fight about who is best qualified to advance these "unfortunate people."

Perhaps the greatest irony is that some early missionaries, perhaps many, understood what was really happening in the Appalachian Mountains during the industrial war. In private correspondence, they expressed grave concerns about "exploitation" and even said that the region and its people would never recover from the industrial onslaught. But the missionaries never spoke against the industrialists and never entered the boomtowns. For one thing, they had come from the same class of prosperous families as the exploiters and many of them shared the same values. Moreover, the robber barons responsible for the daily savagery had attended Harvard, Yale, and other prestigious universities. Who would question them? Like the missionaries, they were there to build a prosperous Christian America, and sadly that might require loss and suffering, if only on the part of the indigenous people.

Missionaries *were,* and still are, decent people with noble intentions, and many of them sacrificed lives of relative comfort to work long and hard in the southern Appalachians. But they were people as blind to their own cultural assumptions as most of us. Despite a century of "uplift," nothing has changed in the Appalachians, because the region's problems are the direct result of land and resource ownership outside the mountains. More than anything else the relentless "uplift" has created a deep reservoir of bitterness. When Woodlands decided to "advance mountain culture," the organization ran headlong into a hundred years of frustration with missionaries.

THROUGH MY first fall in the county, most local anger, at least in and around Franklin, focused on Jim Underwood, who was "networking" throughout the community. Jim talked with people, complimented them, and kindly suggested more efficient ways to do things. He recommended better crops to plant in their gardens. Meeting a person with a talent, he might put him or her in touch with someone with a similar interest. Good intentions aside, people saw Jim's networking efforts as an offensive intrusion in their lives. As one man said, "Somebody's told that guy he's a genius on a mission in Pendleton County. Whoever done that, didn't do Underwood or Pendleton County a favor."

As it turns out, my first impressions—as I watched Jim on Main Street in September—were right. He was an interesting man who had led an unusual life. After we met in late fall, not long after my return from the coalfields, we became friendly enough to stop and talk on Main Street. Born in 1944 in a very small town an hour west of Syracuse, New York, he attended Phillips Academy at Andover, then Syracuse University. At Syracuse he declared himself a conscientious objector during the Tet Offensive in 1968 and then fulfilled his CO obligation by working with Quaker organizations and on government projects. Like me, Jim had rambled around a lot—back and forth across the country, into Texas, Canada, and as far away as Nepal.

The most important moment of his life may well have taken place in the rock climbers' camp at Grand Teton National Park during the summer of 1966. Sleeping under a canvas tarp, he was awakened one morning by a commotion at the other end of the campsite. Bolting up, Jim saw a bearded man brandishing an ice ax as he chased a bear cub. Without a second thought, Jim grabbed his own ice ax and joined the chase. When the terrified cub disappeared into the trees, the two men introduced themselves and Jim's life changed.

The bearded man was Dan'l Taylor, and the story he told dazzled Jim. The son and grandson of highly regarded medical missionaries, Dan'l had grown up in India and Nepal in a small circle of elite Westerners. He had connections with the royal family of Nepal, the U.S. State Department, and the United Nations, and spoke Nepali, Hindi, Punjabi, Urdu, and Russian. At the time of their meeting, he was working toward a Ph.D. in education at Harvard. Dan'l was a visionary, a genius, but like Jim a man of action. What they had most in common, at least at the start of the relationship, was a passion for rock climbing.

With Dan'l's connections, Jim climbed Mt. McKinley in Alaska, Mount Logan in Canada, and a minor peak in the Himalayas. When Dan'l incorporated Woodlands Institute in 1972, Jim was part of the vision, but for the first ten years in Pendleton County, Dan'l simply did not have enough grant money to offer Jim a salaried position. Then in 1980, with a grant from the state and the Benedum Foundation, he appointed Jim a codirector of the technology center.

When Jim moved to Franklin in 1982—after those two difficult years in the North Fork Valley—he bought a small white bungalow at the base of Anderson Hill, less than a mile from my house. I can still remember the first time I went to visit. Stepping inside, I was immediately struck by the small, impeccably clean rooms with a few hand-woven rugs scattered on polished wood floors. An attractive bookcase fashioned from apple crates held titles like *The Third Wave, The Next Economy, Megatrends, Accidents in North American Mountaineering, Country Woodcraft, The Beans of Egypt, Maine,* and *The Tugman's Passage.* A few healthy plants hung from macramé straps and two cats, George and Squeak, slept in sunspots. The tables and chairs, obviously purchased piece by piece at auctions, had a Shaker simplicity. The only sign of disarray was the pile of paperwork on the drop-leaf table that served as Jim's desk against the window and even this was the clutter of a busy man. Jim's home made me think of graduate students—intelligent people with good taste getting by on very little.

Jim's range of knowledge, sheer energy, and willingness to try anything amazed me. Like the institute, he did not seem to have limits or boundaries, but could be whatever he decided to be. He once explained that he had planned his life according to a principle of botany: "In diversity is stability." Beyond being the director of the technology center and an expert rock climber, Jim was a whitewater-rafting instructor, a pilot who had built his own plane, a brewer, vintner, "builder," furniture maker (specializing in chairs), mechanic, gardener, occasional cook, homespun philosopher, computer whiz, welder, and student of Zen.

At any given time, he was in the middle of at least half a dozen projects beyond his work with Woodlands and had another dozen planned. In the yard beside his house, he had planted an experimental plot of bamboo, created an espalier of fruit trees, constructed an elevated garden plot, set up beehives, built a chicken coop, planted hops for beer, and had piled up lumber to build a workshop. Jim was also cultivating several bonsai trees and was especially fond of this project because it blended spirituality with horticulture.

With a touch of self-deprecation Jim referred to his notebook as "my paper brain." He kept it up to date, sometimes to the hour. Ideas, insights, new projects, reminders to call this or that resource person filled the pages—all of it written in a small, neat hand. He lined out completed or abandoned projects and drew slender arrows by those that would carry over to the next day. Even with his "paper brain," he often found it difficult to keep up with all of his ideas. Jim projected ego the way a woodstove projects heat. Each time we spoke I thought of Gatsby, the pure American belief that you can take your life, the future, or even the past into your hands and shape it to your will. Self-improvement. Human perfectibility. Reach down, pioneer, and take hold of thy bootstraps.

In time I would see this as part of the strain between Woodlands Institute and Pendleton County. Below the differences in theology, the distortion of fund-raising, and the suspicions of hypocrisy, belief in progress has always been the fundamental problem between missionaries and people in the southern mountains. Seen from the other side of things, the problem has always been Appalachian fatalism. This is a difficult concept if only because the people in Appalachia are as philosophically diverse as Americans anywhere else. The number of things that you might say "everyone believes" are rare. But a strong current of what most people would call pessimism runs through this region. Many people, perhaps most, do not believe in progress in the grand sense. We live longer, enjoy better health, suffer less pain, travel from one place to another faster, and do not work as hard to feed ourselves and keep warm. Only a fool would deny this. But as W. B. Yeats observed in a poem, "the foul rag and bone shop of the heart" never changes. Money and power always have their way while virtue goes unrewarded. We struggle through a vale of tears. American missionaries see history as a narrative that advances toward utopia. Many people in the southern mountains, Appalachians if you will, view history as repeating cycles. Century after century new actors dressed in new costumes play the same roles. There is nothing new under the sun. Whether this amounts to fatalism or realism depends upon your culture, but one way or another, Jim Underwood, with his belief in progress, was bucking the current of Appalachian thought.

11. Winter in the Mountains

THE SKY is steel gray and the sun is a white blister above the ridge. At dusk, the breeze picks up and it carries the taste and feel of moisture. The temperature has been in the teens on the Pendleton County Bank clock for several days, and the dampness makes it feel much colder.

In the basement at dusk, I settle the fire for the night. As it turns out, Heckle and Jeckle have slicked me. You want to burn wood that was cut a year earlier—or at least a full season. Aged wood burns hotter and faster. Fresh-cut wood still holds sap, which not only makes it burn less hot but also coats the stovepipe and chimney with creosote. This can result in extremely dangerous flue fires, of which there have been two on Anderson Hill this year. These are frightening affairs. Black smoke billows out of the chimney as sparks and flames shoot up like fireworks. The volunteer fire company comes racing up the hill with sirens and lights flashing. A catlike young man climbs up on the roof and swings a long, heavy chain around in the chimney, which breaks up the burning creosote. An entire house can burn along with everyone in it if the fire starts in the middle of the night. A little green wood mixed in with a truckload is all right, but most of the load I bought in September was green.

Out on the lawn, I walk around the house watching the smoke drift out of the chimney. It's white, the color it's supposed to be. As I watch, I notice it coming down, sinking in a wreath around the house. Momentarily, I'm in the station wagon with my dad, and he's pointing to the smoke from the row houses across the street. "It's sinking down," he says. "Change on the way." Looking around the yard, I see smoke from my neighbor's chimney sinking in the same way. I mumble, "Change on the way."

Not long after Becky falls asleep, the wind picks up. It moans as it tears itself against the tin rain gutter at the back corner of the house. My neighbor's German shepherd begins a soft, eerie whine as if trying to match the sound or perhaps sing in tune. His whine sets off the rest of Anderson Hill's doggie chorus: the retrievers baying from up the hill, a high-pitched Sheltie from somewhere behind the house, a few indiscriminate yaps, and then the bear dog's deep bugle from the base of the hill. I fall asleep to dog music.

Before dawn the phone rings and a sleepy teacher tells me, "No school today." After hanging up, I pull the curtain at the kitchen door and look into a white world. The yard is under a foot of snow, and more is swirling down. Here in Pendleton County, real winter begins after Christmas; if we're going to get a blizzard, it will usually be in January or February.

At dawn, I go out into the yard to knock the snow from the bird feeder and the suet holder and clear the ground around the post, then scatter seeds, stale bread, and crushed apples on the ground. Back inside, with a Bach tape on very low, I stand at the window to watch the birds swarm in. Finches, sparrows, nuthatches, chickadees, downy woodpeckers, blue jays, a pair of slender doves, half a dozen grosbeaks, and a pair of cardinals arrive. There is something holy about cardinals in the snow.

I bundle up and head downtown on foot. All of my neighbors are out shoveling their walks and driveways, and I stop to talk with them. Everyone is red-faced and happy, eager to talk. The storm had given us something in common, brought us closer.

Downtown, people walk *in* Main Street rather than on the sidewalks, a disorder that I like. I look for George Dice, but do not see him. It comes to me that he might stay at home on days like this. The snow-packed streets would make Franklin strange and foreign. The summer catalog from Burpee Seeds is in my post office box. Seeing all the bright flowers in the middle of a blizzard is a great pleasure, a promise of things to come.

Trudging up Anderson Hill, the black-and-white Border collie that I have seen crossing my yard since September breaks my thoughts. It's having a happy fit in the snow, diving down, rolling around, sliding on its belly like an otter, as it chews mouthfuls of snow. I stop and laugh out loud. The dog shakes itself and runs off. I turn to look at town, the small white houses of Franklin with smoke rising from their chimneys. The Anderson House is a castle in the snow. An oyster sky touches the mountaintops all around, and the expression "socked in," which the Aleuts often used on the island, comes back to me. One of the things I have always loved about Appalachia is the feeling of being safely tucked into the mountains. The blizzard makes this feeling stronger. I'm happy and at peace.

SNOWSTORMS ARE not pleasant affairs on county farms. At dawn, men fire up their largest tractors and plow through the drifts pulling hay wagons. An older boy, hired hand, or farmwife bundled up like a Russian peasant stands on the wagon pitching out broken bales of hay. Sheep have a hard time in deep snow, which they must swim through, but it's easier on cows with their longer legs.

The first lambs are born in January or February, the worst months of winter. The best market for lambs is in spring, and farmers time things accordingly. Sheep have a gestation period of five months, and so men turn their rams, "bucks" in Pendleton County, into pastures with ewes by late September. The lambs live on the ewe's milk for a good three months. The idea is to have them ready to sell by Easter.

Midwinter lambing season is frenzied. Casting out hay on frigid mornings, farmers watch for ewes that seem ready. As Everett Mitchell, Pendleton County's raffle ticket champion, says, "You can tell they're ready when they start making bag." Everett means that the udders fill with milk and swell up. Like farmers all over the county, Everett takes "ready" ewes into a barn or outbuilding the day he finds them. At times, he misjudges and comes out to find a dead lamb— blood and viscera frozen on the snow.

Most Pendleton County farmers raise Suffolk sheep that have been crossbred again and again to produce lambs rather than wool. The trouble is, most natural instincts have been bred out of the animals over countless generations. Certain ewes do better than others, but some of them do not know what to do when their lambs come. They panic and stagger about with a lamb half in and half out of their bodies. Once the lamb is on the ground, some ewes do not know what to make of their own offspring and will wander away from the struggling newborn, relieved to put the dreadful episode behind them. As often as not, the ewes need human midwives to hold them down, gently tug on the newborn, and then hold the lamb against the teat. When the milk starts to flow, instinct usually does kick in.

But some ewes never accept their lambs. Most winters, Everett will carry at least one orphan into the farmhouse and keep it in a box by his woodstove. He will feed it with a baby bottle just as you would an infant. Orphan lambs become pets and something of a pest. Later in spring, they run up to Everett whenever he appears in the pasture and butt against his legs bleating to be fed.

In January, county farmers often stay up two or three nights in a row midwifing sheep. Greg Bowers, the veterinarian in Franklin, once told me that his grandfather, who lives near the top of Spruce Knob, would move into an old shed with his sheep and try to keep them warm with a small wood fire while blizzards howled on the mountaintop. I have seen farmers fall asleep standing on their feet this time of year. Driving county roads in winter, you might think it's a slow time. Through most of each day, the farms seem utterly still, pastures under snow, and the livestock fixed in place. But inside the barns, it's the mess of being born and dying.

IT'S ONE of those crystal winter nights, a tar-black sky peppered with brilliant stars. We are driving over North Mountain to watch Christopher play basketball, an in-county game between the freshman teams of Franklin and Circleville high schools. Weaving up the mountain, the headlights glide over the winter-black trees on both sides of the road as the shadows loom up then lean back into the dark behind us. I love these mountains on winter nights. I am also excited about watching Christopher play basketball. He won't start and will not get much playing time—he has told me so—but I will enjoy watching him sit on the bench. At the mountaintop, starting down into the North Fork Valley, I decide that I am a typical American father and like the idea.

There isn't much to Circleville—a store, a gas station, and a few homes. This is how the town got its name. In the early 1800s, a German merchant named John Zyrkle built a dry goods store on the North Fork River not far from where the school now stands. As a matter of convenience, other families built cabins near the store and, in time, people began to call the settlement Zyrkleville. Fifty years of American pronunciation turned it into Circleville. Tonight the main street is deserted; two white lights squint in the cold, black air and each sign hangs motionless and dead. On this winter night Circleville seems a lonely outpost in the ice-cold mountains.

The school itself is an old brick building with a great deal of character—a two-story redbrick building with white columns on both sides of the entrance. It's what a country school ought to look like. Tonight, the parking lot is jammed, with more cars and pickups pulling in behind us. Games between Franklin and Circleville are always intense; I have learned that much. But a crowd like this for a freshman game truly surprises me.

Inside the school, we walk down a hall between trophy cases and pictures of the graduating classes from as far back as the 1930s. The gymnasium is very old and there is very little seating room. The bleachers on each side have only three or four rows of seats and the balcony above one side of the gym only creates seating room for maybe fifty more fans. The gymnasium is packed to overflowing, with people standing in the doorways and under the baskets.

The game begins, and both teams play like kamikazes, diving for every loose ball, leaping headlong again and again for each rebound, playing as if their very lives depended upon each basket. The crowd is also very intense and the noise inside the gym is deafening from the very first tip-off. When the first foul is called against Circleville, two men on the other side of the gymnasium rise to shout insults, faces flame-red and contorted with anger. One woman near me holds her husband by the arm as he struggles to come out of the stands and onto the court. I know how spirited crosstown rivalries can be, but this isn't right. People seem close to riot over a freshman basketball game.

Near the end of the game, Coach Smith puts Chris in, and my heart beats faster. He seems a little stiff, but does all right, I think. Magic Johnson is Christopher's hero, and now he attempts one of Johnson's famous no-look passes. It works well enough, but the other player misses the shot.

The ref calls a foul on a Circleville boy, and the outraged crowd is on its feet. Chris had nothing to do with the foul, which was committed at the other end of the court, but he is standing near the sidelines. One Circleville man, not six feet away, yells something and makes a fist at him. Christopher looks frightened and confused. Suddenly, I am on my feet and shouting. Becky keeps tugging on my hand. She is saying something, but her voice is lost in the uproar.

Those angry, flame-red faces filled my dreams for a week after the game and I was nervous and moody. The warm feelings I had about Pendleton County during the snowstorm disappeared, and once again I worried about my children. I had some sense of Pendleton County as a split community before the game. Once, in late November, I had stopped for gas in the North Fork. The attendant was pleasant, talkative, until he asked where I had "set up housekeeping." When I said, "Franklin," his demeanor changed at once. Jabbing a thick finger at me, he snapped, "Those Franklin people think they own the whole county." He glared at me and did not speak another friendly word. What struck me was not just the intensity of his anger, but his willingness to express it to a complete stranger.

And since August, I had overheard other remarks. According to some folks in Franklin, people in the North Fork were "funny." They were "rednecks," "hillbillies," and "always mad about something."

From the North Fork's point of view, the people in Franklin "look down on us," "they think we're hillbilly trash." Adding insult to injury, North Fork people are convinced that prominent Franklin families use that hillbilly vision to justify cheating them out of goods and services. They often speak of the new gymnasium beside Franklin High. "That million-dollar gym was intended for the entire county. But they built that thing right next to Franklin High and it belongs to Franklin," said someone from the North Fork. "If they run out of new textbooks, our kids get the old ones. They fix the roads all around Franklin, and if there's any surplus left over, they fix a few potholes over here." Real or imagined, the list of grievances is extensive, but below practical complaints you hear the bitterness of people struggling to reject the hillbilly label.

The basketball game made me realize how deep the animosity was, and I thought of racism back in Philadelphia. In my old neighborhood, you felt the dreadful strain between black and white like weather. The hatred simmered just below the surface of daily life and always seemed ready to boil over. Feelings in Pendleton County seemed almost that strong.

Gradually, I began to see the county split as a larger and far more damaging version of the split between the Bells and the O'Briens in Piedmont. You can find that social strain in every Appalachian community, but I had never encountered anything like the bitterness in Pendleton County. At first I did not understand, and my Franklin neighbors were of little help. Beyond saying that "it's always been like that" or suggesting it had something to do with how strange "those North Fork people" were, no one knew. In time, I would learn that this too started in the period of industrial war.

IN THE 1880S, as the Franklin families of McClure, Anderson, and Boggs became wealthy, the town prospered. By the turn of the century the entire country was Gatsby's America, and affluent Franklin families, like middle-class Americans everywhere, were determined to announce their arrival. There was a fair amount of urgency and insecurity about this endeavor. America had survived a civil war that almost destroyed us as a nation, and in 1876 we celebrated our one hundredth birthday. We had history and, more than anything else, we felt the need for "culture." Being Americans, we thought we could buy it in a breakneck hurry.

The children and grandchildren of Franklin's millionaires attended faraway finishing schools and then returned to Pendleton County with middle-class aspirations. Understandably proud of their affluence and "sophistication," they built large homes like the Anderson House and filled them with imported rugs, ornate furniture, bone china, oil paintings, and pianos. A literary society, the Pioneers, met in one fine home after another "to discuss literature and history." The Thespians presented plays. There were two hotels downtown, one of them, the Daugherty, was reputed to be the best in the South Branch Valley.

In 1896, Mistress Sally Anderson, a graduate of Stuart Hall in Virginia, established Liberty Hall Female Seminary in a large downtown home. Miss Anderson taught proper young ladies etiquette and the fine arts and Liberty Hall presented formal "evenings" for Franklin's elite families. One yellowed program that still exists announces recitations like "Selling the Farm" and "The Healing of the Daughter of Jarius." The evening also included singing duets and solos as well as a "dramatic comedy" entitled *The Champion of Her Sex*. Each summer, prominent Franklin families gathered at "jousting tournaments" in Thorn Spring Park. Ladies dressed in their finery watched men in smart suits race about on horseback. In short, Franklin nouveau riche families were behaving like nouveau riche families across the country.

But the dynamic was different here, if only in proportion. In the early 1900s, Pendleton County's social structure did not resemble a pyramid but a very slender obelisk with a scant handful of people at the needlepoint top. These county families, most from Franklin, controlled everything—employment, bank loans, land development, new businesses, the legal system, politics, and the newspaper. When the first permanent agricultural extension agent, D. W. McFarland, arrived in 1926, he was astounded by Pendleton County's "feudal" society. The "lords and ladies" from a few county-seat families held absolute power. McFarland had trouble establishing his agricultural programs because "no information was received by anyone except the Feudal Lords, and they dispensed as little as possible." In urban areas around the country or rural locations with higher populations, various families competed for the control of lives and resources. From a grassroots point of view, the struggle was taking place in the vague distance and the power brokers were abstract. In Pendleton County, the rich and powerful were people you knew, and they made the use of absolute power very real and very personal. Once again, this is Appalachia, and as county "lords and ladies" struggled to establish distance between themselves and the imagined lowest class, they turned their neighbors into hillbillies.

You get some sense of this in the county's *Pictorial History*. It's an utterly charming book, and at first glance, you seem to be looking into a Currier and Ives world, free of strife or complications. Men in coveralls pause in hayfields with Father Time scythes or stand beside stupendous fallen trees proudly holding great double-bladed axes. Handsome women bake cornbread in country kitchens or scatter feed to chickens. There are many pictures of horses and horse-drawn carriages and buggies. Milton Dolly stands beside a colossal registered Percheron named Old Champ. Cars appear. One day in 1907,

Mr. Ott Judy sits in his Maxwell—the first car in Pendleton County. He grips the wheel firmly, as if expecting the beast to buck and throw him. People march down Main Street, then a dirt country lane between shade trees, on the Fourth of July. Church groups sit on the grass to have "supper on the ground." The Circleville Coronet band, resplendent in new uniforms, stands in a perfect circle in Circleville. It's a lovely world.

But a closer look reveals something of what McFarland might have seen in the early 1900s. On one page, William Harrison Boggs, wearing a sash and sword, sits upon a Thoroughbred horse. A few pages later, a young black man wearing a floppy straw hat rides an ox across a field. In this picture, the "turkey pluckers" assemble on the steps of Boggs's store. They are a ragged lot and include a boy of about ten. A few pages later, four delicate young ladies in long white dresses stand on the lawn of Boggs's house holding croquet mallets as if they did not know quite what to do with them. They stare demurely toward the ground as gentle ladies should. On December 1, 1914, the twelve county officers stand in front of the courthouse door. They are all confidence, like people who have power and believe that they deserve it. On the opposite page, the "parish farm residents," the poor and unsound, look forlorn.

The most telling photographs are of county schools. In the earliest years of the last century, there were one-room schools all around the county. The children from the Franklin school are dressed like fashion plates. They wear shiny leather boots, sporty "caps," expensive-looking coats with large ornamental buttons. The children from outlying schools like Smith Mountain wear baggy coveralls, dresses made from flour sacks or mattress ticking. In some pictures, the teacher is the only one who wears clothing that actually fits. I should say that these photographs of poorly dressed schoolchildren could well have been taken in hundreds of other rural locations around the country at the time. In the 1920s, conditions on subsistence farms were much the same across America.

At the time a popular form of parlor entertainment among Franklin's elite families was telling stories about the hillbillies in Smoke Hole or Timber Ridge. The sophisticates regaled one another with tales of wild lives and wild behavior. It was all moonshine and fistfights, those crazy, uncouth hillbillies. Franklin men who traveled back into Smoke Hole or Timber Ridge to hunt or fish insisted that the stories were wildly exaggerated. In isolated parts of the county, there were a few outrageous characters, but surviving on a small subsistence farm was too difficult to allow for too much wild behavior. Those who were well informed pointed out that the churches and schools were in good shape and well attended and that there was a strong sense of community in these small places. One Franklin man happened to be in Timber Ridge on the day of a funeral, when the entire community formed a circle around the grave at dusk and sang every hymn they knew. At the end of their repertoire, they started over and kept singing until it was full dark. How outrageous could life be in a community like that?

But the admonitions had little effect on the families that told, embellished, and retold the stories. In fact, the tall tales were remarkably like the stories that missionaries told to their friends when they left the mountains. They were also like the stories by writers in what has been called the "local-color movement."

The local-color movement was another important element in the invention of the Appalachian myth. Once again a glance at American history will help make things clear. In brief, as eastern and northeastern industrialists became affluent, their sons and daughters went to prestigious colleges and ended up with leisure time. Leisure required diversion, which, among other things, meant monthly magazines. In 1850, the Harper brothers began to publish *Harper's* for "a limited class of highly cultivated readers." By 1890, there was the *Atlantic Monthly, Lippincott's, Scribner's, The Century, The Living Age,* and others, all devoted to the same "highly cultivated" group of American readers. The magazines told emerging middle-class families in the Northeast what they most wanted to hear: The "one Christian America" they wanted to believe in existed, and they were at its center. The readers of these magazines loved stories and articles about remote "corners" of America filled with exotic people who were "in America but as yet not of America." Writers who wrote about such things—there were perhaps several dozen—could have traveled to the Southwest or to Alaska or any other remote location to write about an exotic locale, and some of them did. But distant travel was expensive and difficult and the Appalachian Mountains were close at hand. Between the 1880s and the late 1920s, local-color books and stories about the Appalachian Mountains became, as they say, all the rage.

The plots of the stories and novels varied but followed a distinct pattern. A young man of means with a name like Egbert leaves his fine home in Boston or Philadelphia to "sojourn" in the Appalachian wilderness. By happenstance, he encounters a "mountain gal" as lovely as a wildflower—and about as smart—and is smitten. The chaste romance becomes complicated by a drunken father who, in at least one book, swings through the trees like an ape. Like virtually all Appalachian men in these stories, he is a "feudist," constantly drunk on "moonshine" and in the habit of randomly murdering his neighbors. The young man finds himself caught in a dilemma: hopelessly in love, but aware that marriage would be impossible. His mountain gal could never comprehend his sophisticated world of music, art, museums, and cultural refinement. Trapped between the glories of civilization and true love, he chooses civilization, if only because his mountain flower would wither when confronted with the dazzle of high culture.

Through all of local-color fiction, writers constantly set the sophisticated Victorian world in glaring contrast with the cruel, violent, feral world of the hillbillies. In fact, the contrast is so relentless it becomes clear that the literary technique appeals to something beyond a delight in the sensational. Contrasting an imagined Victorian world, of which they believed themselves to be a part, with an imagined hillbilly world helped convince middle-class Americans that they had indeed reached the peak of Western civilization.

Franklin's elite told and retold exaggerated stories about their neighbors for the very same reason. In fact, there was probably more urgency in the county in that people saw themselves as barely escaping the dreaded hillbilly ranks. It was easier for Franklin's affluent families to see themselves as rising if they imagined hillbilly neighbors on the lower end.

As realistic as shoot-'em-up Westerns or Harlequin romances, the local-color books were harmless diversions. At least they would have been harmless if readers had considered them fiction, but people read the books as journalism and reviewers gave them the status of sociology. Indeed, some universities used local-color novels in sociology courses. In turn, as missionaries competed for funds, they gave prospective donors local-color books to reinforce their descriptions of Appalachia.

As the twentieth century approached, prosperous county-seat families would surely have read many of the local-color stories, if only because they filled the pages of the fashionable magazines. Missionaries socialized with the local elite, and indeed considered their homes to be oases in a cultural desert. From the letters missionaries sent outside, it is clear that they thought a few county-seat families had managed to "uplift" themselves. This gave them hope. In return, elite county-seat families were delighted to be recognized as part of the sophisticated middle class and imagined themselves sharing a kind of noblesse oblige with the missionaries. Once again, elements from the dominant culture dovetailed as one need reinforced another. The wealthy families in Franklin pointed to Smoke Hole and Timber Ridge and told one another stories that confirmed both the existence of local-color hillbillies and the elite's great distance from them.

Old families disappear, wealth flows into other hands, as does social and political influence, but the American desire for ascendancy never varies. Missionary fund-raising, the media, and conditions in the coalfields that keep this region economically depressed have kept the myth of backward hillbillies alive. Smoke Hole, one of the most beautiful parts of the county, is primarily a National Recreation Area now. A few families still live down that way, but not enough to constitute a community presence. Now Franklin's prominent families point to the North Fork Valley and more specifically to Circleville to reinforce their middle-class status.

Prejudice is hard to pin down in any community. Ask prominent Franklinites about the North Fork, and they often begin with a disclaimer: "I have nothing against those people . . ." "Some of my best friends . . ." But as you listen, expressions like "those people" and "they" take on a pejorative weight. "Those people are just funny."

Occasionally, someone answers with more detail. As one prominent Franklin matron said, "The sophistication that came here through the Shenandoah Valley just never made it up and over North Mountain." A Franklin man involved with the arts committee and the historical society observed, "We are a cultured people in Franklin. Those people in the North Fork are rednecks. They have no culture."

But people in the North Fork are no less "sophisticated" or "cultured" than their Franklin neighbors. For reasons ranging from chance to personal choice, many North Fork people cling to subsistence life. Families struggle to keep their sheep despite mounting losses to coyotes. People still butcher hogs and cure hams at the start of winter. Men and boys hunt and fish with great passion. In my experience, many North Forkers are less concerned with money and middle-class status objects than their Franklin neighbors. Of course, you can make these observations about farm families all over the county, but what remains of traditional culture feels strongest in the North Fork Valley.

Words like "culture" and "sophistication" can be slippery. I have spent entire days with North Fork families like the Phareses. I've watched them split locust logs into fence posts and drive the posts into the ground with a nine-pound mallet. I've watched them castrate lambs and calves, gather their flocks, medicate stock, and butcher hogs. There is no lack of culture or sophistication here. In their world, I'm unsophisticated and uncultured. I'm not trying to say that subsistence culture is better or worse than consumer culture, but that it's simply different.

That difference, in the opinion of at least some middle-class Franklin families struggling to establish their arrival, turns people in the North Fork into hillbillies. It is very strange to hear someone from Franklin bitterly complain about being labeled a hillbilly, then express bewilderment about why the hillbillies in the North Fork are so bitter. Like the Bells and the O'Briens in Piedmont, Franklin and the North Fork Valley are caught in a social dynamic they do not understand.

12. Spring and Summer

I T CAN happen like this: You begin to notice more light at dusk. At sunset, the treetops on the western ridge take on a reddish hue as the buds swell. A day in late February or early March will break warm. Then, as often as not, it snaps back cold for a few days, only to warm up again. This vacillating freeze and thaw makes the sap run in maple trees. Until the 1940s Appalachian farmers tapped their sugar trees. Families piled tin buckets onto horse-drawn wagons and crossed through pastures—still patchworks of frozen ground and melting snow—into their sugar groves. When the sap was "run'n good," men spent entire nights in the sugarhouse to keep the wood fire burning under the huge pan of boiling sap.

One of Becky's fondest memories is walking into the sugarhouse, an old log building on her neighbor Jacob's land, when Jacob was making syrup. Steam rising from the boiling sap filled the sugarhouse with the fragrance of warm maple syrup. Jacob had a small tin cup that he would dip into the syrup and invite Becky and her brother to sample. Syrup making has almost disappeared, but a few people in the county still continue the tradition. My father-in-law, Jamie Sheets, is among the rare few. His grandfather had a grove of maples and a sugar camp on the North Fork of Deer Creek.

Syrup making ends when the weather settles, but it doesn't always settle into spring. In the southern Appalachians, March can bring the first warm weather or a winter blizzard, but when spring does arrive, there is no sweeter season anywhere in the world. In Pendleton County, coltsfoot, a low yellow flower that occasionally blooms through snow, comes up along the mountain roads. Then the forest floor erupts in wildflowers—hepatica, spring beauty, bird-on-the-wing, wake-robin, snow trillium, bishop's cap, showy orchis, bird-foot violet, and scores of others that I fall in love with every year. The first tree to blossom is serviceberry—"sarvis" in county talk. The hazy white trees dot the winter mountainsides like apparitions in early spring. Within weeks, the redbud trees bloom and then a beautiful variety of dogwoods—lime green, chalk white, and ivory—blossom everywhere. Near the top of South Fork Mountain, the barrier between the South Branch and South Fork valleys, there is a patch of redbud about twenty acres wide. It's a band of pure lavender on the mountainside that makes me almost run off the road each time I drive past.

Robins, bluebirds, and the rest come back. At daybreak, wild turkeys gobble on the mountainsides. The geese return to the rivers. Flocks sometimes fly on moonlit nights. One night that first spring I can remember sitting on the front steps and listening to them honk as they followed the course of the South Branch. The black vultures return from their wintering grounds in the Shenandoah Valley every year. Driving to Harrisonburg one day, I encountered eighty or a hundred spiraling over Shenandoah Mountain like a flotilla of ptero- dactyls. Capistrano has swallows; Pendleton County has black vul- tures. I may write a song about this someday.

In April Franklin town wakes up. My neighbors are out in their yards again, clearing the winter debris, turning gardens over. After a winter of pewter skies and gray afternoons inside, it's wonderful, "a tonic," to be out in the open air and feel the soil under a rake or hoe. The mushroomy smell of soil comes back to town. The IGA market puts out sacks of redwood mulch, which offer a small pleasure as you pass—the smell of western mountains. Both downtown hardware stores, Bowman's and B & H, put spades, rakes, hoes, lawn mowers, green or red wheelbarrows, and lilliputian tomato plants out on the sidewalk. Occasionally a man in camouflage walks into a store or gas station with a wild turkey slung over his shoulder.

As the season advances, Greg Bowers, the veterinarian with an office on Main Street, looks more and more woebegone. Normally neat as a pin in his gray coveralls, he does not shave or change clothes for days at a time. The trickle of newborns that began on county farms in January has become a torrent, and Greg spends entire nights racing back and forth between the valleys, pulling calves from birth canals, putting down some animals, and literally breathing life into others. I have seen him stagger with exhaustion on Main Street.

One afternoon I watched a woman in a thin summer dress— rushing the season—walk out of Bowman's Hardware and march down the street with a tool called a garden weasel on her shoulder. The sunlight turned the bright aluminum tines into a star above her head. Spring had officially arrived in Franklin.

On farms around the county, pastures suddenly fill with cindery black lambs. Beautiful new calves stand against their blocky, phlegmatic mothers. Lambs form small packs and race about—sometimes bucking into the air like tiny antelope. The calves, once steady on their feet, butt heads and chase one another. When Becky was a girl, her father kept Patsy the milk cow behind the house. Jamie bred the cow every year. After the calf was born, he kept it penned for several weeks. When it was safe to turn the calf loose, he took Becky and her brother Bob with him. He pulled back the gate and stepped away. The calf peeked out shy as a fawn and took a few tentative steps into the pasture. A minute later it was racing around kicking its back hooves into the air with the joy of being alive. Becky and Bob would clap and laugh out loud.

Farm families are not much busier in April than they are in January, but the work has moved outside and you see them as you drive past. Men and women are out in the pastures tending lambs, fixing fences, driving stock back and forth, or riding tractors to turn the soil in cornfields. They will have to move the stock back to high pastures, but it's the waiting and watching game again. A spring rain in the valley can be a snowstorm on the mountaintop.

The wild greens come up in April. Until the forties most farm families gathered greens each spring, but now it's hard to find anyone who even knows them. The rare families that still gather them are invariably from small isolated farms. One spring, I had the good fortune to hunt wild greens with Rodney Hoover and his mother.

The Hoovers live "up the Thorn." Thorn Creek, ten miles south of Franklin—where John Vanmeter, the first Caucasian in the county, "got whipped" by Catawba Indians in the 1730s—has two feeder branches, the White Thorn and the Black Thorn. There is no town of Thorn Creek, but the families that live on farms along both branches have always seen themselves as a community. County people often describe their Thorn Creek neighbors as "pretty Dutchy." Rodney, who is in his forties, refers to his army service in Germany as "when Old Uncle sent me across the waters." On summer nights he still wades the South Branch with a torch to "gig" sucker fish with a trident spear. Why specific families cling to traditional Appalachian culture while so many others struggle desperately to escape it has always confused me, but the Hoovers are rare holdouts and, in my opinion, very special. As subsistence life disappears, people like the Hoovers remain connected to nature if only by slender threads. Families like this become more rare every day, and when they disappear entirely, a pastoral vision will disappear with them.

ON THIS warm day—the cloudless sky transparent blue—I walk beside the Thorn with Rodney and his mother. Each of us carries a plastic bread bag for our greens. Mrs. Hoover, a short, gray-haired woman in a plain dark dress, is quiet and shy, looking down or away whenever our eyes meet. So many people associate gathering greens with backwardness or poverty; I think she is uncertain about my interest. But we walk along stopping at plants and, in her quiet way, she tells me what to call them: turkey wing, bird tongue, thistle, narrow dock, rollvuncel—a mysterious old "Dutch" word—lamb's-quarter, and poke. (Poke brings my father back. Out running the dogs in spring, he would stoop to pick what looked to me like a weed. He'd say, "This here's poke. It's good food if you can find enough." He would glance wistfully around as if looking for his lost subsistence world, then toss away the plant and follow the dogs.)

Rodney discovers a few wild strawberries and we eat them on the spot. Smaller than a raspberry, they have a wonderful taste that cultivated strawberries only suggest. "Used to be lots of 'um around," Rodney says, "whole hillsides pretty much covered. Each mountain had a different kind of berry. We had these names—sheep tit, round eye. I've forgotten them now. Deer eat the strawberries up. Too many deer in this old county is what I say."

We come up against a steep mountainside and Mrs. Hoover tips her head back to look up the path. Pointing to the mountaintop she says, "My daddy built his cabin up there on top. He bought a wagonload of boards to finish it. Parked his wagon right here where we're stand'n. It took him three or four days to get the wood up. He'd have the horse drag so many loads up and then he'd spell the horse and drag loads up himself."

Looking up the steep path I say, "My God." Mrs. Hoover smiles.

In parting, she gives me her recipe for wild greens. You wash them, parboil them, then fry them in butter. I find them more interesting than fresh spinach, though not to everyone's taste.

The quintessential Appalachian green is ramps. It's possible to speak of one ramp, but like "grits," the word always seems to insist on being plural, as in, "I dug a mess of ramps" or "Had me some ramps last night." Ramps (*Allium tricoccumare*) are small lilylike plants that grow in deep woods each spring. (Actually they are small wild leeks.) It's best to get them just as the shoots break the ground. You can eat the leaves, but it's the tiny onionlike bulb that you want most.

The Shawnee taught the first Appalachians about ramps. Rich in vitamin C, they are just what you need after a long winter without fresh vegetables. Ramps have a pungent taste somewhere between leeks and strong garlic. Most people fry them as a side dish or add them to home fries or scrambled eggs. There is one drawback to eating them: ramps do to your entire body what strong garlic does to your breath. After eating a healthy portion of ramps, you emit a funky smell through every pore. (When Becky was in grade school, ornery boys would eat a big mess of ramps for breakfast, then wear flannel shirts and sweaters to school. By midmorning, they were worse than skunks and had to be sent home. At least, that's how the stratagem was supposed to work. One old teacher, wise with years, made the culprit sit alone in the basement beside the furnace in his flannel shirts and sweater.) Many families have an agreement that they all eat ramps or no one does.

Each spring in West Virginia, churches, civic organizations, and small communities host ramp suppers. Digging ramps and cooking them in your home has become a working-class practice, but going to the suppers cuts through social divisions. Some ramp suppers, like the one in the Charleston Civic Center, attract thousands. Others in church basements or volunteer fire halls—perhaps a dozen in Pendleton County—draw several hundred. I like ramps, but everyone else in my household hates them. If I'm going to eat ramps, I have to eat them somewhere else and shower a lot. That first spring, I decided to go to the ramp supper in Helvetia, two hours west of Franklin.

This road to Helvetia is more narrow and winding than most. Running high along the ridge top, it passes through deep forest and farmland. The turns are sharp and blind and the drop-offs sheer enough to make me nervous. There are awesome views of farms down in the valleys—small white houses surrounded by pastures that have turned the deepest green. Many trees bordering the fields still have their black winter appearance, but here and there they are pastel and fuzzy with opening buds. In the spring, the light in the Appalachians seems thin and exceptionally clear, not the buttery stuff of summer days. I have noticed the same quality in Winslow Homer seascapes, a kind of distillation.

At a turn, the forested mountainside that drops into a dark hollow on my left is covered with white trilliums and I pull over just to look at them. I don't think I have ever seen this many in one place. I imagine myself lying on my back in the middle of them.

Helvetia is another storybook village. Old "worm fences" surround some pastures. These are fences made of hand-split chestnut laid without nails in a zigzag pattern that suggests a worm's inching progress across the land. American chestnut, a tree long gone from the Appalachian forest, never rots, which is why old-timers made rails with the wood and why some fences still exist.

There are tree-lined lanes rather than streets in this village. An icy-cold trout stream flows through the center and a small bridge crosses from one side of town to the other. I could well be in the Black Forest or Switzerland. In fact Helvetia, the Swiss word for Switzerland, has been called "Little Switzerland" not only because of the mountain landscape but because the community was settled by German Swiss in 1869. The Swiss German language is almost gone, but a few families still speak it at home and some older people still do a Swiss folk dance. Men yodel in polyphonic harmony. It's not as elegant as Bach, but seems almost as complex to me.

They make good yogurt and an interesting cheese in Helvetia. A small restaurant in an old farmhouse serves basic food. The walls of one room are covered with old books. Waiting for the meal, or as you eat, you can page through books and wonder who bought them and why. If you stick to country ham sandwiches or yogurt and fruit concoctions, you'll do fine.

Helvetia is busy today. People stroll up and down the lanes with cameras around their necks and the curio shop is crowded. I first came here in 1969 when I was a graduate student in Morgantown. Half a dozen of us, all young men as I recall, drove here for the ramp supper. I fancied myself an artist and can remember sauntering around this pretty town striking world-weary poses, a well-thumbed copy of *Four Quartets* in my hip pocket. We came upon a house enclosed by a chestnut worm fence festooned with found objects. At first we thought the arrangement was haphazard, but after a second look, someone discovered a theme. All of the objects were bits and pieces of traditional Appalachian farm life—a wooden plow, a broken wagon wheel, a rusted hay fork, a farm wagon seat, the stockless barrel of an old rifle, banged-up tin pots. Someone had arranged the pieces on the rails to lead the viewer around the fence. At the end, by the back of the small house, the artist had stuck a ragged work glove, with holes in most of the fingertips, on a splintered barn board. The index finger pointed to the sky above the distant ridge and on the board, in crude white letters, someone had written, "Ever wonder where it all went?"

We knocked on the door, and to our great surprise a slender, elegant woman invited us in for tea. From the Midwest, she had stumbled on Helvetia as she traveled years before and had fallen in love with the town. Somehow the topic of Appalachia came up and we offered oblique apologies for the culture around us. She had no time for this and said, "You really don't know what you've got here." I felt less puffed up after that.

That was years ago. Walking around town thinking about my first visit, I begin to wonder who I was and what I understood back then. I'm not sure what I made of the woman's fence or the cryptic question on the splintered board. Looking back, it's clear that she understood that traditional mountain culture was special rather than backward and that it was disappearing. How strange for an outsider to come here and see so clearly what had been unclear to me most of my life. When I think of myself as a graduate student in Morgantown, it's like remembering a movie that I saw. I know that boy, but he doesn't seem to be me. Meandering along the stream, I imagine meeting O'Brien, the graduate student, and having a word with him.

On the small bridge, I look down from one side, then the other, hoping to see native trout. The water sparkles with sunlight, but I see no trout. Downstream, along the grassy bank, I spy a patch of forget-me-nots. Some people call these flowers Quaker-ladies. I've always liked that name. These flowers make me think of Becky.

The ramp supper is in a long, low building by the roadside. Country ham, home fries, biscuits or cornbread, coleslaw or salad, green beans, iced tea, lemonade or coffee, and cake. A good crowd fills the hall, and I find a seat next to a plump Mennonite woman wearing a lacy cap and a long dress, the exact pale blue of the forget-me-nots along the stream. Her mouse-gray hair in a bun, she smells faintly of cleanser. She has wire-rimmed glasses and a soft agreeable face as smooth as a doll's. Her mind is as clear as daybreak and so is her life. All evidence aside, I intend to believe this as long as I can. As I sit down, the Mennonite woman smiles. I ask, "How's the food this year?" Holding her fork up like a small scepter she announces, "I shall recommend the beans." Indeed.

The ham, green beans, coleslaw, cornbread, and home fries are merely adequate, but the glorious ramps are spicy and pungent, a taste of the forest in spring. Then I'm off for Franklin and the first of many showers.

IN PENDLETON County, sheep shearing marks the end of spring and the start of summer. At one time, county families sheared their own sheep, but like most of the old ways, shearing is a disappearing skill. Each spring, the few men who can still do this are much in demand, and farmers have to call weeks ahead to arrange a time. I was at Everett Mitchell's farm the day his sheep were sheared.

I set out for his place on Dry Run Road before dawn. After driving through deep woods, I ascend a steep grade, and then start down into farmland. Around a turn, I look down into velvet green pasture surrounded by oaks and maples. The slope of the land is gentle here, as if the farm below rested in the palm of a soft green hand. You know it's Everett's land because he has painted the top ten inches of every fence post white. No other county farmer would waste time and paint like this. Once I asked Everett why he went to so much trouble, and he said, "It's my trademark," and stuck his chin out. At the time I thought it was no answer at all, but now, as dawn breaks, I understand. The fence tops are luminous in the half-light and you ignore the rest of the posts. The white tops seem to float free and they circle the deep green pastures like a string of pearls. Everett Mitchell is a man in love.

His barnyard comes to life: Roosters crow, sheep bleat, cows bawl, the fat tom turkey gobbles, and a wild turkey in the woods gobbles back. I wonder what one bird makes of the other. The white geese, filled with absurd dignity, parade single file to the spring that flows across one pasture. Everett keeps a peacock on his farm. Now it stands on the hood of a junk-pile truck—a smashed-in, rusted cab without windows, no wheels or tires, weeds growing up all around—to cry and spread its wondrous tail. It turns slowly on the rusted truck so that the entire world may see, and calls again. A red fox killed Everett's peahen as it sat on a clutch of eggs last spring and so the cock's display is pointless.

Dennis, Everett's twenty-year-old son, starts his four-wheeler, an all-terrain vehicle about the size of a riding lawn mower, and takes off across the pasture toward a flock of sheep. The farm dogs, Pupper and Sandy, run behind the four-wheeler. Everett and I walk out to the lower end of the pasture. Everett is quick, an animated man full of wisecracks and gestures, what my father would call "a real catbird." He tells me where to stand and to wave my arms if the sheep run toward me. "Not real fast," he says. "You move too fast and it scares them. Run every which-a-way. Oh no, we don't want that."

As ignorant as I am about rounding up sheep, it becomes clear to me that Pupper and Sandy, mongrels my dad would call "your Heinz 57 type dogs," are more trouble than help. They are clearly having a wonderful time chasing sheep, but don't seem to be chasing them in any one direction. As Pupper runs yet another ewe to the far end of the pasture, Everett groans and looks at the sky as if talking to someone up there. He says, "Them two have no idea what's goin' on." If Everett had a cap, he would throw it to the ground.

Despite Pupper and Sandy, we get all of the sheep into an enclosure beside an old shed. At best my help was minimal. The dogs sit side by side against the fence panting heavily. Everett looks at them and then at me. He says, "They think they done something. Just look at 'um." Eyes squinted up and tongues lolling out, Pupper and Sandy do look pleased with themselves. But Everett loves his useless dogs; that is very clear.

Sitting astride the four-wheeler, Dennis says, "Here's Galen now." A pickup turns in from Dry Run Road and makes its way toward us on the dirt road. The man who gets out has sandy red hair and a freckled complexion. He's not that tall but seems large. His shoulders are thick and he tapers to a V at the waist. He moves slowly and deliberately like a serious weight lifter. Everett introduces me. "He's some kinda writer, a-want'n to write stories about how we go about things around here." Galen looks me up and down in obvious suspicion. Like Mrs. Hoover, Galen is uncertain about me, though his reaction is menacing rather than shy. His mittlike hand feels like tree bark. I say, "Pleasure to meet you." He nods slowly and turns back to pull coveralls from his truck.

Galen strips down, carefully folds his clothes, then lays them on the truck seat. Standing in the barnyard in his white Jockey briefs, he makes me think of the he-man action figures Christopher once played with. He catches me staring and I shift my eyes away, concerned that he might—like Heckle and Jeckle—come to the wrong conclusion. It's the poetry of a man in his underwear standing in a barnyard at dawn that makes me stare. Galen grabs his coveralls and steps into them, shaking his head.

Galen's shearing rig resembles the apparatus dentists use for drilling teeth. Slender metal tubes are connected at movable ball joints to create a kind of mechanical arm. The arm extends out from a portable control panel that makes me think of something from the cockpit of a very old airplane. The arm's free end screws into electric clippers that a barber might use. The panel plugs into a small gas generator or, in this case, to an extension cord from Everett's barn. The contraption is remarkably flexible; Galen can move the clippers up, down, or sideways with fluid ease.

The work begins. Everett and Dennis stand amid the bleating sheep selecting ewes or rams. They will not shear the new lambs. They half drag, half carry the struggling animals to a break in the fence that opens into the small enclosure where Galen has set up his shearing equipment. Pupper and Sandy pace nervously against the fence, growling, neck-hair bristling. They want to get in there with the bossman and wrestle sheep, but Everett has ordered them out. The dogs do listen at times. When I was seven years old, I always wanted to help my dad fix the car. He invariably said, "You can help me best by staying out of the way." Here by the fence, Pupper, Sandy, and I are staying out of the way.

The ewes weigh about forty pounds each and offer little resistance. The buck sheep go up to eighty pounds and "have some fire in 'um." They struggle and kick as Dennis and Everett drag them to the opening, but stop the moment Galen takes hold of them. One hand at the neck, the other at the back leg, the sheep go limp at his touch. It's a matter of knowing where to grab, and something more mysterious, I think. I'm convinced that animals sense authority, or the lack of it. I have watched Greg Bowers handle unruly dogs, cats, calves, whatever, just as Galen handles sheep. Galen is in complete control and the animals feel this in his grip.

Bent at the waist, clippers in one hand, an ear, neck, or leg in the other, Galen is all business as he turns the sheep end over end and peels the fleece off in one heavy piece. He often pins them between his knees or tucks a leg under his arm. It's a full-contact operation. The shorn sheep look skinny and clean. Galen shunts each one into yet another enclosure and immediately starts on the next. This job will take all day, even at this pace.

Everett has hung an eight-foot burlap bag—a "gunnysack," my dad would call it—from a metal hoop on the side of the shed. The bottom of the sack touches the ground and a ladder leans against the shed beside it. As Galen tosses the heavy mats of wool to one side, they make a sound that brings to mind wet throw rugs. Everett's farmhand, Harold, trims off mud or clotted feces, then climbs the ladder and drops the fleece into the sack. After a time, with Everett's assistance, Harold lowers himself into the sack. Now Dennis climbs the ladder and drops the wool as Harold "tromps it down." I would not volunteer to have the smelly wool falling on my head, but Harold doesn't complain.

Breaking for lunch, we pause to watch the bucks fight. The rams have already established their dominance order, but once shorn, they do not recognize each other. As we watch, two bucks among the milling ewes catch sight of each other. Both freeze up like statues and stare at each other transfixed. They take a few stiff steps toward each other, stop, and then as if on command, lower their heads and charge. A second before impact, both bucks rise to their hind legs and thrust, making a muted sound on impact like rocks banging together underwater. The bucks stagger off, blinking their eyes and licking their lips. A few moments later, they freeze up to begin another round. Dennis tells me, "It's mostly funny but sometimes you find dead rams in the pasture. Necks broken and whatnot."

Passing the barn, I stop dead in my tracks. This is a new barn that Dennis is still working on. The door is white, freshly painted. The peacock stands before the door in full strut—tail spread, turning in that stiff way. The others don't notice and keep walking toward the house, talking low. They are not immune to beauty but have seen this day after day; for them the peacock is part of the ordinary. Not for me, however. I feel lightheaded. Does the peacock know that the white door is the perfect backdrop for its display, or is this pure chance? One way or another, it takes my breath.

In Everett's kitchen lunch is fried chicken, mashed potatoes and gravy, applesauce, green beans, coleslaw, rolls, and apple pie. Across the table Galen is telling Dennis about escapades on his four-wheeler. For young county farmers, four-wheelers have become what horses once were for cowboys. They talk and boast about them. After snowstorms, they have four-wheeler rodeos—who can get through the deepest snow or up the steepest mountainside.

Someone has told me that Galen killed the first coyote in the county. I ask if this is true, and he says, "That's what they tell me. I don't know."

"Tell me about it."

"Not much to tell."

"That's okay; tell me what there is."

But he looks toward Dennis as if telling him the story rather than me. "This one morning I rode my horse to check fences. It was raining hard. Down in this hollow, I seen something running. First I thought it was a yellow dog. But here it comes out of the hollow and runs along the other side of the mountain. Something about it didn't look right. Dog or no, it had no business around my sheep so I got off the horse and shot it. When I rode up, I could see it wasn't a dog. It had this long foxtail and big eyeteeth. I haven't seen another since. If it hadn't been raining so hard, I don't believe I would of seen that one. They're too sly."

After lunch Everett and I sit on the cool, shady porch to let our food settle. Inside, at our backs, Galen and Dennis talk about barns. Everett's yard is filled with bird feeders and nesting boxes. Two boxes, up high on poles, look like white hotels with endless rooms. The air above the yard streaks with flashing bluebirds and the iridescent green of tree swallows. Countless other birds go by, twit, and chirp. A house wren lands on the rail at the far end of the porch, sings his long, complex song, then hops around to face another direction and begins again. Everett and I laugh out loud. He says, "What a singer. I get one of them little birds every year." I say, "You're a lucky man."

Everett lives in a modern brick house, but a beautiful old farmhouse sits across his pasture. I ask and Everett, obviously pained, tells me the house is empty and has been for some time. It belonged to his grandfather and his father. He was born in the master bedroom. It is uncertain who owns the house now. Everett has a sister and brother who inherited portions of the land, and like so many county people, they moved away to find work. Since Everett's parents died, the Mitchell farm has been a constant source of family discord—heated arguments, bad relations, one court case after another—more heartache than any family deserves. According to Everett, his brother and sister see no point in farming; it's backbreaking work and a losing proposition. In a sense they are right. At best, Everett's farm turns a small profit or breaks even. Some years he loses money. His wife Erma works at the shoe factory south of Franklin. Everett drives a school bus twice a day and sells tons of firewood just to make ends meet. He is convinced that he could do much better if his brother and sister would sell him their land at a reasonable price, or at least let him develop it. They do not agree. If they sell their inheritance, the money will have to be right. Who could find fault with this? But Everett doesn't want to keep the land to make money; he wants to make money to keep the land. As Everett explains things, he loves this farm with a passion that his brother and sister do not understand or share. And so year after year, the beautiful old farmhouse sits empty as the Mitchells file in and out of court. No one's right, no one's wrong, and no one's happy.

In one variation or another, families all over the county and throughout the region share the Mitchell family's dilemma. Court battles over land are common in Appalachia. Occasionally I meet people, like the come-here who thinks of North Fork people as Celts, who see this as another manifestation of Appalachia's blood feud culture: These violent Celts love to fight and since murder is against the law, they slug it out in court. But Appalachia is not unique in this regard; as farm cultures lose the struggle with consumer cultures around the world, family strife and litigation become commonplace. Families keep growing, but the land they own does not. Wrenching disagreements are inevitable. But when family members fight over land in New England, the Midwest, or Provence, it is generally seen as sad. The same thing in America's southern mountains reinforces stereotypes.

Sitting on the porch, Everett tells me other things. He bought the turkey because its gobble belongs in a barnyard. He does not sell or butcher geese, but they also belong on a farm. A farmer should have sheep dogs, thus Pupper and Sandy. The peacock, like the white fence posts, makes the farm more beautiful. It comes to me that Everett has a vision: It's the Appalachian farm as Eden. Don't misunderstand—Everett is no dilettante. He knows farming inside and out, and no farmer in the world works harder. But he is pursuing a dream. My admiration for him is boundless.

The afternoon wears on. The wool sacks fill up and look like monstrous cocoons on the ground. In a week or so, Everett will take them to Monterey, Virginia, and sell them for almost nothing. After he pays Galen, he may lose money on the operation. Despite the work involved, sheep shearing has become ceremony in Appalachia.

Near dusk, Galen is down to three sheep. He has spent ten hours bent at the waist, manhandling bucks and ewes, but now he works faster than when he started in the morning. I mention this, and he says, "It's always like that. When I finally get my rhythm goin', it's time to quit." Appalachian men are self-effacing. Don't boast; just do your job. Galen Botkin bled to death in the snow a few years ago pinned beneath his tractor. Determined to feed his sheep after a blizzard, he plowed into a drift and tipped over.

In parting, Everett gives me a large goose egg. He says, "I like 'um better'n hen eggs. Not everybody does now. You give it a try." Out on Dry Run Road, I hear the peacock cry one last time. "But no queen rises": that line from Stevens comes to mind. Spring has ended.

SUMMER IN Pendleton County is a sweet green idyll. School ends in early June and it's T-ball, softball, the town pool or a swimming hole on the river, bass fishing, 4-H camp, church camp, cookouts, picnics, and lazing around on hot afternoons that go on forever. At the tiny drive-in north of Franklin, love blooms to the sound of movie dialogue and cow moos.

In late April or early May, 4-H kids select the lambs or calves they will work with through summer. Free of school, they spend hours every day grooming the animals and training them to walk in halter. Day after day it's a contest between a stubborn calf or lamb and a determined boy or girl. Sometimes it's hard to see who's winning. The kids will show their animals at the Tri-County fair in Petersburg, forty minutes north of Franklin, in mid-August. A blue ribbon at Tri-County earns a trip to the West Virginia State Fair in Fairlea and hopes of glory.

For county farmers, summer is hay-mania. It's the watch and wait game once again. You want to cut grass at its highest but not in seed. Seeds rob nutrition from the blades, and since cows cannot digest seeds, seeded hay is of little value. You can't cut grass that's wet from dew or rain; it would only rot. Worse, damp bales can generate enough heat to induce spontaneous combustion, burst into flame, and burn down barns. This happens from time to time.

After grass is cut and down in the meadow, it must lie out under the sun until it's just right. Out too long, it loses nutrition. Baled green, "too tough," it rots. When the cut grass is down in the meadow, an unexpected shower means that a blistering twelve-hour day has been wasted. Trying to decide whether to cut or bale, farmers often walk out into the fields and rub a pinch of grass to nothingness between their thumb and finger. They sniff their hand and look to the sky above the ridge before deciding. It takes intelligence, all of your senses, and no small amount of luck. Hay gets cattle and sheep through winter, and if farmers do not cut enough in summer, they must buy it. Given that most farmers are hanging on by the sheerest of threads, a bad hay summer can put a man under.

Hay scenes: Trucks and farm wagons piled high with teetering bales of hay crowd the roads every day. Men with glowing cherry-red faces, arms, and necks walk on Main Street. A farmer rides his tractor through a hay field. The cutter behind him makes a strange, deep sound. He cuts the tractor off and in the heavy silence that descends says, "Lord God, I hate this." He walks back to find a spotted fawn "all tore up," still twitching, maroon blood glinting in the sun. To one side, he sees another fawn, coiled like a comma and absolutely still. "Twins," he says. Walking toward the tree line, he cradles the second fawn in his arms saying, "Your mama oughta know better than hide you in my hay field." He lifts the fawn over a barbed wire fence and lays it down in the shady woods. It stands on shaky legs and stares at him in wonder.

In Everett's meadow, I sit in the shade of maple trees to watch them make hay. The tractor shimmers like a mirage in the oppressive heat, gliding through the grass like a boat through water. I have watched two garter snakes and a groundhog escape the field. The white-hot sun bears down. Pupper and Sandy, filled with doggy self-importance, come my way. Pupper approaches, gives me a sniff, and decides I'm not interesting. Both dogs trot along the edge of the high grass. Another groundhog breaks from the field, and both dogs take off like rockets. Sandy hits the groundhog and both roll end over end. Sandy emerges with the groundhog's throat in her teeth. Pupper rushes in to grab a hind leg. The growling and snarling dogs go round and round as they jerk and tug on the squealing groundhog. The groundhog comes apart, its blue-gray intestines spilling out. It's over. Sandy trots around holding the groundhog high, intestines trailing the ground. Both dogs eat the intestines with obvious relish.

But three days later, sitting in the same spot, all is quiet and lovely. The large round bales sit to one side of their blue shadows. The fresh-cut field is as clean and shorn as a West Point cadet. I smell the perfume of freshly cut grass. Here, as anywhere, we are moments away from loveliness or horror.

THAT SUMMER Jim Underwood invited me to a picnic on his lawn. Come-heres have their own social calendar. A family that lives on a six-hundred-acre farm west of town hosts a spring celebration complete with maypole and sprightly dances. In fall, being of German descent, they host an Oktoberfest that includes a hike up the mountain with exotic beers hidden in icy springs. In the South Fork Valley, another family throws a Halloween party and a Fourth of July celebration. At Christmas, various families have get-togethers. By general consensus, a party out on Smith Creek Road is the high point of the season. Come-heres take these social events seriously. Married couples work on the guest list months in advance and sometimes disagree about who should be invited. Driving home after the affairs, couples talk about who was or was not there.

I turned Jim's invitation down as politely as I could. This had nothing to do with my feelings about Jim or Woodlands, but with my discomfort in crowds.

At the time I was considering writing a magazine article about Woodlands. I had driven up to the Woodlands mountaintop facility one day and had met Dan'l and a number of other bright, energetic people. The Woodlands office was built into the mountainside like a cave and smelled like mushrooms. I really did not understand the institute, but I was interested. Days after I declined Jim's invitation, he told me to stop at the picnic to pick up some Woodlands pamphlets. And so I did.

It is the perfect summer day—bluebird sky and pure white clouds that have three full dimensions above the green mountains. A light breeze keeps the temperature right. Walking through the grade school playground, I pass boys playing a game that resembles baseball.

Jim's house is down the way, where Anderson Hill flattens to level ground, and his long backyard is filled with thirty or forty people. When the breeze dies down, their collective voices rise up the hill in a faint buzz.

When I walk in, Jim is nowhere to be found. Standing on the porch beneath his hop vine, I look out at his friends, beers or drinks in hand, talking, laughing loudly. There is an odd feel to come-here gatherings. It's the Victorian English in India or the white teachers in the Alaskan bush. Some come-heres despise hillbillies and do not hide their contempt. One afternoon at Franklin's public pool a man new to the county disagreed with a local woman over a small matter. He refused to argue, saying, "There is no point talking to you people. You are backward, inbred, and deprived." Like most county people, the woman suspected that many outsiders held this opinion, but she was shocked to hear it stated outright. She found a pen and a piece of paper somewhere and asked the man to repeat what he had said, "So I can write it down." He did just that.

In my experience, most come-heres do not feel this strongly about locals. Most of them are decent, fair-minded people who want to get along with their new neighbors. But the distance they imagine between themselves and county people is what they have most in common. Away from local eyes and ears, among their own element, they talk about how peculiar county people are. These strange Celts and their colorful ways. Some come-heres, like outside journalists, seem to think they are in mythic Appalachia. They expect to find strange hillbillies and do indeed find them. One woman, employed as a social worker, encountered a certain man named Hatfield and described him as "the most murderous man I have ever met." She believed in the Hatfield-McCoy feud fantasy and had found firsthand evidence of Appalachian bloodlust. Another come-here, a self-proclaimed anarchist, deliberately cultivates relationships with minority people. In his menagerie, he includes a black man, a homosexual, an incarcerated criminal, and an Appalachian "Celt." Occasionally, he dresses in mismatched clothing to appear as an Appalachian. It's all quite strange.

In fairness, county people have their own get-togethers where they talk about come-heres in much the same way. The two groups circle one another at a polite distance, and there are few crossovers, especially when it comes to Woodlands Institute.

I fished the South Branch River two or three nights a week that summer and had bass fillets for the table. When I wade down through the middle, casting a small plug toward the bank, the water feels like silk against my legs. Geese, small green herons, kingfishers, and waxwings keep me company all the while. Great blue herons wade the shallows or fly up or down the river, stroking deep and slow in dreamtime. Sometimes I look up to see a doe and fawn standing in the river staring at me. Near dark, when the green and black fuse into violet, small brown bats dip and swirl between the overhanging trees and the surface of the river. Owls hoot at dark and my mind settles.

I often thought of my father that summer but did not call because of my own emotional tangle. Some days the air seemed filled with shattered glass, as if bombs were exploding around me. The world was too bright and I found myself squinting in the light and cringing at sounds. Anxiety roared through my mind like a jet. I have gotten better at dealing with this, but the effort often leaves me exhausted. Once I find a way to be, I try to keep that precarious balance as long as I can. So I did not call, and did not drive back to Piedmont, and told myself I would do so in better times.

This night stands out. Wading along, I see a fist-sized bump sink slowly below the water. It can only be a snapping turtle. Wading to the bank, I lay my rod and string of fish below a willow tree and, with great caution, inch slowly toward the turtle. There he is, his great mossy back, thick head, and dragon tail at the bottom of a deep pool. It's important to note which end is which. When you make your move, the water muddies up, and as a friend once advised me, "You sure as hell don't want to grab the wrong end." Snapping turtles are dangerous. They can take a finger off or gouge out an egg-sized piece of flesh at one sudden strike.

Inching forward, I see him start to crawl away and I plunge beneath the water. Breaking the surface spitting water, I hold the turtle well away from my body by his long, armored tail and shout, "Got you, Mister Mean." The turtle snaps and hisses, biting the evening air in all directions as I carry him to the bank.

Walking back to the car with the turtle at arm's length, I thought of my dad again. My favorite picture of my father is of him holding a snapping turtle by the tail in the backyard of the old house on Greenway Avenue. In the photograph, he appears young and freckled and he smiles. I think he caught the snapper one night fishing for eels. I do not remember eating his turtle, but we must have. In my mind, he is a different person in that picture—happy, confident.

The next day I carried the turtle into the woods and hung him by the tail from a tree limb with stout twine. I shot him twice in the head with a .22, waited ten minutes, then seeing that he was not dead, shot him three more times. These animals hold on to life tenaciously, which is why they have outlived the dinosaurs. Most people consider snapping turtles a pest because they eat trout and bass. I love wood ducks and have seen chicks pop below the surface as snappers grab their legs. Killing these turtles should not bother me, but it does. Snapping turtles are so ugly and mad-dog ferocious, they make a strange beauty of their own. As always, I am caught between ideas. Still, turtle soup, spiked with a shot of dry sherry, is wonderful.

THE FOURTH of July in Pendleton County is pure Americana. There is a parade down Main Street, and the Navy base in the South Fork Valley provides fireworks after dark. People line the road above the base, holding small children in their arms to watch. That first year, back in 1985, I observed the Fourth on the Shaver's Fork of Cheat River in Pocahontas County.

Shaver's Fork is hard to get to. You must walk eight miles of railroad tracks and, after fishing, the same eight miles back. Because of the distance involved, the stream still supports a good population of native brook trout and "native" rainbows. In the strictest sense, rainbow trout are only native west of the Rocky Mountains. But in the 1920s, timber barons planted fertilized rainbow eggs in Shaver's Fork, and the trout have been breeding true.

I park my car at Mace, a small town, and climb the cindery bank through sumac to the railroad tracks. It's an overcast day that might hold rain, but I don't care. As a local friend once told me, "You can only get so wet and you always dry out again." The tracks go up the mountain, but the grade is gradual enough for easy walking. I see my goal up on the ridge, a line of spruce trees that look black. The journey begins as the ties blur together below my feet.

It's like a slide show. Up in the distance the stand of black spruce appears and disappears as the tracks turn. I keep going, mesmerized by the moving ties. In the distance ahead a huge doe, large as a mule deer, stands in the tracks watching me, then kicks off into the trees. I've seen wild turkeys along these tracks. On one trip, a piece of blown-out truck tire across the rail ahead turned into a rattlesnake, an eastern diamondback. I stopped ten feet away and wondered why the snake had paused right there. It came to me that the metal rail held heat. It was a big snake, six feet long, and as wide as my wrist. I've seen pictures of diamondbacks almost seven feet long and thicker than my upper arm.

Finally, I reach my destination. There used to be a town named Spruce here where Shaver's Fork and the railroad meet. In the early 1900s, the town boasted a post office, hotel, pulp mill, company store, bunkhouses, and homes. At 3,853 feet, it was the highest town in eastern America, and the only way in or out was by rail.

Spruce was also a logging camp of about eighty-five "wood hicks." Becky's Grandpa Farmer often talked about these men, and in fact, her Great-Uncle Tweerd, one of Farmer's younger brothers, wrote three books about them. Some were "God-fear'n" Christians who did not curse, drink, or fornicate, but many, if not most, were brutish. For two dollars a day they swung huge double-bladed axes or push-pulled two-man saws for twelve hours. This was six days a week in summer heat or waist-high snow. On Sunday the hicks sharpened their axes to a razor's edge, played bunkhouse poker, or "rode shank's mare" over the mountain to visit other camps. The men stayed on the mountaintop for as long as six months before riding a flatcar into Cass to "blow 'er in," often spending half a year's wages in a day.

As rough as wood hicks were, camp life was governed by rigid protocol. Newcomers—"greenhorns"—did not speak to any of the other hicks unless spoken to. If a greenhorn needed to know something, he could approach an assistant cook—a "cookee"—or the "lobby hog" who cleaned up around the place. On his first day, after washing up, if a new man did not thoroughly rinse the dishpan and put it upside down precisely half on and half off the drain, he was cursed out as a "mossback."

Entering the mess, smart greenhorns kept their hats on their heads or held them. Each hick had his own peg on the log wall. If someone walked in to find another man's hat on his peg, he threw it to the floor and called him out. Taking another man's seat at the table was even worse. An older man who had worked in the Spruce camp told me that a friend of his made that mistake the first day on the job. He sat down ready to eat and a burly hick grabbed his shoulders and threw him against the wall, knocking him unconscious.

Farmer talked about the prodigious meals these men ate. Breakfast was a thick steak or two, half a dozen fried eggs, fried potatoes, "cat head" biscuits with molasses or jam, oatmeal, doughnuts, cake, prunes, and stout coffee. According to Farmer, beans were part of every meal.

Bunkhouse conditions were medieval at best. Fifty or sixty men slept on straw ticks in one room, and everyone was infested with body lice—"graybacks"—which bit and stung. The men rubbed themselves raw with kerosene once or twice a week, but the graybacks returned in force before the day was out. Despite the grueling twelve-hour day, some men had trouble getting to sleep at night for being "et up by them damn graybacks." A large Burnside woodstove heated each bunkhouse, and before going to bed, the men hung wet socks and underwear near the stove to dry. They had not bathed in months and the stench that rose from their bodies and drying clothes must have been overpowering. All things considered, it was a better life than the miners had during the industrial war.

They clear-cut these mountains, gouging, slashing, and destroying everything to get the valuable trees out. At the peak of the logging operation, it must have sounded like a battle on this mountaintop. The battle and the war are long over. In the early 1900s a timber executive stated his company's objectives in Appalachia by saying, "All we want here is to get the most we can out of the country, as quick as we can, and then get out." And this is precisely what they did, taking 98 percent of the profit with them. All that's left of Spruce is crumbling foundations crowded over by sumac, blackberry bushes, and small trees. After a momentary interruption, the forest has gone back to its business. On this overcast day, all I hear is a towhee calling out his "drink-your-tea" song and the wind moaning through the spruce.

Shaver's Fork is ice-cold and gin-clear. Walking along the tracks that run just above the stream, I can see brook trout holding in the current. I'm in no hurry to fish; watching is almost as good. Henry Ford and Thomas Edison fished Shaver's Fork. The old photograph that I have seen, chums side by side with fly rods in hand, was taken twenty miles downstream. Years ago I took my fishing partner Tom Andrews up here. We caught and released trout and walked the tracks goofing around. It was July 4, 1976, America's two hundredth birthday. Sailing ships, the "tall ships," were coming into New York Harbor as part of the celebration. Tom and I talked about Ford and Edison and the tall ships as we walked the tracks. At one point Tom stopped and, pointing his rod downstream, said, "Look yonder, Henry, up river comes a-nutha tall ship. I do believe it is taller than the last tall ship."

"Land o'goshen, Tom, I believe you are right, and why don't you invent the lightbulb."

"Believe I will, right after I capture yon trout. You ought to build cars, Hank."

"Cracking good idea, says I, says I. Lots and lots of autos for the highways and byways of our fair country."

It wasn't a bad way to celebrate America's two hundredth birthday.

At a small bridge I look down to see at least a dozen trout, a few good-sized ones, and then back off slowly. I have been seeing grasshoppers all along the tracks. I snatch one from a bush and drop it from the bridge. A second after it hits the water, a small brook trout shoots out from the shadows and snaps it under.

Twenty yards upstream, I cast a spinner as small as a thumbtack across current and down. The strike is immediate, a tiny trout no longer than my finger. Kneeling down, I wet my hands just as my father taught me, gently remove the hook, and stare a moment. For me, this is the most beautiful fish in the world, with its silver-blue sides and iridescent pink spots. The fins are bright orange tipped in creamy white. I turn him back and sit down on the bank. The only sound is the breeze slipping through the spruce trees above my head and the water music of Shaver's Fork. Somewhere I read that the town of Spruce was the hub of the railroad lines in this part of the Appalachians. I see myself as if from a great height again, this small figure sitting beside a stream. The world seems to rush out and away from my mind in all directions like a beautiful explosion. I'm not certain about the heart of Appalachia, but Shaver's Fork is at the heart of something enormously important to me.

13. Shall We Gather at the River?

THE REVEREND Harry Blackhurst died in 1956 at the age of eighty-six, and his wife, Lula May, died four years later at ninety. The couple had eleven children. Farmer, Becky's grandfather, was the second and the oldest son. He married Bessie Kee, and they had a son named Buzz (given name Harry) and four daughters, May, Catherine, Beatrice, and Ruth—the Blackhurst girls. Beaty, the third Blackhurst girl, is Becky's mother. On this weekend, the descendants of Harry and Lula May will gather in Cass and Green Bank to celebrate family. The Blackhurst family grew up in Cass, but Jamie and Beaty's home is five miles away in Green Bank. Events are scheduled in both places. The four O'Briens have started for Pocahontas County to be part of this. In the backseat Christopher and Shelly are excited. Will cousin Troy be there? How about cousin Rachel? Uncle Berk? Friends come and go in their life, but cousins, aunts, and uncles—not to mention grandparents—are always there.

Becky is excited too, but her feelings are mixed. Grandpa Farmer won't be there, and Gran Sheets won't be in her small home up the road either. The small, perfect world of Becky's childhood is disappearing—one cherished relative at a time—and the next few days will be filled with painful reminders. Beside me in the passenger seat, she stares into the middle distance, and I can see the emotions play through her face as her thoughts flow from pleasant to troubled and back. She is typing on her fingers again. I reach over and take her hand. She smiles, and says, "I'm okay. How about you?" Letting go, I hold my hand in the air and make it tremble. Becky says, "Take walks like you always do. You'll get by."

Reverend Harry Blackhurst (above) and Lula May Burner Blackhurst (right)

These are the dog days of summer. As we twist and turn toward the top of North Mountain, the steamy air wavers, creating water mirages on the road ahead. Cicadas whine in the trees. At the mountaintop looking down, Germany Valley is filled with haze. It has not rained for well over a month, and the pastures down in the valley look parched and yellow-brown. A pickup, a Matchbox toy from this

The Blackhurst family home in Cass, West Virginia

height, creates a tiny plume of dust as it ticks along a dirt road. Late-summer droughts are common in this part of Appalachia, but this one has been the worst in memory.

As we descend Elk Mountain into Pocahontas County, the valleys start to look better. We have moved west of the great Allegheny Ridge, which traps weather fronts as they drift east. Pocahontas County gets more rain and snow than Pendleton does. On this side, the farmers are struggling with drought as well, but it's not as bad. A few miles from Becky's home, Hevener's pasture remains green and lush. Twenty-five or thirty deer, still in summer red, graze placidly in the bottomland. Some evenings you can count over a hundred down there.

Approaching Green Bank, we pass Trent's, a country store I have always liked. The old wood floor is worn smooth, and there is the smell of cheese and spices with just a trace of kerosene. When I stayed at Becky's house before we married, I often heard "Stop by Trent's and pick up . . ." or "Guess who I just saw at Trent's?" Trent's seemed so close and familiar, so much a part of her family's life, it seemed like another room in the house. I remember this scene from years ago: Mr. Trent stands below the wooden front steps near the gas pump while his wife takes him to task about a job he has not completed. Like a husband put upon, he says, "There you are on the steps just a-growl'n."

Green Bank is in a high alpine valley that sits in the mountaintops like a beautiful bowl. In 1951 the federal government established the National Radio Astronomy Observatory here. Just past the sharp turn near Trent's, the radio telescopes, immense white satellite dishes, abruptly appear in a pasture. It's a startling image, but once past the shock, quite lovely—the snow-white telescopes against the green mountains. Both of Becky's parents work for NRAO. Jamie keeps inventory and Beaty has been private secretary to the observatory directors and chief astronomers since the first secretaries were hired. One of the first astronomers she worked for, Dr. Frank Drake, began his search for extraterrestrial life here in Green Bank. This stray fact has always pleased me.

Becky's home is the two-story white house with green shutters at the bend in the road not far from the entrance to the observatory. You can see two of the telescopes across the fields from her front yard. Cars fill the driveway and some are parked out along the road. A crowd surrounds the old sugar tree on the lawn. When I pull in, someone shouts, "Here come the O'Briens!" A few people turn and walk toward the car. The first round of hugs, handshakes, cheek kisses, and backslaps begins. Chris and Shelly run off looking for their cousins. Becky is glowing, her eyes bright and her cheeks flushed pink.

Cars keep pulling in. Someone shouts a family name and the hugging begins again. Aunt May and Uncle Bernie have come all the way from Texas. Bernie, who was a WWII navigator, has brought a little Texas honey for everyone. Uncle Butter—a retired college professor and one of Farmer's brothers—carves wooden apples and mushrooms in his retirement and has brought a box of them to hand out. Aunt Catty and Uncle Berk arrive from Maryland. Berk has always been the family cutup, telling wild stories, doing stand-up routines, and making wisecracks. He has kept us laughing. But Berk has been having serious heart problems and now takes a powerful medication that leaves him confused and frightened. The family draws him in without the slightest trace of self-consciousness. Ruth and Bob McCutcheon, from Washington, arrive and so do their terrific kids. By general

The Green Bank home in the 1970s

agreement, Danny, Ruth and Bob's son, has the most beautiful children in the world. The Blackhurst girls have brought their husbands, children, and grandchildren home.

By late afternoon, it's pandemonium. Relatives fill every downstairs room and stand in small clusters on Beaty's lawn. Inside and out, the high-pitched voices of excited children punctuate the hum of conversation. Aunts pass infants back and forth, talking about whose eyes or nose or chin the baby has taken from the family gene pool. Men retell funny stories, often at their own expense: eating a gallon of ice cream on a bet; the thieving cat that refused to die; turning in a book report written by your girlfriend and getting caught by the teacher; finding a way to see the stars at noon.

While the adults talk, children carry on like the calf Jamie set free each summer. They chase one another around the yard, hide behind bushes, and end up wrestling on the grass. In an amazing display of instinct and timing, a mother snatches her boy as he zips past without taking her eyes away from the person speaking. *You slow down before you hurt someone.* It does no good; at reunions the normal rules of child behavior are stretched, if not entirely abandoned. When the children get too loud, someone growls, "Save that noise for bear hunting!" and laughter ripples across the yard. Grandpa Farmer used to say this, playacting the old curmudgeon. Becky's eyes well up for the first time.

Instinctively, children of similar age find one another and separate into groups. Five- and six-year-olds lie down on top of the grassy hill behind Grandma Beaty's house. Tucking their arms in, they roll down the hill squealing with laughter. At the bottom by Grandpa Jamie's sugar camp, they jump up, stagger around dizzily for a few seconds, and then climb back up for another roll. It's better than a carnival ride.

Eight- to ten-year-olds play whiffle ball by the lilac bush at one end of the yard. Adolescents drift off to talk about how weird their families are. Passing crushes and lifelong friendships begin. Over the years I have watched Chris and Shelly pass from one group to another. In time they will be the adults talking inside the house or on the lawn watching their own kids roll down the grassy hill. This thought comforts Becky. Family continues in defiance of time. This thought only makes me more aware of how fast our lives are passing.

As the afternoon wears on, I run out of things to say and set out for the observatory. Once across the road, I pass through a stand of pines planted as a wall on the observatory grounds. After eighty yards of pasture, I reach a quarter-mile of blacktop, an airstrip the federal government built for the astronomers, who sometimes needed to travel to and from different universities and other observatories around the country. They rarely use it now, but it offers a pleasant evening walk. There is no hunting on observatory land and this has turned the fifteen hundred acres into a deer park. You can count forty or fifty on a walk. After rain, toads and salamanders cross the airstrip. Red efts, immature eastern newts, look like pieces of candied orange peel against the wet blacktop. There are only deer tonight, but I never tire of seeing them.

At the end of the hardtop, I take a short trail to the private road that curves down to the telescopes. As many times as I've walked here, the sense of strangeness never goes away. The huge dishes seem unnaturally white, almost phosphorescent. I stop below my favorite telescope. Its dish is solid metal rather than mesh and the base—like a triangle without a top—is more substantial than the others. Both pieces fit together perfectly, as if art and engineering had come together. The whine of a motor inside the telescope startles me. Then the dish shifts just slightly, pointing toward another star or galaxy. Looking that way, I shrink down to a microbe on a speck of pollen. This calms me.

At dark, Beaty's house has settled into soft voices. Many of the relatives have gone to motel rooms, rented cabins, or to other homes for the night. Perhaps a dozen kids play hide-and-seek in the bushes and down by the sugarhouse, but it's a quiet game—giggles and whispers from the bushes, running footsteps in the dark.

Inside, the action has moved into Beaty's large living room. The Blackhurst girls, their husbands, and some of their daughters—along with Uncle Butter and a few others—sit on the couch and chairs. Two little girls sit on a bedroom floor by the opened door playing dress-up with Beaty's old hats and jewelry. Shelly and Cousin Rachel used to do that. In the living room, one small boy lies sound asleep on the rug, "tuckered out," the aftermath of the reunion's first day.

They have taken the old black family albums out and are trying to resolve some family puzzle. The sisters look to May, the oldest Blackhurst girl and family historian, for answers. May has traveled as far as England hunting down information about ancestors but readily admits to ignorance about many things. The search keeps veering off into vignettes and stories. It's the process rather than the end result that's important here. Becky sits on the couch next to May and I find a place beside her. My wife is so lost in the talk, I'm not quite sure she knows I've come back.

When the photo albums reach me, I lose myself in them. Here is Jamie in his leather football helmet. A few pages later, Beaty appears as a cheerleader. The courting couple stands beside an old humpback car. Jamie wears his blue Navy uniform. Dressed in a skirt and sweater, Beaty still looks like a girl. They are both so happy and so obviously in love. It's the early forties, a time of knee-length dresses with shoulder pads and young women with long wavy hair. Men wear suits with wide lapels and florid ties. Men wear hats; the style and angle are wonderful expressions of mood. I can almost hear the Andrews sisters—"No, no, no, don't sit under the apple tree with anyone else but me . . ." Beaty appears in her wedding dress and Jamie in his Navy uniform. Jamie was scheduled to ship out a week after the

Becky, to the right, in Farmer's arms with parents, grandparents, great-grandparents, baby brother Bob, and a great-uncle

wedding, and the newlyweds had only a few days for a honeymoon. Becky was born exactly nine months and three days after the wedding, prompting a relative to ask Jamie, "Just what was it you thought you were doing those first three days?"

Now Becky appears as a toddler in one of Gran's homemade dresses, her hair done up in Shirley Temple ringlets. A picture of brother Bob at six with a dog named Great recalls a story. One evening at dark, a farmer knocked on the kitchen door to tell Jamie that he had seen Great killing his sheep. There was no question in the farmer's mind. He knew the dog and there were other witnesses. Jamie respected the man. He wouldn't lie or go off half-cocked. Caught between his children and unwritten law, Jamie told the man to do what he had to do. Becky and Bob watched the farmer put Great into his truck and drive away, knowing that he would shoot the dog. Brother Bob didn't sleep that night. When Becky tells this story, it's as if it happened last week rather than forty years ago.

In one picture Reverend Harry and Lula stand side by side. Lula is a broad-shouldered woman who projects great strength. The word

Early-twentieth-century scenes in Cass, West Virginia

"stout" comes to mind. After raising eleven children, she died at the age of ninety. Dressed in black, Reverend Harry is a great belly of a man who obviously loved his food. He was a circuit preacher who rode a long-eared mule to the log churches in the mountains around the town of Cass. The reverend loved to tell jokes at his own expense. Farmer, his oldest son, retold this one: Preacher Jones was out walking one summer day and happened upon Mrs. Smith a-hoeing in her garden. Good day to you, Mrs., and what a fine garden you and the Lord have raised. Kind of you to say so, Mrs. Smith replies, but you should have seen it last year when I was sick-a-bed and the Lord raised it on his own. This is Appalachian religion at its best and the Blackhursts at their best as well.

Reverend Harry's sly wit and self-deprecating manner shines through this family. When Becky was a little girl, the Blackhursts held the reunion at Lula and Harry's home in Cass. She remembers her great-grandparents as sedentary but wide awake and witty. They sat side by side in rocking chairs in a darkened room. Reverend Harry read his Bible every day while Lula wrote rhymed and metered poems. They died at peace.

In the living room, the talk weaves on and on and lulls me into drowsiness. Becky may stay up with her aunts until three in the morning and fall asleep on the couch like a little girl. I say good night.

I SPENT the night in Becky's room, the same bed I had slept in on my first visit. That was in January years ago, not long after we met in Morgantown. I came home with Becky for a weekend visit. Those two days remain vivid; it was my introduction to the small, lovely world of Green Bank. Typical of farmhouses, the upstairs rooms were not heated. Sliding between the sheets on that frigid winter night was like lying down on a frozen pond and every hair on my body stood straight up. Minutes later, under hand-sewn quilts, I was warm as tea. Warming up in an ice-cold room was the sweetest sensation.

In the morning I discovered Becky's high school memorabilia in a closet—yearbooks, scrapbook, certificates of academic achievement, 4-H blue ribbons, a Green Bank Golden Eagle pennant, and a few letters from her last beau. I spent a guilty hour looking through all of this.

Downstairs I walked into the kitchen to find Beaty making cottage cheese. This was a small amazement. It had never occurred to me that people actually made cottage cheese. Later, Jamie took me down to milk Patsy the cow. My first attempt at milking, to my future father-in-law's great amusement, was an embarrassment for the cow as well as me. At my first tug, Patsy turned her mournful face toward me and moaned. I jumped up and apologized, as if caught in some lewd act.

That afternoon I toured the observatory. The tour ended in a small, nondescript room crammed with instruments. The guide said, "This is where we listen to the stars." "What do they say?" I asked. He turned a dial and static cracked through the room. I said, "What does it mean?" He said, "I don't know." This worried me for some reason.

The guide also explained that the astronomers chose Green Bank as the observatory site because it was the quietest location in America. Years later, the "quietest location in America" became metaphor. Coming back to Appalachia meant coming back to deep quiet. The trouble was, I always brought the noise inside my head back home with me.

Before dinner, Becky and I took a walk on Jacob's land. Jacob and Esther live on a farm right behind Jamie and Beaty and you can see their house and barn from the kitchen window. You look out to see thin, wiry Jacob in his coveralls striding across the pasture, occasionally yelling at his cows, or Esther, bundled up in a man's jacket and headscarf, carrying a steaming pail of milk out of the barn.

In time Jacob became an important person to me. He took me deer hunting, and trying to keep up as he climbed the mountains wore me out. Jake knew the woods like some men know their office or living room. He could spot some portion of a deer—an ear or a leg in a laurel thicket—a hundred yards away. As a young man he loved to hunt turkeys. When he got older, he would scatter corn in his lower pasture after snowstorms to help them through hard times. His talk was filled with Appalachian poetry. Like the Hoovers, Jacob was living in an older and better world.

Jacob's pasture is bordered by timber on one side. On that January visit, Becky and I walked across his pasture, across Deer Creek, and into the trees, fantasizing about building a dream home there someday. It was lovely—the winter trees so black and solemn, the evening sky turning orange in the west. We didn't mind the cold at all.

That night Becky took me to the teen dance at the Lodge Hall, a two-story building by Deer Creek where the International Order of Odd Fellows held meetings. The teens brought their favorite 45s— "The Twelfth of Never," "Chances Are"—and someone played them while couples danced. It was one sticky valentine after another. An adult, Becky's dad quite often, chaperoned the dance each Saturday night. Infatuations took a more serious turn when a girl agreed to walk with a boy to the bridge that crossed Deer Creek. About fifty yards from the Lodge Hall, it was almost dark there. Becky and I walked to the bridge that night. It's hard to believe the world was ever that innocent.

On Sunday morning I sat with Jamie, Beaty, and Bob in church. You've seen churches like Liberty Presbyterian on country calendars—a small white church in a grove of oaks. The old skeleton key that unlocked the door was larger than my hand. There were simple oak pews and frosted glass in the windows. The only spot of color was the burgundy carpet on the altar. Becky played the piano while the congregation sang. Mouthing unfamiliar Protestant hymns, I thought Becky had a Norman Rockwell life.

No one does, of course, not even in pastoral Green Bank, where they "listen to the stars." Failed ambition, anger, frustration, divorce, crippling illness, unexpected death, alcohol abuse, mental and emotional turmoil—the tug and maul of being alive is no different in Appalachia than it is anywhere else.

I sometimes think there is a tragedy at the center of every family that never stops reverberating. For me it was my Grandfather O'Brien's suicide. For the Blackhursts, it was Becky's grandmother, Farmer's wife. Bess, born Bessie Kee, died in the state hospital, the kind of place George Dice fears. No one knows what went wrong or even what to call the malady, but in the early twenties, after the birth of her fourth child, Bess began to show signs of depression. Sometime after her fifth and last child was born, she began to withdraw into a troubled world of her own. In his Model T, Farmer (his given name was Allen) would drive Bess to the hospital, where she would seem to recover. Farmer would bring her home, but in short time she would pull away again. Over time the periods of withdrawal became longer and more opaque. Farmer kept a kind of journal at the foundry where he worked. He recorded the daily weather in Cass

*Becky's Grandpa Farmer and Grandmother Bessie Kee
Blackhurst after their wedding, 1916*

and, on occasion, noted family developments or town news (births, deaths, marriages, accidents, fires). He wrote in the first person, but one entry reads, "Farmer took Bess to the hospital in Weston for the last time today." It's the only third-person entry he made.

During reunions these things are often talked about late at night. In Appalachia women, rather than men, seem to be the keepers of dark stories. In a sense, these tales must be retold because they have more to do with who people are and how lives have worked out in families. Although I'm certain it is understood that Becky has told me about her grandmother, I have never been part of those late-night conversations. Some things are too wrenching to talk about beyond immediate family.

But at reunions, I often find myself looking for old pictures of

Bess, wondering what pained her. A slender, pretty woman with delicate features and auburn hair, she stands beside Farmer as a young
man or with her handsome young children. If there is a photograph of
Bess smiling, I have never seen it. Then again, people rarely smiled in
front of cameras back then. Picture taking was a serious business in
that world. In my favorite photograph, Bess wears a long white dress
and has her hair beautifully done up. She strikes a classic pose beside
an ornate wicker chair, her small, white hands lightly touching the
back of it. She appears otherworldly, almost angelic, and this is how I
will always think of her.

THE NEXT day endless talk and laughter continues unabated.
Uncles take the kids down to Deer Creek to catch crawdads and
splash around or off to pick blackberries. There is whiffle ball and
soccer in the afternoon for all ages. The adolescents lollygag around
together. Relatives staying in Green Bank drive to Cass, five miles
away. Relatives in Cass drive to Green Bank. Jamie ferries truckloads
of people up and down the mountains.

In the evening there is baked steak, scalloped potatoes, fried
chicken, country ham, fifteen or twenty casseroles, baked beans, half
a dozen varieties of potato salad, garden salad, coleslaw, pasta salad,
salt-risen bread, rolls. We have tomatoes, cucumbers, green beans,
squash, and sweet corn right out of the garden. Gallons of iced tea,
lemonade, and good strong coffee are consumed. Two tables are covered with desserts—chess pie, apple pie, rhubarb, lemon and butter-
scotch, gooey brownies, fudge, wacky cake, apple pound cake, lemon
cake, German chocolate, Aunt Catty's coffee cake, and a dessert
Beaty makes that is so unbelievably rich it's called sin cake. James
Beard would be pleased.

Aunt May has located a distant ancestor buried in an old cemetery.
Becky accompanies her mother, aunts, and cousins to an abandoned
farm to pay respects. They return in late afternoon with a paper rub-
bing of the faded tombstone.

I spend the second morning of the reunion walking on Jacob's
land. On the way back I meet Jake crossing the creek on his tractor,
which delights me. As always, we talk about "feesh'n." He has not
tried his luck since spring because of the drought, but says, "I'll do a

little sang'n here directly." Jacob hunts ginseng in the woods. He is pulling a flat wagon with a pile of dead chickens on it, and says, "I better get a-going with these dead birds." As if on cue, one of them begins to flop around. Startled, I say, "There's one still alive." Jacob says, "They're all of them dead. It's just a few don't know it yet."

Lying on the bed in Becky's room, I read *Walden*. I forgot to bring books and this one happened to be in the car. Thoreau's wisdom, disguised as common sense, has a calming effect on me. I imagine Henry David and Jacob—two American originals—hoeing beans together. What an amazing conversation they might have had.

I have seen very little of my family today. Chris and cousin Troy played basketball for a time, then carried the battle to the tennis court behind the elementary school. I'm not sure what Shelly has been up to. I don't think I've seen her since we pulled in. The family will come together in the pasture beside Bob's this evening.

Bob lives in a large old house on a ninety-acre farm that borders the observatory. We turn off the hardtop by a bridge on Deer Creek, then drive a quarter-mile of gravel road. The white farmhouse sits behind large maples and is surrounded by pastures that in turn are surrounded by woods. A mountain rises up behind the house. Becky and I lived here for three years after leaving California. Jamie and Beaty owned the house and we rented from them.

I will always love this farm. The large old house sits behind maple trees that keep it shaded and cool in summer. There are white oak floors and wainscoting on the first floor. The ceilings are high and the tall, old windows are filled with wavy glass. When Becky and I lived here, we often looked out to see deer and wild turkeys in the fields. During our first winter, a red fox moved into a thicket behind the house, and we would see it at dusk trotting along the tree line. One morning, after heavy snow, we watched it run across the pasture like a flame. Christopher was six, Shelly three. They had a tiger-striped cat we called Tigre and a small, sweet dog that Christopher named Miss Queen. With Jamie's help and expertise, we raised a large garden in the side yard—lettuce, onions, peas, squash, sweet corn, pole beans; a patch of rhubarb grew in the center. On summer evenings while Becky and I worked the garden, Christopher marched around the yard in a yellow-and-burgundy "Iron Man" costume Gran had made for him. On hot days, Shelly toddled around without a stitch.

Other memories from that time are difficult. The year I taught junior high school was terrible, and the depressive episode that followed was a bad one. I last saw my father at this farmhouse. Now as Becky and I pull into the yard, I see him in my mind, standing by his camper truck looking troubled.

Soon Bob lights a pile of logs. Everyone turns to watch and I slip across the pasture and down into the woods. I know the trails, even in the half-light. During our two years at the farmhouse, I took night walks when I could not sleep and learned to negotiate the woods in almost pitch dark. Crossing the creek, I climb the mountain to a spot beside a boulder where I have hunted deer and sit down. The trees hide the farmhouse, but I can see the orange glow of the bonfire and on the left two telescopes cocked toward the sky like gigantic ears. I try not to think about my father and Marlinton Junior High, but thoughts and images keep playing through my mind.

THIS IS how we came to live in the farmhouse. Becky and I left California in the spring of 1975 and spent several weeks with Jamie and Beaty in Green Bank. I was looking for a college teaching position or a grant to finish the book I had started at Stanford. We drove to see my parents in Philadelphia and look for work. That visit was difficult. I was unemployed, overweight, bearded, and drinking too much. Coming back from older brother Pat's that night, I made my foolish remark about hoping for a grant rather than a job, which prompted my father into his routine—"Das right, boss, we coons don't haft to work. . . ."

Back in Green Bank, I went on with the job search, but nothing turned up. When the junior high position in Marlinton opened at the last minute, I took it. The prospect of teaching seventh and eighth grade worried me. At Stanford, the bout of depression had been serious enough to put me back on medication. I stopped taking Elavil a month before leaving Palo Alto and still felt shaky. But Shelly was only seven months old and Becky, who was struggling with postpartum difficulties, was not ready to start teaching again. Beyond that, I was unsettled by my father's reaction to writing instead of working. I'm not saying I took the junior high job just to make my father happy, but I did want to please him. I wanted to be a good son.

Farmhouse life (Photograph by Bob Irwin)

Jamie and Beaty bought the farmhouse shortly after we came back. Beaty loved the house and thought she and Jamie might do some restoration and move into it sometime in the future. Gracious as always, they offered the farmhouse rent-free with an option to buy. I insisted on at least a nominal rent—$100 a month—and Jamie agreed but added that he would use the money to make repairs and improvements.

Becky and I fell in love with the place at once. As we rambled around the country all those years, our dream of coming home to Appalachia always included a farmhouse, and this was everything we wanted. Two streams bordered the ninety acres. One held small-mouth bass, and the other offered native trout as well as bass. By the time Christopher was five we had been talking about fishing for at least a year and we took our first trip a few days after moving in. Christopher fished for about an hour, then became absorbed with the stream itself. Wading around, he lifted rocks—"opened rocks," he said—and lost himself in the world of crawdads, nymphs, sculpins,

and salamanders. I can remember pausing between casts to watch
him gently "open" a rock, his nose two inches from the water. I could
have been my father watching me at that age. I wanted Chris as my
fishing partner and told myself I could teach junior high and write at
the same time. I would bear down and do it to buy the farmhouse and
keep Christopher with me on the stream. As I think about it, this was
the last time I convinced myself that I could do anything I set my
mind to.

I called my father about a week after that fishing trip with Chris. I
told him about the teaching job and about the farmhouse and invited
him down to fish and hunt. I can't recall exactly what he said, but I do
remember how anxious he was to hand the phone off to my mother. I
wanted him to tell me I was doing the right thing and that he was
pleased with me. I am trying not to make too much of this. Fathers
and sons always disappoint one another. Each one needs a kind of
confirmation that the other does not have to give. I don't think it's a
question of fault but of impossible expectations on both sides. All of
that said, the phone conversation once again left me feeling low.

I began teaching junior high in late August 1975. Marlinton, the
largest town and county seat, is at the other end of Pocahontas
County. At the start of the school year, I got up at 4:30 each morning
to write for two hours before leaving. In memory, but only in memory, the teaching year was a morality play about Appalachia, complete
with melodrama. The junior high principal—a crusty, cigar-smoking
man in his sixties—gave me the "C" class for homeroom. At that time
Marlinton Junior High grouped students into "A," "B," and "C"
classes. The homogeneous grouping was supposed to reflect achievement and did just that. But the groups also reflected and reinforced
the socioeconomic layering in an Appalachian town. The "A" students
invariably came from well-off middle-class families—the sons and
daughters of lawyers, dentists, doctors, ministers, teachers, businessmen, and wealthy landowners. A rung or two down the ladder, the
"B" students were mostly from socially ambitious working-class families. With few exceptions "C" students came from families that lived
in run-down houses and trailers in communities with names like Dog
Town.

Predictably enough, "C" students were unmotivated and far below
grade level in every subject. But that very predictability was, in my

opinion, a serious problem. Certain teachers, administrators, and students thought of children from poor families as "hillbillies" and treated them accordingly. In this regard Pocahontas County is no different from rural communities anywhere; every community has its share of inequality that creates a social pecking order. It's what people do. But once again Appalachian stereotypes make that dynamic stronger. Mountain communities can be unforgiving. Once people label a family "hillbilly," it can be virtually impossible to escape the label. When children with the wrong last name enter kindergarten, the reaction of some teachers and students makes their social status clear and this perception follows them through every grade.

Blaming Pocahontas County schools for this would be unfair. The schools inherited a chronic problem. The teachers and administrators did not create the imbalance or the damaging stereotypes, and most of the professional people I met that year were doing their best to be fair. Relatively few teachers held strong negative opinions about the county's "hillbilly" families, though I might add that it doesn't take many hard-edged people on either side of the imaginary tracks to keep animosity alive.

Looking back, I see that there was far less social tension in Pocahontas County than there was in Pendleton. People in both communities were struggling to reject Appalachian stereotypes, but Franklin's past affluence and feudal control, the lingering superior attitude of at least some families, and the North Fork's bitterness had strained relations to a breaking point. This is clear if only because of what happened in Pendleton County a few years after we came back.

At Marlinton my "C" students were rough kids. One teacher told me, "You've got the bottom of the barrel—or maybe three feet under the bottom." At the time the comment seemed callous but, from an academic standpoint, not untrue. I had sixteen-year-old eighth-graders reading on a second-grade level. One strapping boy glared at me with pure menace for the first two weeks, refusing to say a word. Some of the girls were as tough as gun molls in old gangster movies. They were bitter, flint-hard, and at fourteen had been around the block more than once. At times these kids came to class in the same clothing three or four days in a row. Disheveled, eyes bloodshot, they would fall asleep with their heads on the desk. In time I stopped waking them. For whatever reason, they were not sleeping at home, and it seemed to me they needed rest more than anything else. Some-times students disappeared for a week or longer, then returned with-out an explanation. Asking about the extended absence was often pointless. I remember this exchange with a tall, dark-haired boy whom I will call Robert. Robert rarely spoke a full sentence.

I ask, "Why did you miss so much school?"

Robert shrugs, something I notice he does quite often. I am con-vinced it's exactly what Robert feels most of the time. It's Zenlike.

"Where were you?" I ask.

"Up my uncle's cabin."

"Your uncle's cabin? What for?"

He shrugs again.

"What did you do for ten days at your uncle's cabin?"

"Ate bought'n bread."

"Bought'n bread?"

"Bread you get at the store."

"You ate store bread for ten days; that's all you did?"

"Pretty much."

Robert wasn't dumb, but he was not about to tell me anything real about his life.

I told Robert he would have to have a note if he missed school again, and that if he didn't, I would send him to the principal's office. A month later Robert disappeared for another week. The day he came back he handed me a note that read "To Robert's teacher, Please excuse Robert from his missed days. He played pinball all Sun-day night and woke up with the pinball blues. Signed Uncle Mike."

I began to laugh so hard I had to sit down, but Robert, the perfect straight man, stood there looking dour.

Settling down, I said, "The pinball blues—*that* sounds bad."

Robert gave me a mournful look and said, "Awful," which made me laugh again.

I didn't send him to the office but probably should have.

The principal expected the "C" students, as another teacher later told me, "to walk up one side of Mr. O'Brien and down the other." He was not a mean-spirited man, but probably thought I was a little too smug and, all things considered, he was probably right. The "C" classes routinely terrorized new teachers, and in fact they tested me several times in September. The students would talk back, refuse to do as they were told, leave their seats and walk around, or throw things at one another. Each time they pushed, I pushed back harder. This had less to do with educational theory than it did with primal fear. I wasn't sure I'd make it through the year, but knew that a riot day after day would destroy me. I piled on mountains of busywork and patrolled the aisles like the meanest nun at St. Clement's Grade School. Yardstick in hand, I erupted at every twitch and fidget or sometimes for no reason at all. I never struck a student but made a lot of angry noise and always seemed about to whack someone.

After a month of this, I told the "C" kids a joke that Tom Andrews had told me:

This old farmer goes to the train station with his mule and wagon to pick up a city fella. They load the suitcases, and the city man climbs up to the wagon seat. The farmer walks to the back of the wagon, takes a two-by-four, and whacks the mule a good one on the head. Then he puts the board back, climbs into the seat, and calmly says, "Git up." The mule proceeds. Horrified, the city fellow asks, "Why'd you hit the poor mule on the head like that?" The farmer says, "Oh, he'll do like he's supposed to, but first you got to get his attention."

I told my "C" students I was trying to get their attention. We came to terms.

I knew these kids. Their lives were infinitely harder than mine had been in Philadelphia; my family may have been poor, but I had good parents and a stable home life. But the sense of being trapped at the bottom was the same. Teachers, schools, police, courts, politicians, businessmen—all of the things that represent community—seemed adversarial and foreign to them. In a sense, their families were standing outside Marlinton's plate-glass window looking in. Not given to introspection, they rarely thought about why they were out there but, like my father, had become convinced that's where they belonged. The bottom of the barrel status had become their identity; they were there because that's where people like them were meant to be.

Not all of the "C" kids accepted this. That year I became friendly with two students, a fiery redheaded boy whom I will call Randy Workman and a slight, dark-haired boy I'm calling James Wyatt. Both boys were bright, intense, and extremely angry. I'm not talking about adolescent rebellion—I saw that in other students—but about something deeper and more disturbing. As different as James and Randy were, they were both convinced that the community had stacked the deck against them. Both boys seethed with a frustration that made me think of a burning fuse. Now, given all that has happened, I sometimes think anger may have been the basis of our friendship.

I spent more time with James than I did with Randy. James had straight black hair to his shoulders and what I thought of as gunfighter eyes. There was a wariness about him; he watched everything from some private sideline through narrowed eyes. In conversation there was a slight lag to his responses, as if he chose each word with care. At sixteen, he understood that human relations were essentially political, and did not trust anyone. James stood back, out of reach.

In the fall of 1975 we began to hunt and fish together. Better said, James took me hunting and fishing with him. For all practical purposes, he had grown up in the woods and each trip was an education. He taught me how to smoke groundhogs from their dens, catch snapping turtles, and "finger" fish. At least he tried to teach me the Appalachian art of fingering. We would wade the river until James found a flat rock with some watery space below it. Then he would gently reach under and moments later pull up a writhing bass or chub. When I tried, the fish invariably shot out between my legs and I'd come up with handfuls of water. Shaking his head, James would say, "Well damn, O'Brien, you let 'um get away again. You gonna starve, boy."

I spent a fair amount of time with James's family. His mother had ten children, though six had grown up and left by the time we met, and the family lived in a tar-paper house like my father's home in Piedmont. There was worn linoleum on the floor, a pot of venison stew on the stove, yard sale furniture, erratic mealtimes, and no hassles. James was the youngest child. His parents were divorced. Mr. Wyatt had worked as a wood hick up at Spruce by Shaver's Fork until the operation shut down. Now he was working construction out in Texas and, according to James, "drink'n hisself to death."

Mrs. Wyatt, who worked as a short-order cook in a Marlinton motel, played the guitar and wrote country songs she hoped would make her rich and famous. Her children came and went as they pleased, with no questions asked. When the freezer was empty, James shot a deer or caught trout, sometimes with his hands. His older brother Ronnie was building a car in the side yard from two or three wrecks he had salvaged. Another brother, Will, spent most days experimenting with makeup and hairstyles. Will split his time between Marlinton and New York. In a Long Island supper club, he became Tiffany Star, a popular drag queen. James's sister Darla, who was three years older, always had a girlfriend staying over and the two of them were utterly self-absorbed. They sat or walked around the house lost in nonstop conversation, completely unaware of anyone else. In passing I would hear, "What you need to do is . . ." Passing back the other way an hour later, "No, no, no—that's not it. See, what you have to do is . . ." There was always something going on in that house. Sleeping on the couch one night—James and I would go fishing at dawn—I woke at 3 a.m. to hear Darla and her friend talking in the dark kitchen at the table. All I could see were silhouettes. "Well, if it was me, I'd march right in there and . . ." The small tar-paper house could have caught fire and burned down around them and they would not have noticed.

I loved going to visit James's family. They made me think of the Athabascan and Aleut families that had taken care of Becky and me in the bush. Like our Native American friends, the Wyatts were wonderfully free of middle-class concerns about appearances or propriety. They were on a raft without paddles or rudder and woke each morning to discover where the river had taken them. It was a shipwreck life—the Swiss Family Wyatt—with each person going off in his own direction to forage. They may have been the most tolerant family I have ever met. No one, not even Mrs. Wyatt, criticized behavior or imposed standards on anyone else. Each child evolved into a distinct personality—sometimes admirable, sometimes not— free of pressure or restraint. This is not an endorsement of a random life or an attack on middle-class virtues like forethought and long-term planning but an attempt to view things whole. To see all poor families as constantly wretched and unhappy is to see all of them wrong. There is no perfect way to be in the world. When you choose one life over another, you gain certain advantages at the expense of others. The Wyatts did what they wanted to do, when they wanted to do it. When I was around them, or around my friends in the bush, I became aware of how much time I wasted waiting to live. I envied the immediacy of their lives.

Needless to say, that immediacy exacted a heavy price. The Wyatts were always dodging bullets. The family owned very little and was constantly in danger of losing even that. Always an inch away from "the flat-broke," they had run-ins with merchants and skirmishes with local authorities. Their spur-of-the-moment life set them free in some ways, but trapped them rather badly in others.

James was bitter about being labeled a "C" human being and a hillbilly. Given the way he and his family chose to live, this may seem a contradiction, but James was convinced that the schools in Marlinton had made up their minds before they knew anything about him. I remember this comment one day out fishing: "Who is it gets to say I'm a 'C'? There must of been a stamp on my ass say'n hillbilly the day I was born." He said the same thing in variation many times.

James's instinct for hypocrisy was razor-sharp. There were two sets of laws, one for people with money and another for people like him. The game wardens looked the other way when "fancy people" shot deer out of season or caught too many trout. The courthouse lawyers and politicians were all "crooked as a dog's hind leg," but they "prayed their heads off in church come Sunday." I don't think he was aware of this, and at the time neither was I, but he vented his frustration by openly defying middle-class conventions and breaking game laws virtually under the game warden's nose. James was striking back, trying to get even. His behavior, perhaps his life, was a paradox; incensed at being labeled a hillbilly, he acted the part with a vengeance. I have seen black Americans and Native Americans do the same.

At Marlinton Junior High, teachers were required to march through the grade-level textbooks no matter what. I did my best with 7C because whoever taught my students in eighth grade would expect them to be in sync. But I gave up on the textbooks with my eighth-graders. In the first few weeks of school I had all of the students read aloud in class, trying to get some sense of where they were. The exercise was depressing in 7C, but in eighth grade it was tragic. Watching tough boys blush bright red as they stumbled over words like "Tuesday" or "July" made me cringe. For them, school had been an endless series of humiliations. I did not blame county schools, or anyone else for that matter, but forcing kids like this through eighth-grade books would have been too painful.

In time we became conspirators. At the start of each class we opened our books and I read a page or two. Then we quietly closed the door and together tried to read magazines about hot rods, motorcycles, hunting and fishing, bodybuilding, fashion tips, and country music stars. Some days we listened to George Jones, Tammy Wynette, or Merle Haggard and tried to figure out what the songs were really about. I told them stories and they told me stories and we tried to figure them out as well. Somehow I managed to start a weight-lifting program disguised as reading. Until the principal put his foot down, we took field trips to local garages and watched mechanics fix cars while I asked them how they got started and what was the hardest part of the job and how much they made. We took other trips to the banks, stores, and diners and tried to keep the whole thing quiet, hoping to survive the year without the principal coming down on us.

With two exceptions, my 8C students made it to graduation. I fell apart in February. Seven classes a day, early bus duty, late bus duty, lunchroom duty, and long faculty meetings left me emotionally empty. By the end of the second class each day, I depersonalized. My mouth opened and a voice came out, but I did not know who it was or where that voice was coming from.

Then the county administration decided to save money by not hiring substitutes when teachers called in sick. The other teachers would give up their planning periods and fill in one after the other in a kind of round robin. State law mandated planning periods. It was also against the law for, say, a math teacher to teach physical education or a biology teacher to teach English, and so on. What really angered the teachers was the fact that the administrators had taken themselves out of the loop. They called on the teachers' professionalism: We had to make this sacrifice for the schools and children. But the administrators were not going to sacrifice anything. The teachers were bitter, but said nothing to the principal for fear of retribution.

Petty unfairness annoys me and so I became obsessed with the paternal attitude of the administration. The students were children and the teachers were older children who needed fatherly guidance. All of the frustration in my life seemed to come together in one small bureaucratic sin. I had been treated like a second-rate human being all of my life—so I convinced myself—and this final outrage was too much. As I look back, none of this makes good sense, but at the time it seemed compelling.

One morning at the start of my planning period the principal spoke to me on the intercom, saying that a teacher had called in sick and that his first class—my 8C, as it turned out—was on the way to my room. I can remember sitting there trembling with rage as the kids filed in and took their seats. When the bell rang, I turned toward the window to see the principal strolling the athletic field smoking his morning cigar, as was his daily habit. I'm not sure what happened to me next. Being depersonalized was disturbing, but now that sensation became so complete I seemed to be watching a movie about myself. O'Brien tells the students to sit down and walks to the next classroom. Curiously polite, appearing calm, he asks an aide to sit with his class. Then, shifting emotional gears, he storms down three flights of stairs and fumes across the athletic field. The principal turns to see O'Brien rushing toward him and almost swallows his cigar. O'Brien, a red-faced crazy man, leans into the principal and snarls through clenched teeth, "I will *not* give up my goddamn planning period so you can smoke your goddamn cigar!"

The poor principal, not a bad man in the end, begins to stutter, "But-but-but Mr. O'Brien, Mr. O'Brien, this is insubordination." O'Brien shouts, "Fuck you!" and starts back across the field.

My room was on the third floor, and looking up as I walked across the field, I could see my students crowded at the window cheering and laughing. I wanted to think I had struck a blow for them, but knew better even then. Seeing a teacher and principal carry on appealed to their love of anarchy.

Half an hour later, the principal came to my room and calmly said he would take over while I went to see the superintendent. In the office, I was fairly calm until the superintendent said something—I cannot remember what—that set me off again. I shouted, "Fuck you!" for the second time that day and stormed out of the office. The superintendent, kindly I think, chose to call my remark "a verbal resignation." If I could control myself, the board would let me finish the year, but that was it.

At Marlinton, the school year ended with a field day. The "A," "B," and "C" classes would compete in various athletic events like the broad jump, hundred-yard dash, shot put, and mile race. Once again, I conspired with my "C" students. I wanted them to win beyond all reason. We held strategy sessions and tried to pick the best students for each event. We practiced at lunchtime and after school. In my mind, winning Field Day would redeem the year for all of us.

The day turned into a cornball movie. As the events took place, we held our own, neck and neck with the "B" students. The mile run was last, and we needed to win for first place. The class had selected a girl—I will call her Kay—to run for us, and I was worried about their choice. Kay was lovely: a pert, small girl with a boy's short haircut. Well dressed and impeccably groomed, she was open, sensitive, and always worried about offending people. The class loved her, I think. But at the start of the mile race, that's what worried me. I thought the kids had picked Kay for admirable but unsound reasons.

My fears were confirmed when the race started. The other runners took off like rockets, leaving Kay in the dust. During the first lap, when two runners passed her, I threw my hands up and said, "That's it." But the students around me were smiling and one boy said, "It ain't over yet, O'Brien."

Sure enough, by the fourth or fifth lap, the other runners began to falter. A few of them just quit and pitched themselves onto the grass gasping for air. One boy stopped to throw up, and all of the others ran slower and slower. Kay's pace was slow, but it never varied. On the next to last lap, when she passed the remaining runners and began to pull away, we went a little crazy—jumping up and down, laughing like loons, and for some reason punching one another. We had taken the day.

My elation did not last long. Glancing across the field, I saw a group of teachers, aides, and parents who had come to watch. A few of them were scowling. One woman, whose son was a very difficult "B" student, took the trouble to cross the field and, in a variation of O'Brien and the principal, snarl, "This is the first time I've seen lowlife ignorance win something." I did not think of this on the field, but now I see myself as standing there at that moment in the heart of Appalachia.

I wish I could see something of value in that year. My outburst helped no one, least of all myself. Winning Field Day was another pointless romantic gesture. I still think some of the ideas about making classwork real might have been worthwhile, but I taught—if that's the right word—the way I live, in fits and starts. I had no real plan or follow-up. Most of my "C" students got along with me, but in their heart of hearts they thought our conspiracy was not about teaching or learning but about putting one over, and that's why we got along.

Looking back, I blame only myself. The administration's A-B-C grouping was an honest attempt to let students advance according to their abilities, and while it had unfortunate side effects, the strategy worked well enough. The principal was a plainspoken farm boy trying to do his job. Two years before I taught there, another principal had been so lax and unprofessional that Marlinton Junior High was utter chaos. They had hired my cigar-smoking nemesis to create order first and foremost, and he had done that. The parent who crossed the field to insult me and my students was angry for the same reason that James Wyatt was angry. Above all else, she wanted her children to escape the stigma of the hillbilly label. Her anger was misdirected, but so was James's and so was mine.

The year at Marlinton was a forced march that I would pay for the following fall. In the days and weeks after the school year ended, I may have slept three hours each night. Some nights I walked in the woods behind the house trying to make sense of things. I did not understand my near-violent outburst, and this frightened me. At Stanford the year before I had talked with a psychiatrist twice each week. He rarely came to conclusions, but toward the end of the year suspected that suppressed rage might be the source of my chronic depression. I did not know what to make of this—then or now—and can remember asking, "Rage about what?" He said, "You tell me."

I was troubled with thoughts about my Grandfather O'Brien. I had finally heard his story in Philadelphia the summer before. Drunk or sober, he rampaged through the house and terrified his family. That day at home, he drank whiskey, went out into the yard, and killed himself in that dreadful way. Sometimes a short, fast movie plays through my mind—my grandfather drinks poison, slashes his throat, then jerks a pistol to his temple. He had not just killed himself; he had made a ferocious statement. My grandfather was lashing out at something. But at what? What set of circumstances in his life—or in any man's life—could possibly generate that much rage? I can remember connecting points in my mind on those nights walking through the woods. I drew lines between my grandfather's suicide, the psychiatrist's speculation about suppressed rage, my outburst at Marlinton, and my father's conviction that there was something wrong with me. At times I thought I saw a pattern, but then I would convince myself that I was imposing a pattern rather than discovering one.

From this distance in time, I find myself drawing lines again. There are more points to connect now. James Wyatt and Randy Workman both spent time in prison. Somehow Randy learned that I was living in Franklin and came to visit a few years back. He was the same: angry, intense, ready to erupt. Randy would not tell me what he had done beyond saying, "It was stupid; that's all." In jail for two years, Randy remained defiant. He told me, "I never left my cell the whole time. If they were going to put me in a cage, then I'd by God stay there. I never did go out." In prison Randy wrote poems every day. He gave me a stack of them to read. I wish I liked them more than I do.

James went to prison for killing a man—at least that's what he was convicted of. I must be cautious; there are legal complications and questions about what did or did not happen. But in brief, here is what some people say transpired. Years after we met at Marlinton, James moved into a section of Cass called Slabtown. There were a number of abandoned timber company houses there. A local bully—a man in his forties who stood six feet, five inches and may have weighed four hundred pounds—began to badger him. He pushed James around and made fun of him in front of other people. I'm told the ridicule made James angrier than anything else. One night the man hit him on the side of the head, breaking James's eardrum. Regaining his feet, James swore in front of several witnesses, "You won't leave this town alive." After drinking a lot of beer, the fellow ended up asleep in the back of his pickup truck, and someone struck him on the head with a hammer. The blow was so hard the hammer smashed through the man's skull down to the level of his ear.

The police arrested James, and some say he confessed. After a year in prison, however, he recanted. A lawyer discovered irregularities in the trial proceedings and the state set James free. When I asked if he killed the man, James looked at me through narrowed eyes and said, "No." But whether he did or not, there is an enormous anger in him.

At times I'm convinced that all of the lines from all of the mental points come together in mythic Appalachia. At other times, I don't think so. Reading the region's history, I find descriptions of "fatalistic" Appalachians that could easily apply to my father. One also encounters dark, self-destructive men given to open defiance and violence that match James and Randy perfectly. But I have never trusted easy connections, stories that explain complex behavior too quickly, interpretations that tie up all loose ends. Then again, it's hard to believe that all of the frustration and rage is completely unconnected. As always, my thoughts seem to hover between conclusions rather than becoming fixed.

After being fired, I spent a good part of the summer going to auctions. The farms in Pocahontas County were failing just as they were in Pendleton. Families who were moving sometimes sold chickens and ducks for a quarter or even a dime. I butchered them and filled my freezer. The free-range birds tasted like grouse rather than wet paper. James Wyatt came by with deer hams or trout from time to time. He never told me where they came from, and I never asked. I must have butchered twenty snapping turtles that summer. By the end of July, I was writing for three or four hours each morning and canning garden vegetables in the afternoons.

My parents came to visit that August. I cannot remember how the visit came about, but it overlapped with a fishing trip to Shaver's Fork. I had planned a trip with a young man named Bill Durbin and one of his friends. Bill had taught 7C and 8C the year before I did at Marlinton, and the kids had terrorized him. Despite that, he remained nonjudgmental about the county's poor families and never saw them as hillbillies or as victims. He may have been the only come-here I've met who could do this. In any case, Bill was from Minnesota and would return at the end of August. Fishing Shaver's Fork together was a way to say good-bye. It would be a two-day trip. We would walk the tracks in from Mace, but instead of returning that night, we would sleep on the ground and follow the river out to the top of Cheat Mountain the following day—forty miles in all. Becky would pick us up at Cheat Mountain Lodge, where Ford and Edison had posed with their fly rods.

It was a good trip. We caught and released any number of small brooks and rainbows and saw a few trophies from the railroad bridges. Bill's friend was a broad-shouldered farm boy from Minnesota who spoke with a slight Norwegian accent and seemed smart and fairminded. For two days the talk was easy, and it kept me from thinking about my father. But he would be at the farmhouse on the evening of the second day, and approaching the end of the trip, that's all I could think about. I could not decide what to say about Marlinton. I thought about lying, but worried that it would lead to complications later. As always, my thoughts and emotions were tangled. I did not want to tell him about losing control of myself and being fired because he would worry. But I didn't want him to be right about something being terribly wrong with me. It makes no sense, but at the time I was convinced that telling my father what really happened was admitting he had been right about both of us all along.

I can remember walking the last mile or so of track. Bill and his friend had dropped a little behind me and they were talking about how beautiful West Virginia was. I was so lost in thought about my father, their voices seemed far away. Then as I walked out of the trees, I saw my dad standing by the hard road and stopped so fast I almost fell over.

Bill said, "Are you all right, John?" For a second, I thought I was hallucinating. My father began to wave his hand over his head and shout, "Hey, Fatso! Hey, Fat Boy!" He had obviously arrived early and come to pick us up rather than Becky.

Getting into the car, I remember the smell of whiskey. My father had retired from GE two years before and like so many retired men had started nipping through the days. He had never been a heavy drinker but now saw no reason not to be. Since he was unaccustomed to hard liquor, whiskey did not have the best effect on him.

Pulling away, he said, "So where's all the fish?"

I said, "We let them go."

"I'll bet," he said. Staring into the rearview mirror, he spoke to Bill and his friend. "This guy's a liar. Let me tell you how he does. He goes off in the woods and comes back with stories about all these fish he caught. Then he writes more lies and sells them to magazines."

My father had always had a hard time understanding the concept of fiction. After he read my first published story, he snapped, "You made a lot of that up!"

When I tried to explain about fiction, he said, "Lies, you mean."

I had lied a lot as an adolescent and he thought I was still telling lies and getting paid for it. He went on about this, calling me a "bullshit artist" and asking the other guys to " 'fess up."

In the backseat Bill looked bewildered and a little frightened. As I recall, he didn't say a word. When we dropped Bill and his friend off, I walked part of the way to the porch saying good-bye.

Lowering his voice, Bill said, "That's your father?"

After that my dad seemed to settle. Driving along, we talked about the wildflowers on the road shoulders, saying the names out loud together. Then he asked about teaching and I began to hedge—saying it was fine, okay. He didn't seem about to abandon the topic, and seeing a beer joint up ahead, I said, "Pull in and we'll have a cold one."

He pulled in, but said he wasn't thirsty and would wait in the car. Inside, I drained two beers then came back out. The whiskey smell was fresh in the car again. A few miles down the road, he asked something about teaching, and I said, "I resigned."

"You what?"

"I quit teaching."

"For what?"

"To write."

The rest of the conversation is jumbled in my mind. He talked about "coons" again, about "fictive stories" and lies, and somehow Becky and Christopher came into things. Becky wasn't strong enough—"like your mother"—to raise children. He began to mutter about me being rich or becoming rich by writing lies into best-sellers, and for the first time I realized his feelings about me were more complicated than I had ever thought.

I want to say some things about my father. His life was more difficult than mine. The family was forced out of our old neighborhood by racial violence as black people moved in around us. Over the years, the second neighborhood became even worse. Black men robbed Taren's, the discount store my mother worked in, twice at gunpoint. During the second robbery, my mother watched one of the men savagely pistol-whip the owner. Much of my father's assembly-line work was government contract, and in those early days the entitlement program really did resemble a quota system. The black workers GE hired to get the numbers right understood this. Many of them spent their days hanging around the rest rooms harassing white workers like my dad. Racism is never right, but men like my father do not have the luxury of the long view. Like black Americans in similar circumstances, they form opinions based upon their experience, which is most often bad. My father's fear and hatred of black people, while not forgivable, should at least be understood with this in mind.

It may seem strange, but there is great comfort in fatalism. If you are hopelessly trapped, there is no need to strive and nothing is ever your fault. My father put his head down, prayed, and walked to work every day. The idea that he had no choice kept him going. But if his son, who started with no more than he did, escaped that life, it meant that he might have done the same. His bitter mumbling about me becoming rich—absurd then and now—was not simple jealousy. My father was struggling to hold on to the meaning of his life. I sensed this at the time and understand it more clearly now. My father was a kind, gentle, but troubled man.

The rest of the visit passed well enough. James Wyatt stopped by with trout, and I cooked them for my parents. We had deer steak and eggs for breakfast one morning. Both meals pleased my father. I told him to come down for deer season and to bring one or two of my brothers. I can't remember what he said about this.

My parents had driven down from Philadelphia in the camper truck, an old Chevy with a shell mounted on the bed that my father named The Wanderer. They packed the camper below a maple tree on the lawn and we said good-bye there. Walking back to the porch I turned to wave and saw him standing by the maple tree beside The Wanderer with his head down, looking lost and sad. This was the last time I saw him.

A month after my parents left, I sank into a serious depression. As far as I can tell, the visit had nothing to do with it. I think the year in Marlinton "caused" the depression, but I'm not even sure of that. I do know what triggered the episode. Christopher and Shelly's cat Tigre came down with something. A wound opened behind one of the cat's ears that may have been the result of a fight with a coon or an opossum. Becky and I did our best to doctor Tigre but the wound got worse and began to fester. We could not afford a veterinarian, and when Tigre began to suffer, I decided to put him down.

That year Becky was teaching at Green Bank Elementary School. Christopher was in first grade and Shelly spent each morning with a babysitter while I wrote. After returning from the sitter's one afternoon and getting Shelly down for her nap, I carried Tigre and my shotgun into the woods behind the farmhouse. I remember talking to the cat—rather, talking to myself—saying things like "You've been a terrific cat, Tigs, but I can't stand to see you suffer."

I set Tigre down on a patch of soft moss. He could hardly stand by then. Backing off ten yards, I raised the shotgun to my shoulder and held it on Tigre's head. I closed my eyes and opened them several times and then gritted my teeth and fired. For some reason I did not hear the blast or feel the kick, but I saw Tigre flip into the air and disappear in a patch of skunk cabbage.

I was shaking badly as I walked back, but felt reasonably sound. I told myself that Tigre wasn't suffering anymore and that I had done the right thing. But later that afternoon, I opened the kitchen door to find Tigs standing on the grass with the bottom of his face gone. My mind had no place to put that image. It was like looking at an optical illusion—something that's impossible but right before your eyes. I fetched the shotgun from the closet and shot Tigre again. I buried him under an apple tree in the pasture and sat beside the grave and wept.

I can remember walking room to room in the farmhouse, opening and closing my fists, sometimes lying flat out on the floor waiting for something to explode or break inside of me. Looking out the window that day or the next, I saw Christopher's dog Miss Queen with a black snake in her mouth, shaking it so violently her head blurred. The image roared back over me like the exhaust from a jet. I became an outpatient on medication again.

One afternoon my mother called, and I foolishly told her that I was taking medication and seeing a psychiatrist. I had never said anything about depression to my parents until then. Our worlds were too different, and it would have made no sense to them. The truth is, it made little sense to me. I was also ashamed for not being strong enough to control my emotions and ashamed to admit that my father had been right about me. But when the phone rang, I was in bad shape and said as much.

A few days later, a blistering letter arrived from my mother. I was a disgrace to the family. They had raised me right, and I had let them down. My father had set a perfect example going to work every day and now I could not hold down a job. Psychiatrists and "drugs" were both things I should stop immediately. What I had to do was "Lift up thine eye to the mountains from whence your power comes."

A week or ten days later, my brother David called to see what was wrong. It was the first and only phone call either of us ever made to the other. My parents had gone to visit David and his family. On the first night, my mother went off into a tirade about me in David's living room. Once again I was the family disgrace, hooked on drugs, in a bad marriage, raising my children wrong, and unable to keep a job. According to David, she became so enraged, my father ran out of the room weeping.

Not long after that, my sister Nancy called with a similar account. My mother had called her on the phone. Then my mother called me again and insisted that I stop taking "drugs" and stop talking to "some head shrinker." She snapped, "Here's your father." My father told me to stop taking drugs and talking to a psychiatrist immediately. He said, "Say Hail Marys. It's all you've got." I broke down and said it wouldn't help me. My father began to cry. My mother took the phone back and began to yell again. I hung up.

I began to have troubling dreams about my father. I can only remember images from a few of them: He is sitting on the couch in Philadelphia reading the *Evening Bulletin* engulfed in flames, or standing by The Wanderer under the maple tree on the farmhouse lawn looking terribly sad. That was the image I saw at the reunion and the one that fills my mind right now.

ON SUNDAY morning, we will come together in Cass. In its boom-town days, 1908 to 1922, Cass was quite a town. There were four hundred company houses, a company store that did more than a million dollars in business every year, two hotels, restaurants, a saloon, and uncounted small establishments referred to as "pig's ears," a shack or an old house beyond town limits where hicks drank, consorted, gambled, and occasionally killed one another. The mill ran two eleven-hour shifts six days a week, cutting 125,000 board feet of lumber and filling forty-four railroad cars with pulp wood daily. From Monday morning until Saturday night the band saws screamed nonstop for twenty-two hours each day. On Sunday, the silence that settled into the river bottom must have felt quite strange.

Like boomtowns all through the Appalachians, Cass exploded into existence. In the late 1890s, three families lived in log cabins and worked small subsistence farms along the Greenbrier River in this location. A timberman named Sam Slaymaker came into the area and began a modest operation removing white pine along the river. Something of an adventurer, Slaymaker made long forays up and down the mountains into unexplored territory. On one journey he saw what I saw when I started for Shaver's Fork that day: the dark spruce trees at the mountaintop. Reaching the summit—conceivably the first Caucasian to do so—Slaymaker discovered a seemingly endless tract of valuable red spruce. Unfortunately, Shaver's Fork was not large enough to float logs, even at "freshet" in the spring.

Slaymaker's problem was solved when the Chesapeake and Ohio Railroad decided to build a spur from its main line in Ronceverte that would follow the Greenbrier River and pass through the present location of Cass. In 1900 he began construction of a logging rail line where Leatherbark Creek empties into the Greenbrier just north of town. After completing the line, Slaymaker and a number of East Coast industrialists established the town of Spruce at Shaver's Fork on the mountaintop.

Then, in 1902, the West Virginia Pulp and Paper Company, the same company that owns the mill near Piedmont, opened a mill at the mouth of Leatherbark Creek. That same year the town of Cass, named after Joseph K. Cass, chairman of the West Virginia Pulp and Paper Board, was incorporated. Six years later, two thousand people lived in Cass, and three thousand loggers frequented the town from the camps in the surrounding mountains.

In the early 1900s, Cass was as raw and violent as any coal town. The wood hicks rode flat cars off the mountaintops into town two or three times a year. Prostitutes—"bats" in local speech—met them at the depot by the company store. The men stayed in a pig's ear, drank until they passed out, then woke up and started over. Fighting was entertainment. Wood hicks wore shoes studded with sharp spikes to give them traction on logs. The point of every fight was to get your spikes on the other man's face.

Farmer and Bess, Becky's grandparents, lived in the "Patch" in the bottomland next to the Greenbrier River. The company bosses had beautiful homes up on Big Bug Hill. Their wives were fashion plates who tiptoed from the train to their homes with their noses tilted up like goats. Today, walking through the ghost town that Cass has become, I imagine Bess on her way to the company store with her daughters. The last few times Farmer picked her up at the hospital, she would seem fine until they reached a certain turn on the mountain about a mile from home. At this point, she would often begin to

The Blackhurst-Burner family in Cass, 1917

pull away. Cass must have looked like a shattered hornet's nest on the ground, angry hornets boiling out. When I think of Bess in boomtown Cass, I imagine wood hicks brawling in a muddy street, the buzz saw screaming at the mill, Ford and Edison strolling beside Shaver's Fork, and Bess Blackhurst looking for another world.

Becky's mother grew up in Cass. Farmer raised his family on his own for many years. He worked in the foundry as "a molder of metals," as Aunt May wrote in the family history, six ten-hour days a week. He rose at 4:30 a.m. to begin washing the laundry by hand, cooking breakfast, and preparing food for the evening meal. Farmer bought everything at the company store and often ended up with fifty cents after settling accounts on payday. He read the Bible every day and remained optimistic until he died at the age of eighty-five.

Appalachian towns can be unforgiving in more ways than one. In second or third grade, Beaty was assigned a part in the Cass school play. A costume was required, and when the teacher asked if her mother would make it, another child blurted out, "*Her* mom can't do that; she's crazy." Beaty carried this as a girl in Cass. It's how my father grew up in Piedmont, but it did not have the same effect. All of Farmer's children—Reverend Harry and Lula's grandchildren—not only survived; they prospered. They went to college, found good jobs, made good marriages, and became devoted to their children and grandchildren. A deep commitment to extended family and to home in the Appalachian Mountains is part of their heritage. Reverend Harry and Lula May's descendants remain unpretentious and free of hard feelings about hillbillies.

Today we are gathering in the Cass Community Center. The building was once the Cass Presbyterian Church, where Grandpa Farmer taught Sunday School and many of the aunts and uncles and cousins were married by Reverend Harry. Large family tree charts and family pictures are on display. After an opening prayer, we remember relatives who have passed away since the last reunion. Candles are lit and members of the immediate families come forward to speak about their loved ones. Aunt May brings us up to date on her genealogical discoveries. She's been as far as England on this quest. Beaty, Becky's mother, gives us official reunion news—who has volunteered for various responsibilities for the next reunion, which activities still need volunteers, and how much cash is in the reunion account. That completed, the children and grandchildren of the Blackhurst girls present a slide show of family events from the past sixty or seventy years— birthday parties, graduations, weddings, funerals. Some of the cousins have formed a choir and sing songs like "Goin' to the Chapel," and "In Your Easter Bonnet" during the slide show. It's a warm and moving presentation and Becky sheds a few tears as the family reminisces. Then, someone hands out gifts to the oldest and youngest in attendance, also to the relative who has traveled the longest distance. I keep looking at the food tables against the wall: the family cooks have outdone themselves again.

After the meal, they take the official reunion pictures. Cousin Eugene sets up his camera on a tripod and about a hundred people crowd together under the maple tree. We assemble in eleven individual family groups—the descendants of each of the eleven children of Reverend Harry and Lula May. Our mob—the children, grandchildren, and great-grandchildren of Grandpa Farmer and Bess—fills the wide stone steps in front of the church. There are about forty of us. Then an aunt must have a picture of just the O'Briens. Someone else wants a shot of just the Blackhurst girls or of just the great-great-grandchildren of Reverend Harry and Lula.

As always I go for a walk around Cass. The old company houses are mostly empty, though families do live in some of them. Walking between the rows on the wooden boardwalks, you pass dark, abandoned houses that are occasionally interrupted by one freshly painted with bright flowerpots hanging on the front porch. I cross the Greenbrier River, twice the size of the South Branch in Franklin, on an ancient concrete bridge that is crumbling in places. I look back across the river at the old company store building which still sits on the hillside above the river. Below the company store is the train depot, the railroad tracks, and the parking lot filled with cars belonging to tourists who have come to Cass for a train ride. A local grocery store owner convinced the state of West Virginia to buy the lumber company after it closed down in 1960 and to turn the property into a state park. The handsome old Shay engines pull passenger cars filled with tourists to the top of Bald Knob, the second highest point in West Virginia, every year from late spring until the autumn leaves pass their peak in the fall. Most of the children attending the reunion have taken a ride on the train sometime during the weekend, and relatives of all ages love hearing the haunting wail of the train whistle as it echoes up and down the narrow valley.

I decide to walk down the railroad tracks to the old mill, or what remains of it. It looks like an extremely large warehouse and makes me think of my father's ruined high school in Piedmont. The roof has fallen in and the entire structure sags to one side as if sinking back into the ground. There are rusting machines surrounded by weeds, scraps from the leather belts that ran the giant saws, broken boards, shattered glass. One day I found the brass casing from a spent 30-30 and a belt buckle not far apart. The ground is covered with a kind of industrial loam. It's mostly rotted sawdust, but you find splinters of wood, bent nails, bits of cloth, and pieces of brown or green bottles that once held patent medicine. Poking through a handful is like a minute archaeological dig. Sumac, blackberry bushes, milkweed, locust, and sycamore saplings grow inside the shell of the building, and there is a smell of ash and urine. The forest that the robber barons clear-cut is beginning to grow back.

When I return to the community center, the extended family is scattered about involved in various stages of leaving: packing leftover food, putting children in car seats, cleaning the community center, and saying good-byes. Most of the Allen Blackhurst family is planning to meet back at Beaty and Jamie's for a lazy evening of visiting, eating leftovers, maybe watching some old home movies, looking at some more family albums, and making the annual visit to the Arbovale Cemetery to pay respects to Reverend Harry and Lula, Grandpa Farmer, Grandmother Bess, Uncle Buzz, who was tragically killed in a plane crash while in the Air Force at the age of twenty-nine, and other friends and extended family. The reunion is winding down. On Monday, most of the family will be leaving. Good-byes will begin in the kitchen, move out to the back porch, travel across the lawn, and continue at the car windows. If the drivers would move slowly enough, they might go on down the road.

WITH SUMMER near its end, Becky begins her start-of-school anxiety. Both kids are shopping for school clothes. There are hot nights in the yard watching an orange moon rise above the ridge over Franklin. I can remember thinking that we had been home one full year and how it had not been the nightmare I worried about in Oswego or the paradise I wanted but, as always, something in between. Many of the things Becky and I wanted in our family life had been realized: Being close to grandparents, aunts, uncles, and cousins. Sunday dinners at Grandma's, cider-making with Grandpa's old hand press, truck rides up into the mountains on summer and fall days. As we suspected, or perhaps hoped, Franklin was a wonderful small town and we had terrific neighbors on Anderson Hill. On one side of the yard a magic fence sprouted tomatoes, yellow squash, zucchini, and cucumbers thoughout the summer. Our neighbor on that side, Howard Lambert, was a good gardener and a pleasure to talk with across the fence. He was a good storyteller with a quick wit.

Christopher was spending a lot of time with Judy Hott's boys in the house next door. Eddie had become his fishing partner and he shared a passion for sports with John. Judy Hott had become a second mother to him. Shelly had two girlfriends in the house right behind us. On warm afternoons I would look out the kitchen window as I washed dishes to see Shelly and her friends playing recorders, like three of the nine Muses, or Becky and Judy sitting on the grass talking family, hugging their knees like schoolgirls. All of this felt right to us. It's what we wanted. Good West Virginians have their eyes fixed on what's truly important: family, good sense, getting by.

I was less worried about Chris and Shelly, though I still had misgivings about limited courses and activities at the schools. I blamed no one for this. Rural schools, in West Virginia and around the country, have low enrollments and that usually means low funds. Beyond this Chris was comfortable at Franklin High. Fishing the South Branch together, I would look downstream to see him in the soft evening light as focused on the river as he had been "opening rocks" as a little boy.

Shelly was buoyant most of the time, and she had friends at Franklin Elementary School. I took her fishing a number of times, and while she enjoyed the river, there was no passion there. But we went on "dates" to the mall in Harrisonburg and would sit on benches making up stories about the people passing by before going to see a movie. On spring and summer evenings, we took drives on the back roads with a pot of water looking for wildflowers to bring home and arrange. We sang as we drove along, an old Harry Belafonte song about leaving a girl in Kingston Town being our favorite. One evening, two adolescent boys drove past as we walked out of a field with ironweed and yelled something in a falsetto about posies, just to remind us where we were. Shelly said, "Why did he yell like that?" and I said, "Because he's a jackass and that's what jackasses do." It wasn't important to either of us. More than anything else, I wanted my kids to make a better compromise with their lives than I had made with mine. They both seemed happy.

I had made no progress on my Appalachia book. I wrote two proposals—one about the coalfields—and the agent rejected both out of hand. At the time, I thought it was because he wanted the clichéd vision of the region but now I see that it was my own confusion. I was struggling to reject stereotypes about the people here but did not explain why the stereotypes existed or, for that matter, offer another view of Appalachia. This may seem like a contradiction, but the problem was I knew West Virginians too well. I knew them, but in the same intimate way that I knew my family, not as research subjects or characters but as individuals. For the longest time, that familiarity blinded me. My fishing partner Tom once said, as he released a bass, "You know, a fish don't know a thing about water till you pull him out of it." It would take time to pull myself out of Appalachia.

When I think of myself at the start of the second fall in Pendleton County, I'm struck with irony. There I was looking for a place that I have never escaped and never wanted to. Appalachia is less a specific location than a frame of mind, a set of misconceptions mistaken for the truth. The people who work hard to reject the misconceptions and the people who buy into them share opposite sides of the same delusion. Mythic Appalachia would affect my life and all of Pendleton County a little later that fall. Woodlands Institute, the county, and, of all things, a hurricane were about to come together.

14. Juan in Appalachia

THE LATE-SUMMER drought extended into fall. Farm wells dried up all over the county, and springs that had been active for more than a generation simply stopped. The volunteer fire companies in all three valleys rushed from one brush fire to another, and on Anderson Hill, my yard had turned to yellow stubble. By the end of September the talk in post offices and county stores focused on high school football and the desperate need for rain.

That fall, some of the talk almost certainly focused on Woodlands Institute as well. A new rumor was making the rounds: The institute wanted to take over county schools. Once again, it's hard to say exactly when or where the rumor began, but the story may have started after a school board election. One school board candidate said that Dan'l Taylor-Ide offered to pay his campaign expenses in exchange for his support on the board. According to the candidate, Taylor-Ide also said that he and a friend in Charleston had plans to turn Pendleton County schools into an experimental system that Woodlands would control.

As always, not everyone believed the rumor. Some people did not think it was possible to exempt county schools from state law. Others wondered why Dan'l, or anyone else, would want the schools to begin with. Operating funds were depressingly low. The buildings were old and the educational resources were limited. Beyond that, the state was pressing harder for consolidation of the Circleville and Franklin high schools, and that was going to be a hornet's nest.

After our conversation at his picnic, I saw very little of Jim Underwood through summer and fall. He had started a construction project ten miles north of town and was spending most days on the site.

At the time, Woodlands Institute did not officially employ him, but this was only a technicality. No one had signed up for his earth shelter workshops and the grant money was gone. Despite this, Jim still shared the Woodlands vision and in fact was on the institute board.

The drought persisted into October, and there was concern about the opening day of small-game hunting season on the second Saturday of the month. All of those hunters marching around in the woods smoking cigarettes presented a real threat of forest fire. I overheard several men say that the Department of Natural Resources, the DNR, had canceled the season. This turned out to be a rumor with no substance whatever. As a game warden told me later, "Cancel the hunting season? You must be kidding. We'd have a statewide riot on our hands."

Rain, rain, rain—the word began to sound like a chant. "Whole damn county's gonna dry up and blow away," as an older man said in the post office lobby one October afternoon. George Dice had a theory about the drought. When I drove him into town from the IGA or from the post office to his house, he carried on about the weather. "It's those daggone scientists, I tell you. They shoot missiles up through the sky and put things in the air and water. They've got everything fouled up so bad it won't be fit to live on earth no more." George thought the end was in sight. He sometimes said, "God'll even things out here directly."

I took long walks along the South Branch River every night that October. The drought had left the river so low it was hard to find good fishing water. The bass I managed to catch in late September tasted muddy, and I see no point in bothering fish unless I plan to eat them.

Leaving the house at dusk was pleasant most evenings. The soft light was fading in the trees and the crickets and katydids had started up. The sky above the valley's west ridge was sometimes streaked with salmon and pink, the backlit clouds inflamed. On home game nights, a sphere of hazy light rose above Franklin High on the east side of town. The crowd noise rose and fell like surf in the distance. Some nights I could hear the Panther marching band deconstructing one tune or another. At breaks in the music, the clicking drumsticks echoed back from the other end of the valley, as if some ghost band was marching around in a dark hollow down the way. It was a pleasant October evening in an Appalachian town.

When I walked past Howard Lambert's German shepherd, the dog lunged against the fence snarling and barking like something from another world. I gave up trying to sweet-talk the dog; this only made it more ferocious. The shepherd set off the Anderson Hill doggy chorus: yips and barks from the dark yards all over the hill. I recognized most of the dogs by then and felt less a stranger in Franklin town. Each night I found myself anticipating the bear hounds at the base of the hill. When they began to bugle, my father came to mind. He loved the sound of his dogs running a rabbit. In my mind, I would see him standing next to a thicket smiling.

I was never far from some memory of him that entire year. Looking back, I can see myself walking around in one of those riddle pictures Christopher used to bring home from preschool. Find the kittens that Jack Frost has hidden. At first, you only see trees in fall color, grass, and clouds, maybe a little house with smoke curling from the chimney. Then as you study the picture, the first kitten appears in a curlicue of smoke, than another emerges from a cloud. There is one in the trees, another in the grass. After you find them, it's hard to see the landscape. In a sense, Pendleton County was like that: It was filled with small things that made me think of him.

The night walks were wonderful. It was so quiet downtown I could hear the bank clock groan and click as the minutes changed. In late September a barred owl moved into town, no doubt hunting rabbits on lawns. That's unusual, I think. In my experience, barred owls are secretive birds that rarely come out of deep woods, but this one had perhaps because of the drought. It's the owl that calls "who cooks for you?" I listened for it every night and walked toward the call but never saw the bird.

Minutes away from downtown, I was in real country—pastures, woods, brilliant stars above. Opossums, coons, and skunks crossed the road. The silhouettes of deer flashed so quickly in the trees I wasn't sure whether I saw them or just imagined that I did. The road I took ran close to the South Branch for a while. In one deep spot, the only deep spot for miles, a family of beavers had moved in near the end of September. Some nights I would see one pushing its dark V across the water. One night at that same deep spot, I walked up on a family fishing for eels. It was a man and a woman and two children sitting around a Coleman gas lantern. The smell of bourbon—like apples and wood smoke—laced the air. It brought back memories of eel fishing with my dad. He used a coal oil lamp and we sat in a sphere of yellow light, while the night bugs and bullfrogs made jungle noises. For a moment I was there, a boy beside him on the riverbank.

On moonlit nights, I walked a dirt road through a pasture into the woods and sat on a rock to watch for deer. This was right across the river from Franklin and perhaps a mile away. From that vantage point, the houses and buildings looked as though they had been scattered against the mountainside by some gigantic hand. I could see no pattern. Without planning to, I managed to be at that same spot just at dark several times. As the house lights snapped on here and there, I imagined myself inside a jar of fireflies.

Back then I was trying to understand Franklin as an Appalachian town but having no success. In fact, I could not quite see the town as a single community. The Franklin that McCoy, the bankers, lawyers, doctors, businessmen, well-off landowners, and all of their socially prominent wives imagined was not the same town some angry North Fork people hated. Black county residents living on Entry Mountain went shopping in a Franklin only they imagined. County come-heres saw a quaint, provincial town. The poor standing outside Franklin's plate-glass window saw a community beyond their reach. The Appalachian town that Underwood and Woodlands Institute planned to advance was something else again. That Wallace Stevens poem would come to mind—

> Twenty men crossing a bridge,
> Into a village,
> Are twenty men crossing twenty bridges,
> Into twenty villages,
> Or one man
> Crossing a single bridge into a village.
> This is old song
> That will not declare itself . . .

In the last week of October, I found a letter from my mother in the post office box. I did not open it for several days. In Oswego, a letter my father wrote to Becky had triggered an episode of depression. I was anxious and thought it best to wait.

Here is a history of how relations with my family unraveled. In 1979, two years after my confession about the psychiatrist and "drugs," a friend from Philadelphia came to visit me in Hampton, Virginia. She had been in the old neighborhood on an errand and happened to pass Taren's discount store. Remembering that my mother worked at Taren's, she stopped in. My mother was working that day. They chatted for a minute or two and then my mother expressed her great disappointment in me. I had been raised like all of her other children, who were doing wonderfully, but I had let the family down.

I don't think I said anything to my friend but I was livid. My mother had stood in a public store telling a virtual stranger that I was a failure. Days later, I got over my anger but began to understand a number of things. In a variation of my father's despair, my mother had turned necessity into virtue all her life. This entailed shaping reality to meet her needs. My father loved his factory job because it was the job my father had. The neighborhood was perfect because they could not escape it. She did not think she had said or done anything wrong. I had broken relations with my family for no reason. This had nothing to do with the comforting delusions we all nurture to get by; it was a manufactured reality. That was all right. My mother's life had been difficult and she had to do this to keep going. She had probably pushed all thoughts of her angry letter and of the tirades about me from her mind and now truly believed that I had broken relations "out of the blue." Her confusion was probably genuine.

I understood that my mother could not change, but that I couldn't either. I had been in and out of clinical depressions for ten years and this had become part of who I was. I blamed no one, but could not see how to hold my family together, write, and survive depression while I contended with my family's censure. My mother had no reverse gear, no sense of truce. The steely will that had held the family together through hard times now would keep us apart. Making the break, I was sad rather than angry. I told myself that, at least for the time being, I was only doing what I had to do.

I opened my mother's letter on October 28. The date stands out only because of what would happen to the county a week later. There was no terrible news, just more of my mother's bewilderment: "We've done nothing. Why do you hate us? Your father blames himself." I sat up a good part of that night writing letters to my father and throwing them away. I picked up the phone once or twice, then put it back without dialing the number. I was not in the best shape emotionally before the letter arrived, and now I felt desperate.

AS WELL as I can remember, I first heard about Hurricane Juan on October 30. Walking out of the Pendleton County Bank, I noticed an old junker car parked at the curb with two squirrel tails tied to the antenna. The car had not been there when I went in. Up close, I could tell the tails were fresh; they were still soft and supple, and the cut glinted red. As I ran my fingertips down the fur, a voice at my back barked, "Hold it right there, buddy."

A lanky young man stood behind me with his finger and thumb cocked like a pistol. I had met him half a dozen times on the South Branch "a-feesh'n for supper" and we had become friendly, though I never learned his name.

Gesturing toward the car, I said, "Got you some squirrels."

"Just this morning," he said. "In the early bright."

He talked about hunting on Elk Mountain, and that led into a story about being up there years before with an uncle and seeing squirrels migrate—"hundreds of 'um jump'n through the trees." He kept talking, but my mind drifted into a memory: My father and I kneel on a frozen field at the edge of dark trees. He spreads the toes of a gray squirrel I have shot and tells me how to tell a resident squirrel from one that's migrating. Migrating squirrels wear the fur off their toes. He tells me the same story about hundreds of squirrels leaping through the trees.

As we parted company, the young man turned back and said, "You got yourself braced for Don Juan?"

I must have looked confused because he went on to explain that a hurricane was headed for the county. I said, "Better get home and board the windows up."

That night I watched Hurricane Juan on television—this ragged pinwheel of clouds spiraling counterclockwise up the Appalachian chain. Hurricanes are occasionally devastating in Appalachia. The cyclonic winds generally do not come this far inland, but when the moisture-laden system encounters the cooler mountain air, it rains unbelievably hard. In these narrow valleys, the watershed can be sudden and murderous. The small runs and streams on the slopes fill quickly and the water rushes down to the rivers in the bottom. Within a day after a downpour, a torrent plunges through the V notch, ripping out large trees, smashing barns and homes, killing stock and people. Truly bad floods have literally erased small towns along the rivers. It's part of life here. But a flood was the last thing on my mind that October.

Hurricane Juan arrived on Thursday, October 31. There was no high wind and no rain, but a strange fog filled all three valleys. Fog isn't unusual in the Appalachians. Patches can be as opaque as milk on mountaintops, which makes for dangerous driving on these twisty roads. But it's most often a brief and very local phenomenon. I had never seen fog that covered an entire county or one that lingered day after day.

I could not see the river. Sounds were distorted. When a deer crossed the road just ten yards ahead of me, I could not see it. It sounded like women in high heels hurrying off. I was disoriented and began to feel anxious, but on the way back, the view of Franklin suddenly changed my mood. Kids dressed up as goblins and spooks for Halloween were on the lighted porches of the old homes. Parents waited on the sidewalks. The fog made everything as soft and filmy as a dreamscape and this made me light-headed with pleasure.

Two days later, on Saturday night, I went to an "Appalachian fiddle" presentation at a small church on Main Street. I rarely go to events like this, but the come-here responsible for the presentation, Paul Goland, was a friend who had asked me to attend. Given the peculiar weather, he was worried about a poor turnout.

We sat in the last pew and I became edgy as the people filed in. Beyond the usual discomfort I feel in crowds, I did not know what to make of "Appalachian cultural presentations" back then. Organizations sponsor events like this, featuring fiddle players, ballad singers, and/or storytellers, all through the southern Appalachians, but "Appalachians" rarely attend. The church was filling up with come-heres, a number of my friends among them, but there were almost no locals. "Appalachians" do not turn out for these evenings because the presentations have virtually nothing to do with real mountain cultures. A man from the American Folklife Center in Washington, D.C., had come into Appalachia—an invented region—to play Appalachian music to a church filled with non-Appalachians. This cultural hall of mirrors also had its start near the turn of the century.

In the 1890s "high church" missionaries, mostly unmarried women with degrees from Vassar or Smith, "finished" their education with a sojourn in Europe. At least some of these missionaries belonged to the Episcopalian or Anglican Church, but the designation "high church" had more to do with their upper-middle-class status and the colleges they attended. In London these women were much taken with the folk art movement—Ruskin's ideas that flowered with William Morris—and with the settlement house movement, where Oxford students "learned to sup sorrow with the poor." At the time, missionizing Appalachia was also at a high point. When these bright, energetic women returned to America looking for meaningful lives, mythic Appalachia, the settlement house, and a mania for folk arts merged.

Old fiddle tunes and ballads did exist in the southern Appalachians at the time, but so did a rich variety of contemporary music. In the 1890s, those old disappearing art forms were of marginal importance to mountain cultures and since then they have become even less important. But that aside, "high church" missionaries who had fallen in love with "folks" and the settlement house vision added another label to the list of identities for people in the southern mountains: the hillbillies, highlanders, Celts, mountaineers, and Appalachians were now rustic "folk." Given this, they were surely producing "folk art" that should be preserved, and high church missionaries took this as their mission.

At times, this created what can only be described as cultural delirium. The founder of one settlement school, Olive Dame Campbell, traveled to Sweden and was much impressed with Danish folk schools. Returning to America, Campbell established the John C. Campbell Folk School in North Carolina to teach and preserve "all that is native & fine" in Appalachian culture. To this end, she taught Appalachian children dances like the Danish March and the Ander's Hop and songs like "Gustaf's Toast" and "Anders, He Was a Lively Lad." She also taught them Morris dances and sword dances more or less created by folk art enthusiasts in England.

Appalachian people, like most turn-of-the-century rural Americans, wove cloth, made rustic furniture, and whittled wood into toys and tools. Some of the settlement schools brought in better looms and carpentry tools, instructors from outside, new patterns, finer yarns, and new designs for furniture. With a little market research, the school leaders found out what would sell best outside the mountains and then had Appalachians come to work for eight hours a day producing "folk art." Like missionaries generally, the settlement school teachers were well-intentioned people who worked hard at great sacrifice, but they were clearly inventing a "culture" that charmed them.

The largest part of the invention, the region of Appalachia, took place in 1897 not long after "high church" missionary William Goodell Frost became president of Berea College. Berea College, in the mountains of Kentucky, was founded in the 1850s as one of the first racially integrated, coeducational colleges in America. Until the Civil War, the school was well funded, but in the decades after the war, wealthy donors began to support black schools like Hampton Institute. In fact, when Frost assumed the presidency in 1892, Berea was within two years of financial collapse.

By this time, wealthy industrial families in the North and Northeast had become terribly concerned about the "purity of our Anglo-Saxon blood." It's a complicated story, but in brief, influential middle-class people, especially on Ivy League campuses, thought America had ascended to the peak of Western civilization. More than that, we had done so—in a dreadful misunderstanding of Darwin—because of our superior Anglo-Saxon blood. The first wave of Jewish immigrants was coming into the country at the time and people worried about their children and grandchildren marrying Jews and polluting the nation's blood.

Inventing yet another identity for the inhabitants of the southern mountains, they decided that the people were "pure Anglo-Saxon stock" and, as such, an undiluted reservoir of the blood that made America the greatest country on earth. Mountain blood, as the fantasy went, was pure because the Anglo-Saxons who settled the region had been completely isolated, which of course made little sense. The region had been settled by Scotch-Irish, Irish, German, and English families that had often intermarried, and the robber barons had started to bring Polish, Italian, and black people into the mountains. If one took New York City or Boston as a standard, the gene pool in the region was probably more homogeneous, but the idea of "pure Anglo-Saxon blood" was ridiculous.

But William Goodell Frost, a person of high moral standing, recognized an opportunity when he saw one. An intelligent, energetic man who counted the presidents of Ivy League colleges among his close friends, he began a fund-raising campaign that focused on New England.

Frost was a compelling and tireless speaker. On campuses, in private homes, and in lecture halls, he described people in the Appalachian Mountains as "our contemporary ancestors" who had fallen into a "Rip Van Winkle–like sleep." As these beguiling people woke, they would need help dealing with the modern world. In effect, Frost was telling affluent Americans, who had just discovered their past, that their great-great-grandparents were still alive and that they were as rustic and childlike as they had always imagined them to be. The gracious people in the churches and lecture halls could care for their ancestors and preserve America's pure Anglo-Saxon blood by donating money to Berea College. The pitch was irresistible. It was also utter nonsense.

Frost maintained that the Rip Van Winkle sleep resulted from extreme isolation, and, like so many misconceptions about the region, there was some truth in this. In the 1890s only a few poor roads led into the southern mountains and this kept communities isolated, at least to a certain degree. But the region was no more isolated than hundreds of rural locations around the country at the time, and in the late 1960s regional scholars concluded that extreme isolation was yet another missionary fantasy. Examining the historic record, rather than relying on the standard myth, researchers discovered ample evidence of extensive contact with East Coast cities. In letters, diaries, and deeds dated as early as 1850, families listed among their possessions pots, pans, rifles, silverware, clothing, boots, shoes, rugs, books, pianos, and countless other items manufactured in Richmond, Baltimore, Washington, and other cities. When people demolished old log cabins, they often found newspapers from Baltimore or Pittsburgh used as chinking between the logs. In a letter written in the 1860s one visitor recounted his attempt to get beyond civilization by climbing to the last cabin on a remote ridge only to find the owner in possession of a goldfish and an aquarium. How isolated could the region have been?

Beyond this, Appalachian cultures had changed substantially since the 1750s. Subsistence cultures, which value tradition first and foremost, change much more slowly than consumer cultures, but they do change. If one thinks about it, change is the very engine of consumer cultures and, given this, traditional cultures may seem backward, but this is simply a difference in cultural values. And there is always the question of how much real progress, as opposed to change for its own sake, the rapid change in consumer cultures provides. It is interesting to note that American anthropology, just beginning near the turn of the century, labeled their studies of other cultures "the childhood of mankind." This is profoundly ethnocentric.

A fine writer, Frost published several articles in the *Atlantic Monthly*. In the first article, he declared the "mountainous back yards of nine states the God ordained region of Appalachia," and with this he completed the American middle-class invention. One can trace the process in clear phases. Each new layer of invention was generated by the immediate needs of outside missionaries, and each was accomplished with the best of intentions.

Berea College became the center of Appalachian "folk art," and "Appalachians" became romantic "folk" as well as slack-jawed hillbillies. This is the Janus image that the American middle class creates for minorities—the razor-totin' nigger out to get white woman/kindly Uncle Remus; bloodthirsty savage updated to drunken Indian/Tonto the Earth poet; the gene-deficient monstrosities of *Deliverance*/ quaint Anglo-Saxons playing their fiddles.

I don't think I have ever understood the middle class, smug in their assumption that everyone should be like them, but at the same time oddly insecure. They sense a hole at the center of their lives, which they try to fill with something earthy or authentic. Blues, Native American Earth wisdom, Appalachian fiddle playing—it's all a search for the genuine. At times I do see middle-class American culture as shallow, but then I have never really escaped my working-class background, and that perception is itself shallow. My phenomenologist fishing partner in Oswego, Dave Harbert, and I sometimes argued about this while we fished. I never understood how one person's life experience could be more authentic than someone else's when nothing is "authentic" to begin with. Harbert insisted that some lives and activities were infinitely more real than others. In fact, his pursuit of subsistence hunting and fishing began with this assumption. Apparently the come-heres attending the Appalachian fiddle presentation agreed with Dave and were there for an "authentic" Appalachian experience.

That night Jim Underwood came into the church and sat directly in front of me. His face was inflamed as if he had spent the day working outside. More or less forced to watch him, I was struck once again with his remarkable self-consciousness. When Jim tipped his head to one side to whisper to someone beside him, that simple movement was infused with drama. Settling back into the pew, he was the very essence of a man settling back into a pew. It was uncanny, as if Jim were playing the part of Jim Underwood in a movie. I concluded that we were both extremely self-conscious, though Jim, unlike me, seemed to be enjoying himself.

Paul Goland said a few words and then introduced Alan Jabbour from the Folk Life Center in Washington, D.C. A tall, slender man, Jabbour appeared Lincolnesque in the soft church light. He spoke so kindly and with such gentle self-deprecation that I liked him at once. When he began to play the fiddle, the small church filled with a strange, otherworldly sound. That old music is based on a twelve-note rather than an eight-note scale. It wasn't bad at all.

When the performance ended, the audience was jammed up at the church door. After three days of mist and fog, it had finally started to rain.

SUNDAY

It's morning. I'm at the living room window, drinking coffee as I watch the deserted bird feeder and listen to Bach Variations on the stereo. The Master makes his argument against disorder, turns it inside out, adds some filigree, and moves it forward. In my mind I see myself talking to my father on the phone. The two of us begin to weep. The beat of the rain never varies.

MONDAY MORNING

On Jack Mountain twelve miles south of Franklin, county school superintendent John Bowers bolts awake an hour before dawn to the sound of rushing water. It is so loud Bowers thinks the water is running under his bed. He gets up, but the floor is dry.

Bowers quietly walks into the next room and sits in an easy chair. Snapping on a light, he listens with deliberation. He was not dreaming: The sound fills this room as well. Two small runs flow near the farmhouse and they flood the yard a few times each year, but he has never heard them make this much noise. If it's this bad on top of Jack Mountain, Bowers wonders about the South Branch River down in the valley bottom.

He dresses, throws a long black topcoat on, grabs a Pendleton County Farm Bureau cap and walks out into the rain and dark. Bowers is a short, dapper man with snow-white hair and quick intelligent eyes, but the long dark coat and low cap make him look like a gnome. At the bottom of Jack Mountain, he pulls to the left against the guardrail of a small bridge and rolls the window down. He sticks a very long flashlight out into the rain and points it to the river. The lead-gray water seems to boil in the circle of light.

At about this time on Timber Ridge in the North Fork Valley, a man in an Army fatigue jacket and black ski cap walks to his pickup truck. John Mallow does not like to hunt turkeys in the rain but does not mind all that much either. The weather will keep the dandified hunters in bed, and he will have the woods to himself.

Steady rain falls in front of his headlights. The wipers beat back and forth. It has not let up since Saturday night. Near the top of Elk Mountain, Mallow drives into a waterfall. The windshield becomes opaque and he slows to five miles an hour. Later he tells friends, "I never seen it rain like that before. Big as half-dollars some of them drops."

Mallow turns onto a dirt road and stops at the edge of deep woods. The downpour pounds the truck's cab for another five minutes and then suddenly stops. As the light breaks in the trees, he watches the forest floor, hoping to see a gobbler drop down from its roost tree. In one spot, the ground splits open before his eyes and water bubbles up and out like a spring.

Grabbing his shotgun, Mallow gets out of the truck to investigate. Standing a good ten yards away, he watches the flow get stronger. A little to the right, the ground splits again and a larger spring erupts. He hears a third erupt in the dark woods and this one sounds huge.

Mallow hurries back to his truck and starts for home. Later when someone asks, "Was you scared?" he says, "Not exactly. I'd just seen about enough for one morning."

The school buses begin to arrive at Franklin High. Superintendent Bowers, now looking the part in suit and tie, talks with the school bus drivers in their coffee room at Franklin High. He knows these men and trusts them. Farmers struggling to make ends meet, they know the land and watershed. The men talk about the speed of the rise, how fast the water's coming up, and this worries Bowers.

A little after eight Jim and Janet Underwood walk into the high school to meet with Yar's teacher, Joe Garber. Garber is a delicate man with a penchant for Day-Glo orange ties. As the three of them sit at Garber's desk discussing Yar's course of study in the gifted program, there is a lot of noise in the hall and kids begin to slam locker doors: Superintendent Bowers has canceled school. Garber tries to go on with the meeting in the middle of the chaos—kids running up to his desk to ask questions, the noise level rising—but it's impossible. They reschedule the meeting an hour later at Garber's office in the old McCoy House downtown.

My kids come home. In his basement room, Christopher plays his *Purple Rain* album loud enough to rattle windows. I hate this album even more now, but find myself singing along again. It's like being in purgatory. I keep going to Christopher's room, sticking my hand in and lowering it down, down, down.

Shelly's girlfriends come splashing across the backyard. Laughter erupts from her bedroom. All three girls walk around the house eating bowls of Froot Loops.

In his quarters next to the courthouse, Ruskin Murphy, the county jailer, is cooking breakfast for a prisoner in the cell above him. It's scrambled eggs, sausage links, toast, juice, and coffee. He carries the tray up the stairs, unlocks the heavy door, and calls good morning to the young man in the cell. He's in for DWI with complications and will stand trial today. Murphy, a heavy smoker, lingers by the cell and lights another Pall Mall. He chats with the young man about the rain and his upcoming trial, tells him he hopes it goes okay. It'll be over with, anyway. Murphy gets along with his prisoners, or most of them. A year ago this wild boy was pulling cans of beer up to the cell on a fishing line hanging out the window. He had friends down in the parking lot. In the ensuing scuffle Murphy broke his finger, but that kind of trouble is rare.

Murphy is on the Franklin rescue squad. Back in his quarters with coffee, he lights another Pall Mall and places his monitor, a black box slightly larger than his pack of cigarettes, on the table. It's been cracking with calls since he woke up and they are coming in faster all the time. Most weekdays are dead quiet. With so much rain, at least some calls might be expected but not this many. More than that, the calls are coming from all over the county, the ridge tops down to the valley bottoms. Dennis Miller, the county emergency director, works over in Virginia and Murphy is second in command.

Murphy drives across Franklin to the nursing home, Emergency Station One in Pendleton County. As he walks through the doors, a passing nurse says, "Boy, am I glad to see you. The emergency phone has been ringing off the hook." The phone rings at that very moment and Murphy thinks, Something's way out of line here.

THE MEETING with Garber over, Jim Underwood walks down Main Street to the low water bridge and looks at the South Branch River. It's up and over the bridge, raging with frightening power. Jim is unconcerned and even laments the fact that the wild water has come at the wrong time of year. In a warmer month, he would be out there in a kayak or canoe having the time of his life. He starts back home.

I'm driving down Anderson Hill to get the mail and escape the house. It is still raining. The relentless gray spears drive into lawns, and drum on the car roof. Dyer Avenue has become a shallow stream with a quarter-inch sheet of water gliding down. I see that all of the side streets have become streams. Main Street is a larger stream. All of the water is rushing down to the South Branch.

George Dice flounces into the post office lobby talking to himself. "It's all or nothing around here," he says, "drought or flood." He stands there dripping water, singing under his breath, "Ain't nobody's business if I do." It's a Billie Holiday song—at least that's how I came to know it. George sings it under his breath a lot, sometimes in anger, and I often wonder what he has in mind.

He turns in my direction, saying, "Hello there."

"It's O'Brien, George."

"Say, you wouldn't be going my way, would you?"

"Which way's that?"

"Up to the house."

In the car, George says, "Don't this beat all? This here rain, I mean?"

"It's something, all right."

"Is the river up as much as they say?"

"I don't know. I haven't been down there."

"They say it's God-awful."

"You wanna go see?"

A vague smile crosses George's face, and I realize I have said something stupid. He says, "Let's go have a look."

Approaching the low water bridge, I begin to hear the roar, even with the windows closed. I feel something inside my chest, a kind of pressure that comes in waves. At the bridge I say, "My God!"

George shouts above the roar, "Tell me what you see!"

"It's like—it's like boiling chocolate milk. There goes a willow tree; there's a shed. I think that's a dead sheep—wait, I don't think the sheep's dead, I think it's trying to swim. . . ."

George tips his head back and opens his mouth like a man seeing a vision.

AT HIS drop-leaf table, ordering materials for his earth shelter building project, Jim Underwood has been listening to his monitor. Like Murphy, he is puzzled by the calls to pump out basements on the mountaintops. Flooded basements in valley bottoms, especially near the rivers, are fairly common after heavy rain, but flooded basements on the ridges seem strange. He calls Rescue Station Two in the community building near the town park to let them know he's on standby. Minutes later, as the calls increase, he drives down.

Emergency Station Two is a very small room next to the bay where the fire truck is parked. As Jim walks in, the conversation stops. The other men, four or five of them, look at him, nod, and look away. The men do not like Jim and make no attempt to hide their feelings.

On top of the file cabinet, a scanner squawks and flashes nonstop as calls from all three valleys are monitored. After listening for ten minutes, Jim feels an adrenaline rush. Something unprecedented is taking shape out there in the rain, and he is determined to play some part in it.

Hurrying back to his old white Volvo, Jim drives toward the nursing home and makes a mental note to get in touch with Ron Kirk. Ron is not on the rescue squad but the two men have been friends since meeting several years earlier at a cave rescue. Like Jim, Ron is a rock climber and a come-here. Though not a member of Woodlands, Ron—as Jim's close friend—seemed to share many of the institute's views. Like Jim, Ron was also a man of action and something of an adventurer. One afternoon not long after Jim moved to Franklin, calls had come in on his monitor about a spelunker trapped in Nut Cave near Moyers. When Jim arrived, Ron, who had heard the calls on a scanner, was already there and so was a large man named Mike Steele.

Steele, a former sailor from the naval base in Sugar Grove, was a quiet, earnest man who saw himself as the skills team's silent partner. Taking charge, Jim recruited Ron and Mike, then fashioned a number of rope and pulley devices from his climbing gear. With Steele as anchor at the cave mouth, Jim and Ron descended and brought the man out. Kirk and Underwood had been so pleased with the rescue they often talked about forming an elite rescue unit—the "Pendleton County Tactical Skills Team." The team did not officially exist, but they had stationery made up—gold paper with a round logo at the top. A lightning bolt filled the top half of the circle and, separated by a climber's knot, a raging fire filled the bottom. "Pendleton County Tactical Skills Team" appeared in bold print. Jim was convinced that the skills team would be needed before the day was over.

At the nursing home Murphy and another volunteer are manning the emergency phones and the shortwave radio. The calls pour in, and by now some of them are telling of urgent, even life-threatening, situations. Jim tells Murphy that the skills team is ready to go. Murphy simply nods and answers another call.

When Jim stopped at the nursing home again later, he overheard a call about Kimble's Trailer Court twelve miles north of Franklin. The South Branch had trapped three old men and the water was rising fast. The situation was desperate, and Jim asked Murphy to send the skills team on the mission. Jim told Murphy that he had a canoe and climbing equipment, as well as the necessary skills, but Murphy could not seem to make up his mind. As Jim and Ron located the canoe, paddles, wet suits, and other gear, they became more and more frustrated with Murphy. In their view, lives were at stake and this was no time for indecision.

For Murphy, the largest difficulty was assessing the situation at the trailer court. Squad members from Upper Tract, three miles on the other side of the court, had already been dispatched. Had those men reached the trailer court? Had the old men been rescued or were they dead by now? A North Fork boy had already died in a pointless rescue attempt, and Murphy did not want to send Jim to the trailer court unless there was a good reason. When Murphy tried to call Upper Tract on the ham radio, the frequency was jammed.

Beyond this, Murphy had spoken with the rescue squad in Randolph County, west of Pendleton County, and they had promised to send a large, seagoing boat. When he mentioned the possibility of a canoe rescue attempt, the squad member in Elkins had been incredulous. The idea of putting a canoe into a flood of this magnitude seemed crazy. Dennis Miller, the Pendleton County emergency director, had called from Virginia, and his reaction to a canoe rescue was the same. Miller told Murphy not to send Jim, or anyone else, into the flood in a canoe. But Jim kept coming back to volunteer. Murphy was bewildered.

At stations around the county, rescue squad members overheard Murphy talking about the canoe rescue over the scanner. They also thought the idea was insanely dangerous, and in their view, Jim Underwood, typically, was grandstanding. The squad members had spent the morning and the afternoon responding to emergency calls. They had pumped out basements, carried furniture from homes, driven cattle and sheep through high water, pulled stalled cars out, and transported people to houses on high ground. There was nothing dramatic about most of this. The men were wet and tired and they would be on call all night. In their view, Jim had done nothing all day except wait for an opportunity to appear heroic.

A good part of this reaction was culture-bound. Appalachian men affect a Gary Cooperish demeanor, the strong silent American who does not boast or brag. As Jim "networked" through the community he was seen as boastful. His daily efforts to "advance mountain culture" might well have been applauded in another cultural context, but in Pendleton County, men thought he was "strutting like a turkey." Setting out on a canoe rescue in a raging flood was, in their view, more of the same.

Shortly after dark, Bill Ruddle was filling his pickup with gas outside Thompson's Motor Lodge on the north end of Franklin. As he stood there, nozzle in hand, he saw Ron Kirk's Land Rover speed by carrying Underwood and a canoe. As the taillights disappeared around the turn, he muttered, "There goes a couple of jackasses."

BECKY and I had spent the afternoon rummaging through drawers and closets for candles, matches, and flashlight batteries. I discovered an old kerosene lamp hanging from a nail in the garage and, after cleaning carbon from the glass dome, I placed it on the kitchen table beside several packs of matches. Right after dark, I began to worry about our supply of food and candles and set off for the IGA market. On the way I decided to cruise down Main Street just to see what I could learn. By then I knew that Franklin was in the middle of a major disaster.

It was like Saturday morning on Main Street, cars and trucks kept streaming past. People hurried up and down the sidewalk with worried or pained expressions on their faces. When a pickup abruptly stopped in front of me, I slid to within a foot of the rear bumper. A middle-aged woman had stepped off the curb, forcing traffic to a halt in both directions. Standing in the rain, with her hair all wet and plastered to her head, she began to talk with the man in the truck. They were both looking for other people. Her voice breaking with emotion, the woman said, "Have you seen any sign of Frank?" The driver answered, "Not since morning," and then said, "I'm looking for Ann." The woman shouted, "Check out the school. The grade school. People are sleeping on the floor up there." Horns began to blow, the woman darted back to the sidewalk, and traffic began to move again.

The IGA was overcrowded. People in dripping rain gear stood talking in every aisle. Stopping to pull a cart free, I overheard a man tell someone about Brandywine in the South Fork Valley. He said, "They're going to evacuate the whole town. They're worried about that dam out there." I had fished at Brandywine Reservoir many times. The dam was solid earth and I could not imagine it giving way.

Walking down the aisles, I tossed in one thing after another—chocolate chip cookies, diet pop, canned peaches, anything that would not require cooking. The people whom I passed were telling flood stories. I heard about barns collapsing, livestock being swept away, roads going under, cars flipping over, pets drowning, and people trapped in their homes. At first the stories frightened me, but then I could no longer quite believe them. They seemed too unreal. Then at the checkout counter, I overheard a woman telling the cashier "Brandywine's gone. The whole town's been washed away. That dam busted." I was frightened for a second, but then found myself smiling. It seemed a perfect illustration of small-town gossip. You walk in one door and they are talking about evacuating a town. Come out another door and the town's been washed away.

Approaching my driveway near the top of Anderson Hill, I slowed almost to a stop. A large, wet skunk was creeping up the road in front of me. I had known that a skunk lived near the house for some time. When I went walking at night, I often caught its scent. I assumed it lived down in the gully under a tree root or large boulder, but had never actually seen the animal until then. The encounter pleased me, and I said aloud, "We meet at last." Then it came to me that an animal living near my house was heading for higher ground, and once again a wave of anxiety rose in me. In the driveway, I stood in the rain and watched the skunk disappear into the underbrush above my yard. I tried to remember if my father had ever told me anything about skunks moving to higher ground.

The lights went out not long after I returned from the IGA. The dark house excited my children. They lit too many candles and invented reasons to go off into the other rooms with the flashlight. My daughter's friends had gone home earlier, but my landlord's daughter, Emily, had come to spend the night. I cannot remember who came up with the idea, but we began to play charades in the living room. I was struck time and again with how lovely the children were in the candlelight—their shadows waving and dancing on the walls and ceilings. My mind kept going back to the O'Briens in Philadelphia. Hard times were like this in my father's house—candles and a coal-oil lamp. My brothers and sisters and I loved it, and my children did too.

At one point, while the kids whispered about a new skit in the dark kitchen, I got up and opened the front door. Usually the town lights create a fuzzy glow just above the rooftops below my house. Now it was as black as fresh tar. The South Branch was at least a quarter mile away, but I could hear it thundering through the valley bottom. Closing the door, I decided to keep my worst fears to myself.

. . .

THE ACCOUNT of the skills team canoe rescue is harrowing. Within minutes after Bill Ruddle watched Kirk's Land Rover leave Franklin, a landslide stopped it. Tons of earth, rock, and vegetation, made sodden and heavy by the rain, had come down from a sheer rock face to cover the road. If the skills team had left town ten minutes earlier, the Land Rover would have been under the slide.

The three men waded through waist-deep mud and got around the slide. They might have jogged the next five miles, but not with a canoe. As luck had it, a young man in an old truck appeared on the other side of the landslide. He was desperate to get to Franklin and so they struck a deal; Kirk would drive him into town while Underwood and Mike Steele transported the canoe in his truck.

Mike dropped Jim and the canoe off perhaps a mile from the trailer court, where the South Branch had overtaken the road, and then returned to the landslide to pick up Kirk. The three men reunited at the water's edge something over an hour later.

In that part of the South Branch Valley, near Ruddle—a village named after one of Bill Ruddle's ancestors—the river is normally about thirty yards wide and five feet deep. Now, the South Branch filled the entire valley bottom and might have been three hundred yards wide and twenty or thirty feet deep. More than that, it was plunging through the valley and filled with debris—house trailers, parts of houses, large trees, chairs, tables, dead cows and sheep, countless plastic milk jugs, bits and pieces of things shattered beyond recognition, and refrigerators that seemed to bob merrily down the current like gigantic fishing corks. It was as if half the homes in the valley had cracked wide open and spilled their contents into the river.

At the water's edge, Jim shouted instructions over the thunderous roar, advising Ron and Mike to check their ropes and pulleys. Then he established a seating order; because of his size, Mike would take the middle seat. Ron would sit in the bow, and in order to direct the canoe, Jim would take the stern. Lifting the canoe from the road, they pushed off into the muddy water. Hoping to keep the canoe against the steep bank, Jim shouted for them to paddle hard on the right, but the moment they entered the current, the three men began to struggle. As the canoe moved faster and faster, the current kept pulling it out toward the center. In less than fifty yards, trees or logs had almost rammed into them half a dozen times. This clearly was not going to work.

Pulling up against a steep bank—the side of a hill actually—they climbed out and Jim devised another plan. This time they edged back down the hillside into chest-deep water and the men held on to the side of the canoe with their right hands while they grabbed branches and pulled themselves along. It was a curious form of locomotion— half swimming, half walking—that worked well enough until they reached a turn in the river. There, for some reason, the current became much stronger and they were forced to climb out again.

As the men stood talking in the driving rain, part of the hillside twenty yards ahead suddenly collapsed. Had they been standing there, they would have gone under with it. After exchanging long looks with Mike and Ron, Jim suggested another plan. This time, Mike would wait on the hillside with the canoe, while Jim and Ron walked through the woods to the site of the trailer court.

After his teammates left, Mike climbed on top of a large boulder and stood there with the canoe rope wrapped around his hand. Fifteen minutes later, a gigantic tree rushed past in the current, jammed a branch into the bow, and flipped Mike into the flood like a rag doll. He went under, came back up, and managed to climb into the canoe, only to be thrown out a minute later when another tree rammed the stern. Under for a second time, he unraveled the rope from his hand and clawed his way up the hill out of the water, lacerating his palms and tearing out fingernails in the process.

After stumbling through the dark and rain for perhaps an hour, Jim and Ron reached a point not far from the trailer court. The water was not only on the road but near the top of one power pole that somehow had managed to remain standing. The power poles rose a good five feet above the house trailers, which meant the court and the men had been swept away.

Reuniting in the woods, the three men started back toward Franklin. It was rough going. Their flashlight batteries were dead. It was pitch-dark and still raining very hard. The land rose and fell into gullies, and they often tripped and went tumbling to the ground. At one point as they stumbled along, the air was filled with a humming sound, and then the darkness exploded into blue light that gave everything around them the look of a photograph negative. A stepdown transformer had blown, and for a moment they wondered what would have happened had they been in the water. Then, minutes later as they started into yet another gully, the land suddenly flattened out onto a small terrace. From the darkness below, a bright light snapped on, temporarily blinding them. A man said, "You have to go back the other way." As it turns out, they had walked right onto the roof of a small garage built into the hillside. The owner of the garage and a woman in her early twenties were standing in knee-deep water right below them.

The three men climbed off the roof, and Jim briefly explained about the canoe rescue, adding that they would continue back to Franklin. The young woman, whose name was Frankie, did not want the men to do that. Her house was on high ground a hundred yards away, and neighbors had gathered in her basement to wait the flood out. All things considered, Frankie thought that the skills team should do the same. Jim and Frankie argued about this. Jim thought the team might be needed in Franklin but Frankie was convinced that going back out in the flood was crazy. In the end, Jim agreed to at least stop by the basement to warm up and have coffee.

In Frankie's basement, two men and two women stood around a woodstove talking low while small children ate peanut butter sandwiches on the floor beside them. A Coleman gas lamp hanging from one of the basement rafters threw a circle of powdery light around the gathering. In what surely must have been a singular moment in their lives, the four adults turned at the sound of the opening door to see three men in wet suits—"Frogmen, by God!"—walk in out of the flood. Embarrassed, Ron and Mike stayed back, but Jim walked to the stove.

As he approached, the four people shifted to make room, and at first, no one spoke. Then, rather cautiously, one man asked Jim what he was up to. Jim explained about the canoe rescue in some detail and ended the account by describing the electrical explosion as "the prettiest blue light I've ever seen." The people around the woodstove exchanged wide-eyed glances but said nothing.

The heat felt wonderful, but after half an hour, Jim decided to move on, and for the second time that night, Frankie argued with him. It was dangerous out there. Their first attempt had made some sense because, at least at the time, they thought they might rescue someone. Since this was no longer true, said Frankie, they should wait until the water went down.

Once again, Jim said that he wasn't afraid of the flood. Frankie believed him, but from her point of view, a sane person was afraid when there was something to be afraid of. They argued on. Jim said, "Someone else might need the skills team tonight." Breaking into tears, Frankie shouted, "Well, you can't help no one if you're dead."

An older man, one of Frankie's relatives, entered the debate. He had lived his entire life right across the road from Hammer Run and the South Branch River. The water rose up fast, he said, but it went down fast too. As politely as he could, he asked Jim whether going back out right now made sense. If they waited two hours, the water would drop—he guaranteed it.

Jim saw no reason to go on with the argument. The skills team would have to go. He thanked the people again, and then as an after-thought, asked if any of them had rope. The older man, whose farm was about fifty yards away, did indeed have rope but he did not understand. When he asked why they wanted rope, Jim said he planned to "shoot a line" over Hammer Run, in order to "hand over hand" across the water. This confounded the man. Why couldn't Jim wait until the water dropped and then just walk across? Jim explained once again about not being afraid and about being trained, but the older man still did not understand. He thought—but did not say—If this fellow is going to kill himself and his friends, I want no part of it. Looking down at the floor, he said, "I don't have no rope." The skills team left the basement.

And so, two cultures had met face-to-face in the middle of a disaster and the gulf of misunderstanding remained as wide as ever. The people in Frankie's basement saw themselves as part of the natural world. They had learned to survive by getting out of the way, finding the high ground and waiting for better times. You survive by acqui-escing. Men like Jim Underwood believed they should have dominion over the world. It was to be subdued. Mountains must be climbed. Jim saw the flood as a challenge the world had thrown at him.

I WOKE at 7:30 to a quiet house. Something felt wrong about the morning, and it took me a minute to realize that the roar of the South

Branch was gone. The flood was over. Everything would be normal again.

A few minutes later, my friend Eve Firor stopped to pick up her daughter Emily and she seemed troubled. While we waited for Emily to gather her things, I asked Eve whether the flood had left us anything in the valley bottom. I meant this as a small, conversational joke, but instead of answering, Eve grimaced and stiffly shook her head. She leaned toward me and whispered, "People died last night."

Shortly after Eve's departure, I drove downtown. Main Street was completely deserted, which was very strange for a Tuesday morning, but other than that, everything looked fine. Above the low water bridge, however, a few homes, foundations and all, had disappeared during the night. Below town, the land had turned pale brown and everything seemed inside out. For several moments, I did not know what I was looking at. It was not just a matter of not recognizing a familiar scene, but of not understanding the landscape as part of the world. My gaze jumped rapidly among collapsed buildings, mounds of twisted junk, huge craters, gaps in tree lines, and vast fields of river rock. But the landscape had no balance. It was like looking at one of Pluto's outer moons.

I drove down the dirt road toward what had once been Franklin's town park, and pulled up behind half a dozen vehicles on what remained of a blacktop road. The thick steel poles around the tennis court were bent and flattened against the ground like soda straws. A grassy field where I had watched boys toss a football around days before was now a moonscape of gray boulders. I walked past car-sized craters filled with foul-smelling muddy water and around towering junk piles packed with things like lawn mowers, shopping carts, hay bales, basketballs, bras, a dead kitten, and unbroken lightbulbs. Hundreds of dead fish—suckers, bass, river chubs, and trout—littered the ground. In muddy pools here and there, live ones still gasped and flipped about. Crayfish, a few almost the size of small lobsters, scuttled around in aimless circles, holding their claws up high, as if still trying to fight the water. Most of the blacktop road had been erased except for one small section of macadam, which twisted up into the air in defiance of gravity like a detail from a Salvador Dalí painting. At the time, fifteen or twenty people were walking around in the bottom.

I spent most of that morning driving the roads in and around

Franklin, trying to find an end to the disaster, but each rise or turn offered only another view of devastation. Within a short distance from town, each road was blocked by flood debris, a mud slide, a damaged bridge, or a place where the blacktop and the earth under it had been gouged out by the floodwater. The last route I tried was 220 North. Within two miles, a mud slide covered the road. Pulling hard to the roadside, I got out of the car and walked around the blockade, heading north. After a while I stopped and looked up and turned around in the road. The sky was hazy, but I could at least see it now. Birds were calling back and forth from the trees on the mountainsides. My father told me more than once that birds sang at the end of storms. Remembering this made me unreasonably happy. I came to a break in the trees that offered a good long view of the valley. It was all the same: smashed homes, barns, and trailers, the same light brown mud as far as I could see.

Returning to the park, I got out to walk around again. By then, there may have been sixty people there. A tall thin man came striding through the slow-moving people. Dressed in mismatched clothes, smiling unselfconsciously, he bounced lightly along like someone on a Sunday stroll. I could not take my eyes from him. Stopping at a pile of debris, he pulled out a metal rack from a refrigerator and smiled with pleasure. Rack in hand, he waded into a pool of muddy water and began to seine out fish.

We had no power, water, phone service, or any way to find out if relatives and friends who lived outside of Franklin were alive or dead. Becky stood at the phone, mechanically dialing and redialing trying to reach her parents in Green Bank. She got busy signals, recordings, or crackling static. In the absence of information, rumors ran wild: everyone in Circleville was dead, hundreds of others had died around the county, Riverton had been erased, Brandywine had been erased, the National Guard was on the way, the National Guard was not on the way, no one beyond the mountains knew what had happened to us, everyone beyond the mountains knew what had happened but did not care how many hillbillies had died, and Jim Underwood was dead.

On Tuesday night, there was a community meeting in the showroom of Sites Garage on Main Street. Flashlight beams swayed back and forth against the walls and ceilings. The room was packed, filled with dark faces and the smell of wet hair. I ran into Jim, who leaned close to me and whispered some dreadful fact or statistic about the flood and then grinned broadly. I was so startled to see him alive I could not speak. He seemed buoyant, in fact extremely happy, which made no sense.

"A few days after the flood," he explained, "I realized I was having a ball. You have to understand; I have exceptional skills and abilities. The flood gave me a chance to use them." I don't think Jim was taking pleasure in the disaster but was simply being honest. For a rock climber—and for some combat veterans I have known—ordinary life seems slow and tedious.

The National Guard arrived on Wednesday afternoon. By Thursday, Red Cross, FEMA—Federal Emergency Management Agency—and the Salvation Army had set up headquarters in school-rooms and offices around Franklin. Camouflage trucks and jeeps moved up and down the roads constantly, and we now lived with the staccato, batting sound of helicopters. In time, we learned that the entire eastern half of the state had been devastated. Thousands of homes, businesses, and public buildings had been destroyed or seri-ously damaged. Entire herds of cattle and flocks of sheep were gone and millions of dead turkeys littered the landscape. Forty-seven peo-ple died in West Virginia. Pendleton County lost seventeen, the high-est figure in the state, and that is wrenching in a rural community in which everyone knows someone who died.

Every night the emergency officials held open meetings in the community building and the word that best describes the meetings is "groping." The officials spoke a government language about "maxi-mizing potential" and "utilizing resources." County farmers talked about "hay bales soaked so bad I can't move them with my tractor" and "dead cows stuck in the mud." The gulf between them was quite wide. This scene comes back: I'm walking through the Franklin Elementary School auditorium, which is filled with people. FEMA has set up thirty small tables, and an official sits behind each one talking with a county man or woman on the other side. At most stations, county peo-ple stand in lines waiting to be heard. I stop at a table as a FEMA woman asks an old man in faded coveralls, "Tell me what you lost."

The man quietly says, "Everything."

"What does everything mean?"

"It means everything."

"No, no, no," the woman says.

The old man looks as frightened as a schoolboy in front of the principal. The woman leans over the table toward him and begins to speak more slowly and much louder. I hear the words "verifiable" and "depreciation." The old man blinks and licks his lips.

FOR THREE DAYS, I sorted donations sent in by relief agencies. A ten-foot mountain of used clothes had been assembled in one of the firehouse bays. My job was to stand at the edge of the mountain and pull things out. Shoes and boots in one pile; winter coats and jackets in another; shirts, jeans, hats, baby clothes, all had to be sorted out. In the next bay, the county church ladies organized the clothing on long tables lined up end to end. People came in and took what they needed. This went on ten or twelve hours a day.

In the opinion of many people who worked in the emergency center, the recovery in Franklin was far more tense and confused than it should have been. Chaos reigned because Jim tried to direct the recovery and he was constantly rebuffed. Local accounts of confrontations fall into a pattern. Dennis Miller, after being trapped outside the county for two days, returns not only to the turmoil but to a power struggle with Jim. In Miller's account, Underwood keeps jumping between him and Charleston, countermanding orders and issuing orders of his own. Jim meets people as they walk into the emergency center and advises them to ignore Miller. He walks into the office of the extension agent making demands. A day later, he orders the state police to take direction from him and no one else. Walking into a meeting of the county's ministers, Jim describes himself as the Quaker representative and tells the clergy members what they should do. On top of Shenandoah Mountain, Jim orders the state road supervisor to close the roads that the supervisor and state police have just opened.

A few encounters approached violence. Others left people speechless and confused about what to do. From a local point of view, Jim's activities during the recovery carried more of the same missionary assumption: *They* were too backward to make decisions on their own. I should say that all of this is from the local point of view. Jim's only comment about the encounters was "There *was* no tension."

Several months after the flood, Jim said to me, "For a while there we saw a golden door open. We had a chance to set things up in a better way. I'd be in charge of housing and emergency services. Dan'l and Jennifer would take education. Henry [Dan'l's brother, an M.D.] would handle all of the county's medical services. For a few days, we thought we had it. But then the door closed."

As Jim spoke about this, I saw his talk as boasting mixed with whimsy. Though perfectly sober, he was sipping scotch at the time and was in an expansive mood. The people who overheard Jim say similar things during the recovery took it quite seriously and became angry. "We're knocked flat on our backs," one resident said, "people have lost whole farms and family members, and this jaybird's trying to take our county away from us." County people saw Jim as "try'n to make himself look like a hero." Jim saw himself as a "Maccabee" who wanted to serve his community. It's a difference in cultural perceptions. And so it comes back to missionaries and Appalachians once again.

The recovery, or at least the most intense parts of it, began to wind down. The crowds at the emergency centers thinned out, and then the centers closed one after the other. The showroom in Sites Garage shut down first. I can remember seeing an occasional National Guardsman or bureaucrat on Main Street well into December, but the Guard units and most of the agency personnel left the county near the end of November.

The county began to look normal again. The huge piles of debris disappeared. The small runs near the ridge tops, which had been first to jump their beds, cleared and settled. The county's three rivers sometimes ran at strange angles across pastures, but the levels had dropped to normal and the water looked steel gray rather than chocolate brown. Many of the homeless moved into temporary house trailers brought in by FEMA. Others stayed on with family and friends. A few families moved back into homes and trailers that I thought had been abandoned for good. Yards were still under mud, and sometimes trailer foundations were temporary constructions of logs and river rock, but wood smoke issued from the chimneys again and lights came on at night. In Franklin, storeowners put Christmas decorations in their windows, and my Anderson Hill neighbors put strings of lights on their houses and shrubbery.

One mid-December afternoon, as I walked out of the IGA loaded down with groceries, George Dice approached me for a ride downtown. After George settled into the car I said, "First I've seen you since the flood. You been hidin' out, George?"

"No sir-ee. I had no business in all that mess so I stayed home where I belong."

"Smart thinking," I said, and added, "It's over now. A thing of the past."

"Maybe yes and maybe no," George said. "Sometimes the Lord will send us reminders to live right. Now you take . . ."

I took great comfort. There I was driving my friend around town again and he was talking philosophy. County life seemed back to normal.

15. Advancing
Mountain Culture

B Y THE summer of 1986, a year and a half after the flood, I
thought the county had completely recovered. Wading knee-
deep in the river, I would sometimes pause between casts and
try to imagine the gentle South Branch thundering ten feet above my
head, drowning seventeen people, smashing barns and houses into
splinters, tearing out entire groves of trees that had lined the river-
banks. It seemed impossible despite the fact that I had actually seen
the flood. I remember thinking that the world had no memory of the
disaster and had just gone on with its business, and I thought county
people had done the same. Then one August afternoon, walking out
of the library with an armload of interlibrary loan books, I met a minister's wife walking in. Her husband was a missionary, though I never
knew which denomination. We knew one another, sort of, and
stopped to pass the time. A short woman with short brown hair and
glasses that made her eyes appear large and bright, she was one of
those Christians afflicted with optimism. When I said something
about the flood being forgotten, she lifted her finger like a school-
marm and said, "Not so." I raised my eyebrows and she continued.

"Oh, I have my regulars," she said. "A woman that lost her husband, a man that lost his farm. Every time it starts to sprinkle, I listen
for the phone. Sometimes it rings at three in the morning. I pick up,
and a man or woman whispers in this little child's voice, 'Can we
talk?' And do we *ever!* We talk about kids, family, canning, shooting
deer, what's going on in this crazy county. We talk about everything
under the sun except that it's raining and the rivers are coming up
again. We just have a grand time in the middle of the night."

Her wrenching story was so at odds with the buoyant telling. I had been reading about AMA missionaries and was struck again with the paradox of Appalachian history—good-hearted missionaries creating profound problems while they helped unfortunate people. I liked the missionary's wife despite her numbing cheerfulness and all the more for teaching me something I should have known: For some county people the flood will never end.

By that summer Chris had found his place in Pendleton County. He had bright, interesting friends, loved playing basketball, and was doing well in school. Chris had exchanged letters with Angel for over a year and even went back to Oswego for a brief visit. I am not sure which young lover first saw the impossibility of their relationship, but by the end of his sophomore year, Chris considered himself an eligible bachelor. Romance was a problem. The girls he felt drawn to were attached to boyfriends they had met in grade school, but he saw the difficulty as a matter of low numbers and limited options, which was the best way to see things. Chris seemed happy and I worried less.

Shelly had become one of the "flag twirlers" who dress in sequined outfits and spin banners at parades and football halftimes while the band bludgeons popular songs. She had stopped writing poems. Or at least I had stopped finding the discarded bits and pieces on scraps of paper. That was all right with me. Most of the poets I have known were not happy people, and I wanted Shelly to be happy. One fall afternoon I sat in my car on the road above the high school athletic field to watch the flag twirlers, in their civilian clothes, practice routines without the band. They would listen to a teacher for several minutes and then, each face a mask of concentration, march through an intricate pattern that I could not decipher. I'm not foolish enough to think adolescence is a carefree time, but there they were, unmarried, undivorced, unaddicted, and childless, marching around in fall light and silence. I could not imagine anything that lovely being detrimental.

County people remained extremely angry with Jim Underwood and Woodlands Institute long after the flood. It was rumored that a foundation had given Jim a grant to write a new emergency program, and people saw him driving around town in a new Toyota. Jim denied receiving a grant, but given the community's conviction that Jim had created unnecessary turmoil during the recovery, the rumor infuriated some people.

As always, tempers began to cool as time passed and people went on with their lives. Then in the late 1980s, the bitterness and resentment flared again when two Woodlands publications surfaced in the county. One document, *Three Options for Community Development,* proposed raising fallow deer on a large scale, establishing a Woodlands bottling company to sell county spring water, and turning Pendleton County into a vast retirement complex administered by Woodlands. Another attached proposal suggested "shipping the unemployed out of state" on fleets of buses.

Proposing to import deer into a community of farmers who consider deer a major nuisance or suggesting the sale of spring water in a county that suffers with serious drought was not the wisest public relations move. The same thing must be said of proposing to "ship" the unemployed out of a state that struggles with a declining population. Beyond this, some people found the language in the proposals unsettling. In an introductory paragraph, the institute writer describes the Appalachian Mountains as "a major barrier to the transfer of ideas from the world outside," and goes on to say that "the people of West Virginia are increasingly bypassed by the commerce of ideas, development and modern life. What is apparent is that West Virginia needs a vehicle to bring ideas into the state." This is, of course, the explanation of the Appalachian "problem" that missionaries invented in the 1880s. It places the blame for the region's difficulties on backward culture created by imagined isolation rather than on industry and corrupt politics, an idea that has long been discredited.

Concerning the state's high unemployment, created primarily by the coal industry, the Woodlands writer states, "One solution worthy of consideration is setting up a vast employment agency to ship unemployed West Virginians outside the state to jobs and places that are growing and do have the necessary forward momentum. . . . What is being talked about is a planned migration similar to Ireland during the potato famine. . . ."

The proposal to market spring water begins, "One of the greatest resources in West Virginia that has not been adequately harvested is water. Coal has been harvested. The air has been polluted by chemical plants and steel mills. The mountain slopes have been harvested for timber, but water has never been adequately utilized." But the very problems the Woodlands writer purports to address were created by the successful "harvest" of coal and timber. To speak of harvesting spring water just as coal was harvested or of "shipping" people out of state is disturbing.

But what troubled county people most was the fact that Woodlands planned to radically change the community, as a Franklin man said, "behind our backs." Residents had learned about the advancement proposals virtually by accident. A part-time employee secretly carried the document out of the office and gave it to a Franklin storeowner. She told him that Woodlands had countless other proposals to "advance" the county and that some of them were frightening.

The Franklin storeowner made copies of the proposals and gave them to friends, who made copies and passed them on to neighbors. In short time, the institute's "secret plans" for the community became the hottest topic on the gossip network. When people spoke in country stores, post office lobbies, and parking lots, or on farmhouse phones, they talked about weather, cattle prices, high school sports, and hunting, but conversations invariably returned to the institute's plan to "take over." What would happen to Pendleton County? Would people wake one morning to discover that half the springs belonged to Woodlands? Would buses for the unemployed line up outside some makeshift office on Main Street? Would bulldozers begin to clear entire mountainsides for retirement complexes? What other advancement programs was the institute drafting and when would residents know about them? Pendleton County's preoccupation with Woodlands began to resemble community paranoia.

Whether the county's mounting anxiety was warranted or simply more Appalachian counterreality, the community's fears seem less bizarre in light of the region's history. The pattern of outside agents working hand in glove with politicians that began more than a century ago remains a fact of life in West Virginia. Families in small communities can wake up one morning to discover the mountain outside their kitchen window being strip-mined or learn that their small town has become an industrial waste site. With the right connections, anything can, and often does, happen in Appalachia. County people had not forgotten the picture of Jim Underwood handing the institute award to retiring Senator Jennings Randolph, and as the eighties ended, Dan'l Taylor-Ide was spending more and more time in Charleston. Returning to Pendleton County, Taylor-Ide often spoke of conversations with "Jay" or other prominent politicians. As locals saw things, the state and the Benedum Foundation had granted Woodlands $600,000 to teach a technology that the institute never understood. If Charleston and a foundation would fund something that bizarre, they would fund anything.

As always, bitterness circled back to the same questions: Why had Woodlands come into Pendleton County, of all places? All of the institute's money for salaries, property, and programs came from foundation or government grants and donations, but what were the grants and donations based upon? Many county people thought they knew. As Reid Waggy, a former Franklin mayor, said, "These people are making a lot of money by going outside to describe us as a bunch of damned hillbillies who can't put their socks on in the morning without them." Other people found the idea of Pendleton County as mythic Appalachia and of themselves as backward hillbillies so ridiculous, they dismissed the notion out of hand. How could anyone walk around in a pristine mountain landscape, talk with local people, and then conclude that Pendleton County was part of woebegone Appalachia?

Then in September 1987, a feature article about Woodlands appeared in the *Roanoke Times and World News*. In the piece, the "substantial evidence" of a new species of bear the institute had announced in the *Pendleton Times* became "the startling discovery of a new bear species . . . that was noted worldwide." But in his letter of explanation, Dan'l had agreed that the bear existed in a Nepalese zoo. Beyond that, no zoologist knew anything about the institute's discovery. The mystery deepened.

In the same article, Taylor-Ide, referring to the institute's "Scholars Program," describes the best students in West Virginia as "hillbilly kids and normally they wouldn't get a diddle. And not only does our program get them special consideration from admissions officers, but they almost always get financial aid as well."

After mentioning "whiskey-making," Taylor-Ide went on: "Mountain people are uniformly stubborn, independent, and conservative when it comes to new ideas. I don't care if it's the Blue Ridge Mountains or the Himalayas, they share characteristics you'll find all over the world. . . . Mountain people will continually astonish people from the plains, for example with their willingness to walk. People come here to the Appalachians and are amazed to see mountaineers who think nothing of tramping all the way to the other side of the moun-

tain just to find a good blueberry patch. Same thing in Nepal—you'll
find people there who will walk for three days just to go to a festival
where they can hear music and get drunk. . . . Around here [Pendle-
ton County] they can tell you where you've been just by looking at the
dirt on your shoes. . . ."

Describing the suspicious nature of mountain people, Taylor-Ide
observed, "You see, they were usually pushed up here generations
ago. For one reason or another, they couldn't make it in the Piedmont. . . . People from outside are the bad guys, the ones that took
care of your grandpap. That's why they've got such a long memory for
hostilities. . . ." The observations were followed by references to the
institute's need for funds.

But these descriptions of county or state people made little sense.
With very rare exceptions, West Virginia's top students, like straight-
A kids anywhere, come from professional families. Many of them are
the children of doctors, lawyers, teachers, college professors, successful businessmen, and other professionals. Putting aside the question
of how much help students like this need, and the fact that 98 percent
of them go to college no matter what, describing them as "hillbilly
kids," with all of the implications about grinding poverty and backwardness this stereotype carries, hardly seems appropriate. Beyond
that, was Taylor-Ide's contention true? Would prestigious American
universities refuse to offer West Virginia's brightest students "a diddle" without the institute's intervention?

In fact, county people are no fonder of walking than Americans
anywhere. Indeed, since the advent of all-terrain vehicles, they probably walk far less than health-conscious city people. Families sometimes pick berries at reunions for nostalgic pleasure, but berry
picking as serious food gathering disappeared here in the 1940s, as
it did in rural America generally. The idea that people, even at
reunions, would walk miles to a berry patch rather than ride is outlandish.

County people cannot tell where you have been by the dirt on
your shoes, and to say this presents a cartoonish picture of the community. The people who settled Pendleton County, and the Appalachians generally, came here for the same reason that immigrants have
always come to America: freedom from persecution and the promise
of a better life on their own land. When the Germans and Scotch-

Irish arrived in the 1750s, the Appalachian Mountains represented the western frontier, which had just opened for settlement. Farmland was virtually free to families willing to clear the timber and that is why they came into the mountains. There is no historical evidence to suggest that the ancestors of the people now living in Pendleton County "couldn't make it" in the Piedmont or that they ever wanted to.

West Virginians do not have a longer memory for hostilities than other Americans. The stereotyped assumption that they do stems from the invented Hatfield-McCoy "feud." Appalachians have learned to be suspicious of outsiders—this much is true. But they have become suspicious because outsiders, especially fund-raising missionaries, often leave the mountains to describe them as backward hillbillies. In his description of Pendleton County, Taylor-Ide was justifying the very suspicion he found peculiar.

From a local point of view, Dan'l was not describing Pendleton County but doing what fund-raising missionaries have done for over a hundred years: inventing Appalachia. What is most surprising about his portrait is how little the missionary invention has changed in all that time. Since the late 1960s, in what has been called the "Appalachian Revision," regional scholars and a few outside writers have systematically deconstructed the fantasies about the region. Well-regarded books and articles have documented the obvious causes for Appalachian troubles—outside ownership of land and resources and the political corruption that results from this—and the missionary vision of backward people in backward culture has been thoroughly dismantled. But twenty years of research has had no effect. Reading the Woodlands documents, one finds the myth intact. In that missionary view, the "Appalachian problem" has nothing to do with exploitation or corrupt politics but with the people themselves. The barrier of the Appalachian Mountains has kept the region isolated from modern life, and enlightened missionaries must serve "as conduits between these people and civilization." The peculiar whiskey-making folk who are seething with hostility over "grandpap's" murder, strangely fond of walking, and in possession of atavistic knowledge about mountain soil might well have been lifted from the pages of a local-color novel. Once a myth becomes established in the collective imagination, dislodging it becomes virtually impossible, especially when influential people find it useful.

Through the late 1980s in Pendleton County, as people complained and worried about the institute's plans to "tell us how to live," the community erupted in one dreadful fight after another. One fight began in the county emergency organization when Underwood and Kirk asked the membership to officially recognize the skills team as an independent adjunct. When the membership voted no, the two men refused to concede. The fight became vicious—men threatened one another, made obscene phone calls, and resigned en masse. Franklin continues to have difficulty maintaining an adequate rescue squad.

Months later, another fight erupted over whether Kirk would or would not be given a portion of Franklin's town park. Kirk had managed to get funds to build a very small factory that would manufacture rock-climbing equipment, and the county commission, eager to encourage development, had donated some land next to the town park as a construction site. Apparently Kirk was unhappy with the site and, according to residents of Franklin, there was hushed talk about trading part of the town park for the offered land. Legally, the park belonged to Franklin rather than Pendleton County, and if a trade was to take place, the town council had to approve it. According to Franklin residents, secret phone calls had been made and a rushed, quiet town meeting was scheduled to "ram the deal down our throats before anyone knew what was going on."

In any case, people heard about the proposed swap and about the meeting, which they packed to overflow. Once again, people stood up to call their neighbors liars and to accuse them of helping Woodlands take over. Of course, no one could prove this. Kirk was not a member of the institute, but in local opinion, he was Jim's partner. During the town council meeting, the two men sat close to each other, just as they had during the near violent meetings about the tactical skills team. More than that, another member of the Woodlands board who was also the town mayor, a man named Bruce Minor, was at the very center of the proposed land swap, and Jennifer Taylor-Ide attended the town meeting as a reporter for Mr. McCoy's newspaper. Everyone denied everything, but county people could not fail to notice the same personalities reappearing in the community fights. As one Franklin woman said, "If you ask me, it's Woodlands Institute. The trouble always goes back to the same place." Whether the prevailing opinion was right or not, the fights were seriously eroding community trust.

Whether the fights were about specific plans the institute had to "advance mountain culture" or whether they resulted from Jim Underwood's "networking" under that general mandate was often debated. Underwood and Dan'l and Jennifer Taylor-Ide denied any knowledge or involvement, but few people believed this. It was indicative of the profound difficulty "Appalachians" have had with missionaries since 1880. People here always sense missionary condescension and manipulation but never get to confront the problem because missionaries smile and give vague non-answers about just being here "to help." This creates great mistrust and endless confusion. Why are the missionaries *really* here and what, exactly, are they trying to do? Confusion aside, most county people saw the fights as part of an ongoing struggle with Woodlands over the direction and control of their own community.

In the middle of the turmoil, Jim Underwood bought a second home and Dan'l bought a third. The institute cosigned for at least one loan for one of its members. This meant that should the member fail to make payments, grant money—some of it from taxes—would repay the loan. Needless to say, this added to local bitterness. As a Franklin woman said, "They get to spend Monopoly money. We have to spend the real stuff."

At the end of the 1980s, Woodlands owned almost an entire block of homes on Main Street, as well as houses and land around the county. In at least one case, a homeowner refused to sell to the institute, so a third party purchased the home and then resold it to Woodlands. In one situation, Woodlands acquired a large grant to open a "teen center" in a house next to two other properties. This puzzled locals for several reasons. There was ample space for a teen center in the basement of the new public library and in the community center. The rooms there were empty most of the time and would have lent themselves to a teen center. Why not spend the grant money on recreation equipment? Beyond this, it was common knowledge that very few county adolescents would have anything to do with an institute program. Putting aside the question of whether this was reasonable or warranted, even Woodlands had to know this, or so county people thought. Nonetheless, the institute bought the house with grant money and, to no one's surprise, the "teen center" failed because county teenagers did not show up.

By 1990, Woodlands had been in Pendleton County for eighteen years and, as residents saw it, an organization that no one trusted was generating millions in grants to "advance mountain culture" based upon a vision of local residents as Appalachian hillbillies, too backward to help themselves. County people bitterly rejected the identity and did not believe Woodlands had the ability or even the desire to advance them. Despite this, foundations, elected officials in Charleston, and the editor of the *Pendleton Times* supported the organization. County people were caught in the Appalachian Catch-22 that began in 1880: If you're labeled Appalachian, you're too backward to know that you're backward. It was maddening.

In the spring of 1990, a front-page article in the *Pendleton Times* announced that Democratic Governor Gaston Caperton would be the featured speaker at a Woodlands ceremony at the institute's mountaintop facility in the North Fork Valley. The announcement sent a wave of frustration and confusion through all three valleys. Why was Caperton, whom many residents had voted for, endorsing an organization that had created so much anger and turmoil in their community? In Appalachia, people always feel a great distance between themselves and their elected officials, but this was almost unbelievable.

The afternoon Caperton arrived in the county, I walked off the hill and started for the woods to hunt mushrooms. The bear dogs at the base of Anderson Hill started to carry on as I passed, and for some reason kept at it. I could still hear them bugling as I walked down along the river road and came up to an old building where half a dozen men were working. A man standing on the roof with a crowbar in one hand was looking toward the baying dogs. As I passed, he said rather absently, "They've treed the governor."

Around this same time, a process was set into motion in Charleston. Citing economies of scale as a rationale, officials in Charleston began pressing for consolidation of the two county high schools. This would mean that the North Fork Valley would lose its high school in Circleville and that the students would have to attend Franklin High. The thought of losing their high school and sending their children into a community where they felt people would treat them like hillbillies outraged some North Fork families. Others, for many reasons, simply did not want to lose their high school. Before the school board election in 1990, North Fork Valley residents became remarkably organized. Every eligible voter in the North Fork received a phone call encouraging them to vote, and a shuttle service to the polling places was provided on election day. As a result, the North Fork Valley took a 3–2 majority on the school board for the first time in Pendleton County history. All three North Fork candidates had campaigned on one issue: Stop Consolidation. Since that election, the North Fork majority had voted en bloc at Chairman Phares's direction on every issue.

Then, in January 1992, a wrenching community fight erupted and this time the bear broke cover. The trouble began when Democratic State Senator Jae Spears called Pendleton County school superintendent Dr. Alan Canonico on Thursday morning, January 16. According to Canonico, Spears called to congratulate him about Pendleton County's exciting news: Dan'l Taylor-Ide had just left Charleston after meetings with Governor Caperton and Senator Sondra Lucht, chair of the state education committee, at which it was decided that Circleville School, in the North Fork Valley, would become a new "break the mold" experimental school. The state would grant Pendleton County waivers that would exempt the school system from West Virginia law and give Woodlands Institute control of Circleville School. In Canonico's version of events, Senator Spears had been beside herself with excitement; Spears was not talking about something that might happen but about something that was a fait accompli, except for minor details. According to Canonico, "The money was *on* the table." The problem was that parents, teachers, and county administrators knew nothing about this plan.

After hanging up, a bewildered Canonico called Calvin Thompson, the principal of Circleville School. Thompson knew nothing about the business, but said a teacher named Jane Wilkins, a member of the local elite and close friend of the Taylor-Ides, had, just that morning, handed him some kind of school plan that Woodlands had put together. Thompson had not had time to look at it, but said he would drive over North Mountain to show Canonico the plan.

Within an hour, the superintendent was called by Jennifer Taylor-Ide. According to Canonico, Jennifer called for a special meeting of the school board. Canonico liked Taylor-Ide; he felt she was a bright, energetic member of the Franklin PTO and a wonderful resource for county schools. But for all the world, he could not understand why Jennifer thought she could call a special meeting of the school board. As politely as possible, he explained that even the superintendent could not call a special board meeting; that was the chairman's prerogative. Although Taylor-Ide and the board chairman, Dr. Robert Phares, later denied communicating with each other, Phares called the superintendent minutes later to announce a special meeting of the board on January 21. This was five days away, the shortest time between the announcement of a school board meeting and the meeting itself required by law. Not only was something happening, it was happening at breakneck speed.

When Canonico saw the school plan, he thought it was a mix of intriguing ideas and at least a few concepts that had been tried unsuccessfully during the sixties. The institute's school would do away with grades, textbooks, tests, examinations, and report cards. Grades 1 through 12 would be replaced by four "academies." Terms like "integrated, thematic curriculum," "student-centered teaching," "inherently meaningful," "learning experts," and "brain-based learning" appeared throughout the document with some frequency.

If there was an "innovative" aspect to the plan, it was Jennifer's description of the school's relationship with Pendleton County: The system would provide health centers for the community as well as the students. School buses would double as public transportation and cafeterias would become restaurants where adults would pay monthly fees for color-coded meal cards. In time a Woodlands preschool would replace Head Start, and the school would also serve as the center for senior citizens. The public library would "pointedly accommodate" the schools. "A strong entrepreneurial component" would establish "linkages between local government and business. . . . Students' work is displayed everywhere. . . . Libraries . . . Storefronts . . . Local newspapers . . ." Students from the Woodlands school would write regularly for the *Pendleton Times* and serve on county committees. Among the requirements for graduation from the fourth academy would be "An Autobiographical Thesis, Who Am I?" Chapters would include such topics as "an examination of personal religious beliefs." In short, the institute's school would change Pendleton County in dramatic fashion.

Canonico had no serious objection to the plan itself, but he was angry about the way things were happening. Canonico, a short, silver-haired man in his fifties, had taken the superintendent's job two years earlier, in 1989. He had no hard feelings about Woodlands. Many county people, of course, felt differently, and made no attempt to hide their feelings. The superintendent wondered if a tornado had touched down in Pendleton County.

County anxiety veered toward panic. The talk about the institute's interest in county schools, which many people had dismissed, suddenly took on substance, and this made the more disturbing rumor about Woodlands "taking over" Pendleton County seem all too real. In fact, if one read the institute's plan carefully, it looked as though the school would indeed "run the county." County people feared losing control not only of their schools but of their community. More than that, they were convinced that a typical Appalachian political process had been set in motion: An outside interest had secretly enlisted a few local elites and made arrangements with politicians in Charleston.

But who could county people turn to? Canonico had been cut out of the power loop and therefore could not help. Approaching Phares about a conspiracy that most people thought he was part of made no sense. Should they call Governor Caperton? Dan'l Taylor-Ide had just spoken with the governor and the chair of the state education committee. Given the call from Senator Spears, one had to assume they had come to some agreement. Expecting support from the *Pendleton Times* seemed foolish as well. The widespread anger and frustration with Woodlands had been common knowledge for eighteen years, but to many McCoy just seemed to ignore the community's concerns. Time and again he had given the institute front-page space to announce anything, from inflated descriptions to sensational discoveries of new bears in zoos. Jennifer Taylor-Ide was writing the articles about school board meetings for the paper.

On Friday night the community's gossip network kicked into overdrive. People made copies of the Woodlands plan and shared them with their friends, relatives, and neighbors, who then made copies of the copies. The Woodlands "takeover" became the sole topic of conversation. On Sunday morning, ministers read portions of the plan to their congregations. On Monday at the shoe factory, workers abandoned their machines to crowd around a young woman named Sherry Moyers as she read sections of the Woodlands plan aloud. By Monday afternoon, people had taped homemade signs on storefronts all over Franklin.

Tuesday, January 21, broke clear and icy cold in the county. Late in the morning, we learned that Beaty, Becky's mother, had suffered a heart attack. Becky and Shelly came home from school (Chris was a junior at Virginia Tech), hurriedly packed a few things, and began the trip to the hospital in Lewisburg, about two hours away, but it was agreed that I would stay and attend the meeting. I had arranged to ride over North Mountain into the North Fork Valley with a teacher friend of Becky's and sat waiting on the cement steps in front of our house just after dark. It was cold and still enough to hear the trees cracking in the woods above the house. Presently a barred owl started hooting up along the ridge and I remember thinking about leitmotifs in my life. My father and I are standing knee-deep in the Capon River listening to an owl around the bend. I stare down Main Street trying to locate the owl that had moved into Franklin just before the flood and now listen to one on a winter night. I was thinking of my life as music. Nonsense, really, but I had been listening to Bach.

Going down the other side of North Mountain, our car was part of a steady stream of headlights weaving through the winter trees; another stream of headlights flowing south along the valley bottom merged with ours at Judy Gap. I had never seen that much traffic on a county road.

Between eight hundred and nine hundred people jammed the tiny Circleville gymnasium. Every folding chair and bleacher seat was taken. People stood shoulder to shoulder in the aisles, packed in tight at the door and spilling out into the hall. Phares and the four other board members sat behind a long lunchroom table at the front of the gym. The Taylor-Ides, another Woodlands member, and Canonico sat on folding chairs a few yards away. Phares called the meeting to order and introduced Jennifer.

Blond and attractive in a thick green sweater, Jennifer took the podium and rather ironically talked about putting on and taking off hats and changing identities as she did. She was a member of Woodlands and a Pendleton County mother. As the county saw things, this was a serious part of the problem. Jennifer explained that there was no plan, merely some ideas to talk about. She introduced Dan'l.

Dan'l amazed me. The anger and tension in the small gymnasium was something that I felt on my skin like heat, but he seemed unaffected. Slight, with black hair, dressed in a sport coat, plaid shirt, and cloth tie that made me think of prep schools, he began with a small joke: Perhaps the school should have charged admission, he said. A small admittance fee from a crowd this large would help balance the budget. Dan'l paused for polite laughter from the crowd, but the silence was deep and heavy.

He explained that everything had happened by chance. He happened to be in Charleston talking with Governor Caperton and happened to run out of things to say. Rather casually, he brought up the topic of exempting Pendleton County schools from state law. Caperton rather casually called the chair of education and arranged a lunch. Dan'l had another casual conversation. There was no concrete plan.

Virtually no one in the gymnasium believed the Taylor-Ides. Over the years Woodlands had made so many extraordinary claims and offered so many improbable explanations that the organization had no credibility in the county. More than that, the idea that everything had simply fallen together was unbelievable. Many people were offended by the fact that the Taylor-Ides would stand in front of them and offer an explanation that they found preposterous. As a Franklin woman observed, "Just how dumb do these people think hillbillies *are*?"

After Dan'l sat down, county residents came forward to attack the Woodlands plan and question his honesty for more than three hours. As the meeting staggered toward an end, a fundamentalist Christian minister named Mike Watson came to the microphone and asked everyone who opposed the plan to stand. Virtually everyone in the gymnasium rose at once. Watching Watson, I wondered if he knew that he was taking part in a war with outside missionaries that had begun in the 1880s.

Walking out of the gym into the icy January night, people thought the institute school plan was behind them. Jennifer had formally withdrawn the plan. But the issue would not go away. Until April, school board meetings—and other meetings about the plan—continued to draw crowds as large as seven hundred.

According to state law, county school boards had to submit an approved "building and curriculum plan" by the second week of May. If the state superintendent accepted a county's plan, the legislature approved an appropriate budget to facilitate it. If the Pendleton County Board did not submit an approved plan to Charleston by the second week of May, the county's school system would be granted no operating funds and would therefore become bankrupt. In that event, the state could—and in some people's opinion *would*—take over county schools and put someone else in charge. Given the connection between Dan'l Taylor-Ide and Charleston officials, some county residents imagined another open door for a Woodlands takeover of the schools. In any case, school board chairman Phares kept tabling the motion to vote on the county building and curriculum plan but refused to explain why. If he did this through May, Pendleton County schools would have no operating funds for the coming year—that much was certain. People feared the North Fork majority would allow this to happen, simply to stop consolidation. Most North Fork families did not trust Woodlands Institute, but a few people were so angry about consolidation that they would, as one South Fork Valley man said, "dance with the devil to keep Circleville High open."

Community trust had been shattered and viciousness set free in the county. Old, unrelated rivalries were ignited. The Taylor-Ides and state officials, meanwhile, kept insisting that nothing was going on. The article in the *Pendleton Times* about the first large meeting in the Circleville gymnasium was astonishing. According to the article, the school board met to discuss "innovative education." The writer failed to mention the more than eight hundred angry people in attendance or the outrage they voiced for three straight hours. This was like writing an article about the *Titanic* that focused on the ballroom music while ignoring the iceberg.

The editor of the *Charleston Gazette,* Don Marsh, who knew about the controversy, vigorously defended Dan'l and insisted there was no story in Pendleton County. But in early February the *Washington Post* sent a reporter and a photographer into the county for three days to cover a story that the editor of the state's largest newspaper insisted did not exist.

Which end was up and which down? Hoping to find an answer, I drove to Charleston in mid-February and spent two days talking with senators, representatives, the governor's assistant, and at least one janitor. The legislators, who apparently rode the same turnip truck to the state house each morning, knew nothing. After two or three interviews, the legislators seemed to know me before I introduced myself. I was hustled out of offices and doors slammed behind me. Straightforward questions provoked anger, no end of doublespeak, and occasionally hysteria.

Lying awake in my motel room by the sludgy Kanawha River, I kept trying to add things up. The idea that nothing except casual conversation was taking place in Pendleton County made no sense. Beyond that, I could not believe that people as bright as the Taylor-Ides and county board chairman Phares would conduct one urgent meeting after another unless they were trying to accomplish something important and had firm support in Charleston. Why create a firestorm and then feed it month after month without substantial reasons to believe that something would come from the effort?

The interviews I did manage to conduct only muddied the water. Each new encounter presented an updated revision of events, with everyone backing up, changing stories, or reinventing positions. Lying on the bed at the motel I remembered something from Alaska. Hunting on the tundra, I occasionally walked onto muskeg, land that seemed to be Jell-O covered by a thick hide of moss. I staggered and fell a few times and flailed about trying to regain my feet and for a frightening second or two it was as if the entire world had turned to Jell-O. Nothing held in place and there were no fixed points of reference. That is how it felt inside the heart of the heart of Appalachia.

Wandering from one incomprehensible interview to another, I often felt something like vertigo. Late on the second afternoon I mistakenly took the freight elevator up from the basement. For some reason, elevators in at least one part of the statehouse go up from the basement to floor 1, floor 2, floor 4, then, at least according to the labels, floor 3. There was a janitor on the service elevator with me, a skinny man who looked and, remarkably enough, sounded like my Uncle Jimmy from Piedmont. I asked him, "How come we go up to get to a lower floor?" Looking at me balefully, he said, "I don't have any idea. I stopped trying to figure these assholes out years ago." He was the only person who made sense to me all day.

At that time I was reading about the turn of the century in the southern mountains, the horrendous land swindles and the mine wars, and I had brought half a dozen books from home with me. Awake on the motel bed until early morning, I would read for fifteen or twenty minutes, then lay the open book on my chest, struck with how little Appalachian politics had changed in a hundred years. As coal and timber companies took farms—over half the state in the end—and as the brutality of the mines careened toward Armageddon, editors, elected officials, and local elites insisted that nothing was happening or that their backward neighbors were entirely responsible for the violence. In the early 1900s, West Virginia governors—former or future coal executives—refused to meet with the miners. They had been quietly meeting with coal company representatives all along and everyone knew this, but the elected officials denied everything. The governors and legislators would "stay out of the controversy and let the system work." Lies this bold-faced and transparent shattered the trust; as small communities lost their moral systems, neighbors turned against one another. I had just left this in Pendleton County. I am not saying that the outrage of the industrial war in Appalachia compares in magnitude to what was taking place in Pendleton County, but that the assumptions of backwardness and the political behavior arising from this assumption have not changed. Sometimes, as I lay in bed with a book spread open on my chest, drifting in and out of sleep, turn-of-the-century Appalachia would fuse with present-day Pendleton County into a very strange play. In a surreal mix of past and present, all of the actors—missionaries, coal company representatives, local elites, politicians, newspaper editors, and abandoned Appalachians—kept stepping in to act the same parts again and again. I thought of Faulkner's remark about the past not only not being over but not even being the past. Appalachians will never escape their history; it is the water we swim through every day. For the first time, I thought of Appalachia as a relationship between power and voiceless people rather than a specific place.

Back in Pendleton County, it came down to the school board meeting in mid-May. Would chairman Phares table the vote on the county plan and plunge the system into bankruptcy? Or would he request a vote, get a 3–2 rejection, and then a 3–2 approval of the Woodlands plan? In either case, people were convinced, they would lose their schools, and if the vote went the wrong way, there might well be a riot. Frustration and anger had passed the boiling point months earlier and the bitter talk had taken a sharper edge. As the final meeting approached, some threats began to sound less like venting steam and much more like predictions.

Downtown on the afternoon before the May meeting I bumped into a man I knew. An outdoorsman and something of a rough customer, he offered some advice about the meeting that night: "Better sit by the door on this one."

"How come?"

"This one could blow up."

"You think so?"

Leaning toward me, he whispered, "Let me put 'er this way: they ain't gett'n our schools."

"What's gonna happen if the vote goes wrong?"

"Never you mind about that," he said. "You just be sitt'n by the door."

Walking away, he pointed at me and repeated, "They ain't gett'n our schools."

He was a serious man and I took him at his word.

The meeting was scheduled for 7 p.m. in Franklin's elementary school and I left the house early to walk down the hill. It was one of those soft May evenings in the county—an azure sky, wispy clouds on the horizon, and the trees on the lawns filled with robins burbling to themselves as the light faded. I could hear unseen geese flying the course of the river in the valley bottom, their faint honking moving steadily upstream, and I remember wondering why life had to be so difficult in a place so lovely.

As expected, the grade school auditorium was packed beyond standing room. This had become a familiar scene—lots of angry people jammed into a room, crowded around the hall doors, spilling out into the parking lot, and more angry people walking toward the building. I squeezed in near the end of a long table and began to look for the man I had talked with that afternoon. Presently he pushed through the crowd at the door, followed by two other grim-looking men. I could not tell whether their faces were red from scrubbing up for a trip to town or from drinking. Were the three of them together? Did they deliberately fan out in three different directions or did I imagine this? My stomach tightened like a fist.

The meeting began with an odd, formal feeling. People stood to ask polite questions or quietly plead with the school board to do the right thing by their children. One sensed restraint as well as tremendous strain. Any number of people wanted to give Phares a piece of their mind, but losing their schools, and in a sense their children, was much too important for a display of temper. I noticed people, especially women, trying to hold Ronnie Vance's eyes. His was the swing vote on the board. People in this part of the country, Appalachians if you will, place great faith in personal relationships. Those crooks in Charleston would do whatever they could get away with, no matter what county people wanted. Phares and John Smith, another board member, in the prevailing opinion, had made up their minds. But Vance was undecided and his neighbors wanted to hold his eyes before he voted. I could almost hear people thinking, *Ronnie Vance, you look at me now. We know one another. I'm worried about my kids. Do the right thing for all of us.*

I remember thinking as I sat there about how much I liked these people. They made me feel like a boy in Piedmont surrounded by my relatives. I loved the music in their talk, their unpretentious common sense and fundamental decency. Everyone was behaving with dignity, and this was no small accomplishment given the fact that many county people felt they had been lied to, misled, insulted, and left without a voice for five months. Near the end of February the principal of Upper Tract Grade School, a man who had just moved into the county, was talking on the phone with his mother in the Midwest. Distraught, he told her about the unbearable tension and about the community's fear that Woodlands would take their schools. The principal's mother said, "This is America; things like that can't happen in this country." But things like that can and do happen in Appalachia.

In many ways the worst part of the struggle was the vague awareness of the larger culture hovering over the county's shoulder. Appalachians always know smug America is out there, ready to turn our hard times into cartoonish melodrama: those feuding hillbillies at it again. But the five-month fight had resulted from the invented myth and attending labels placed upon us rather than from imagined backwardness. The handful of families in the North Fork were fiercely determined to keep their children away from a town and school that would treat them like hillbillies. County people packed meeting after meeting because they did not want to lose their schools and their children to an organization that considered them "hillbilly kids" who would not "get a diddle" without Woodlands. For a moment, if you can, trade places with these people. If these were your children, would you fight about this?

Phares calls for a vote. There are two yes votes right away. Phares votes no and so does Smith. Vance is trembling. As everyone watches, he votes yes and most of the seven hundred people jump to their feet cheering and hugging one another. The schools have their funding. After five dreadful months, it is over. I remember wondering what the celebration was about. What had been lost or won? If Woodlands had taken over the schools, would that have been good or bad in the long term? I don't know the answer to this. As I got up from the table, I thought that maybe the hardest part of our lives had started. People would not forget what had been attempted or what their neighbors had said about them. The bitter feelings caused by mythic Appalachia were much worse now and the Pendleton County split was wider.

Within a matter of months, Dan'l and Jennifer left the institute. Woodlands remained in the Hiner house on Main Street for a few years but recently relocated its offices to Harrisonburg, Virginia. When Dan'l resigned, the institute became something else, and a strange chapter in Pendleton County's long and difficult history ended.

16. Bringing It All Back Home

O N A SUMMER evening, I am walking down Main Street toward the low water bridge, headed for the woods on Town Mountain across the river. Tonight, Franklin's lilliputian downtown seems as still as a photograph and at this moment I am the only thing that moves. These days I spend most of my time dwelling on the past. I am on Main Street, but in my mind I'm that boy sitting on the porch swing at Grandmother O'Brien's the rainy day we left Piedmont. Then, without transition, I am serving mass in old St. Clement's while my dad sits watching in a pew behind me. Now in the small bakery near GE, the one-armed German man squeezes a doughnut with his chrome pincher until jelly forms a ruby on one end. A jet thunders up from the wildlife refuge swamp. In the small backyard the satin-black eel nailed to the grape arbor turns lapis blue as my father pulls the skin down with his needle-nose pliers. Memories like this play through my mind like filmstrips, most often without sound. I have entered old age, I think.

Lately two memories return more often than others. In one, my father and I walk down Island Avenue while the union goons in the car that slowly follows shout obscenities. In the other, we eat lunch in the old station wagon while out rabbit hunting that November morning, my dad closing his eyes to repeat the machine movements that he dreams about. Like so many remembered stories, these two have changed shape and meaning over time. When I was small, the Island Avenue scene was a fixture in my daydreams. Alone in the cellar, I would act it out again and again, changing the ending to change the

story's meaning. In one variation we walked back to the car and, like
the Lone Ranger and Tonto, beat up the two men. In another, I ran
home to get my dad's deer rifle. At gunpoint, the men cry and repeat
apologies, calling my father Mr. O'Brien. But years later when that
story came to mind as an undergraduate in Morgantown, I did not
want to change it at all. I thought he had done the wise thing by walking quietly away. At that time the point seemed to be my father's gen-
tleness. Sometime later in Iowa, struggling with depression, I would
become frustrated, almost angry, when I remembered Island Avenue.
By then I had become convinced that my father should have done or
said something just to let the union goons know he was alive. In Iowa,
I thought that if my father had not been so thoroughly defeated, my
own life would have been less troubled. I am no longer sure about
this. I do not know where my father's troubles end and mine begin.
And if I start to lay blame, where do I stop? With my father? His
father? Me? It all seems pointless. Now when Island Avenue comes
to my mind, I cringe with the pain my dad felt that day but make
no judgments or come to any conclusion. It is just something that
happened.

In my early thirties, when I thought about having lunch in the station wagon that November day, I sometimes imagined stepping into
the memory like a movie director. When my father closed his eyes to
repeat his robot motions, I stopped the action to lecture, sternly
telling him to dream of other things and to make a better life for himself. Now the lecture seems absurd to me; my father *was* his life. Had
he lived another, he would have been another man and who would *I*
be walking down Main Street on a summer evening?

Stopping to look at the stuffed owls in the *Pendleton Times* window, I see my father's face transfigured in my own, and I am suddenly
struck with a vision of my father walking down Greenway Avenue
through the shimmering hot air, that troubled preoccupied expression on his face. That is how I look right now.

Passing Bowman's Hardware Store and the parking lot, I walk into
the shadow of the courthouse and the aroma of the county jailer's
evening meal, a small-town intimacy that pleases me. A block later I
stop midway on the low water bridge to look up and down the South
Branch. Enos Horst, who occasionally fixes my plumbing, has released
his chalk-white pigeons for their evening flight over town; their wings

whistle like silk above my head. As I watch, two birds land on a large rock downcurrent, step to the edge for quick drinks, than flap off to rejoin the flock wheeling above the courthouse. The Presbyterian church bell begins to toll seven and I look in that direction, struck again with Franklin's loveliness.

After all of my worries moving in, Franklin has worked out well enough for my children, though living here has not been without complications. Chris became a small-town West Virginia boy—fishing the rivers, playing basketball, listening to rock and roll with easygoing, unpretentious friends. Tennis fell by the way, but I don't think he ever felt the loss. In the end Franklin High was a good school for Christopher. He graduated at the top of his class, and we celebrated by fishing for striped bass on Smith Mountain Lake in Virginia. Out on the water, we popped a bottle of Mumm's champagne and drank to "snakes in heaven"—a toast Chris came up with when he was five.

That summer, 1988, Cornell accepted Chris, and this became one of the complications. Once on campus, Christopher was surrounded by bright, confident students, whose natural assertiveness ran contrary to his Appalachian sensibilities. Like so many boys from the southern mountains, Chris was quiet and somewhat self-deprecating. No one was rude or unkind to him, but he was intimidated and frightened every waking moment. After an agonizing series of phone calls, he came home.

Our relationship was strained for several months as Chris and I slipped into a variation of my father and me. I blamed myself for not instilling more confidence in my son and for bringing him to Appalachia. I realized that his return from Cornell might well have been more complex than this. Chris *was* a small-town boy from Appalachia, but that's not all he was. Students from all parts of the country quit college and go home. But I remain convinced that being "Appalachian" was at the heart of Christopher's difficulty on the Cornell campus. I blame myself. Chris blamed no one and insisted that he was making a choice about *his* life. In one heated exchange he said, "You've been a certain kind of person all your life and now you want me to go to a school like that." He was right about this. I have always felt apprehensive about middle-class aspirations—that desperate yearning for "sophistication," the right clothes, speech, church, car, or house. I'm far less concerned about these things now than I was as a young man, but at times I still feel a little uneasy about social distinctions. Don't misunderstand—Cornell is a wonderful university and I wanted Christopher to have the kind of education a school like that would offer. Part of my fatherly ambition had nothing to do with some fantasy about ascending the social ladder. But to be honest, I was also taken with the prospect of Christopher on an Ivy League campus. In my daydreams my son was attending class in an ivy-covered building or playing tennis with Binks and Swoozy outside that building. Chris was right: I was more affected by the signs of arrival than I was willing or able to admit.

In time, we came back together. Christopher went to Virginia Tech, loved all four years, and graduated magna cum laude. In Blacksburg, he met a fine young woman named Marci and they married in 1993. They live in Grottoes, Virginia, a very small town in the Shenandoah Valley an hour and a half east of Franklin, and plan to stay close to the Appalachian Mountains. We still fish together. I will ask your indulgence, but I find my son plainspoken, empathetic, and genuine. Putting aside the complicated notion of "Appalachia"—and whether there has ever been such a place, these are traits I have always associated with good people from the Appalachian Mountains.

During her high school years, even as she twirled flags at football halftime shows, my daughter hated small-town Appalachia and was determined to escape for the "real" America of malls, theaters, and restaurants. In fact, Shelly did escape. She married an intelligent young sailor from the naval base in Sugar Grove. After two years in Japan and two years in Texas, she is now settling into a suburb of Washington, D.C. In Texas, Shelly discovered—to her own great surprise—that she missed the Appalachian Mountains. Now on summer nights, she deliberately sits on her front steps listening to crickets because they make her remember home in West Virginia. My daughter grew up in the mountains; Appalachia is home even if she doesn't want to live here. She has become like some of my friends who can only love the region—if love is the right word—from a distance.

As for me, after missing the southern mountains most of my life, I no longer think of Appalachia as home. This is what I mean: Back in graduate school an English professor occasionally joked about *Paradise Lost,* wisecracking that paradise, by definition, had to be lost. The realities of dealing with other personalities, angelic or human, would make any location less than paradise. The earthwise, authentic mountain folk whom I missed as I rambled around the country have become the very real people living around me. Sometimes I think I want more than the world has to offer. Since leaving college in Morgantown, and through all of those years of travel, I felt an uneasy distance between myself and wherever I was. It was as if I watched communities and people from behind a glass wall. Rambling around the country, I thought the wall would dissolve when I came home to Appalachia, but as much as I like mountain cultures and love this landscape, the distance and the wall remain. Twenty years ago I read a poem by an obscure poet whose name I have long forgotten. A few lines went *"Craggy mountains, grassy plains, or rolling seas are all the same to me. My home is in my head."* Going one step further I might say, my home is the memory in my head.

I'm not unhappy in Appalachia. I still find Pendleton County lovely in all four, or perhaps five, seasons and Franklin remains the prettiest town I know. County people, like people anywhere, can be opinionated, provincial, petty, or gracious and remarkably kind by turns, but I admire them most of the time. The rich, earthy metaphors and the poetic rhythms in Appalachian speech that I first heard as a boy in Piedmont still delight me. And there are scenes of Appalachian enchantment that I live for: snowstorms in Franklin, pretty girls walking on side streets after dark, my neighbors coming out of church in their finery, October mornings on Main Street, pausing on the low water bridge to watch the pigeons take their evening drink, or now, this moment, stopping at the entrance to my favorite oak woods on Town Mountain. The dirt road ends and a logging trail angles between oaks and maples, then disappears farther up the mountain. With dusk coming on, the evening light slants down between the trees in columns onto kelly-green moss and banks of ferns. Skippers flit through the columns of light and I can smell mushrooms and sweet decay. As if on cue, a deer picks up my scent and makes its loud chuffing sound of alarm, then crashes off unseen. The quiet settles back into the woods and onto my shoulders like benediction. It's the dream my father gave me. I will walk the logging trail to the mountaintop looking for chanterelle mushrooms and think of him.

Today is the fourth anniversary of his funeral and of that day in Piedmont. Since then, I have struggled to understand what being Appalachian meant to him. In a sense it's the same effort that I began on the steps my first night in Pendleton County, but his passing turned research into a quest. My father's death made my own less an abstraction in the unseen distance. It would happen in the next hour, tonight, or in several days. I would be in the world and then gone, like a lightning strike. Coming home from Piedmont I felt desperate to understand my father's life, if only to better understand my own. Time was short and the woods were on fire.

I grew up listening to parables. My father understood the world as linked stories. In turn, I understand Appalachia in these stories. In 1912, a coal baron named John C. C. Mayo invited the missionaries from a settlement house to dinner at his new mansion. Mayo, one of the rare coal operators actually from the region, was known for his outrageous manipulation of the legal system, and by 1907 he owned or controlled 700,000 acres of land and had twisted the laws to get the mineral rights on uncounted other acres. Like all coal barons, Mayo ruthlessly controlled and abused the miners and their families in his fiefdom. Disease, brutality, starvation wages, and corruption were commonplace in his coal camps. The settlement school missionaries knew this, but never spoke out or interfered in any way. After dinner at Mayo's mansion, a young teacher named Elizabeth Watts wrote to her mother that the settlement schoolteachers "had a glorious time staying at the home of John C. C. Mayo, a self-made multi-millionaire, a coal company being the cause of it. They have just moved into a $500,000 house that has taken seven years to build and is perfectly wonderful. They had sense enough to have interior decorators who knew [their] job and both Miss Rue and Miss DeLong say it was wonderful. They had beauteous things to eat with three butlers to wait on them." Gatsby had taken Daisy on a tour of his mansion and won her heart.

Henry Ford, who loved to fish for native trout here, financed a mission school and referred to the students as "my Anglo-Saxons." When Ford came to visit, the administrators, understandably eager to please their benefactor, had the students dress up in Appalachian outfits. A group of them met Ford at the train station and drove him to the school in an oxcart, kept only for that purpose. The children talked by-cracky English and performed "real" Appalachian dances while the great man smiled fondly and handed out dimes.

When I drove through the coalfields my first year home and stopped to watch the Homecoming Day parade, three pretty girls walked toward me. They had fixed their hair in outlandish pigtails, blackened out their front teeth and sewn phony patches on their designer jeans. When I asked them what they were supposed to be, one girl, who had been laughing a moment before, looked toward the ground in embarrassment and said, "I guess hillbillies."

Dan'l Taylor-Ide once ran for the Pendleton County School Board and, like many politicians, made a number of speeches promising miracles. After one speech, a county man stood up to ask, "If you're so smart, what are you doing in Pendleton County?"

During the five-month fight over Pendleton County schools, I attended a Woodlands Institute support meeting in the basement of a North Fork Valley church. The meeting attracted about a hundred people and at times it veered toward violence. Sherry Moyers, the young woman who had read the Woodlands school plan to her co-workers at the shoe factory, was there to learn all that she could. Coming out of a rest room she was confronted by three North Fork men who refused to let her pass. After glaring in menacing silence long enough to terrify her, one man snarled, "Now git back over the mountain where you belong, bitch." At the end of that meeting a North Fork Valley woman who supported the Woodlands plan "laid hands" on the county superintendent because he would not support a plan that the vast majority of county parents violently opposed. I turned to a woman sitting beside me and asked why she thought there was so much anger and tension. She said, "It's in our blood; we're Hatfields and McCoys. We fight." It is possible to induce culture.

One writer has described Appalachia as a colony within the borders of North America, and this helped me understand more clearly. If one thinks about it, colonies involve outside ownership of land and resources, a puppet government that sends profits back to the seat of power, the myth of backward people in need of advancement, missionaries to give exploitation a benevolent appearance, and a few prominent families to accept the myth and administer the colony. All of this has been in place in Appalachia since 1900.

Colonies also demand a colonial identity: peculiar, substandard human beings with peculiar ways who are seen as murderous savages, cretins, or childlike little brothers who need our guidance. In Appalachia, virtually everyone is affected by the hillbilly stereotype, though not in the same way or to the same degree. Some people bristle with anger and are quick to take offense even when none is offered. In a variation of black Americans "cut'n shines for whitey," I have met West Virginians who act out the hillbilly stereotype in broad caricature. Remarkably enough, others shrug the stereotype aside and go on with their lives as if it did not exist. Most "Appalachians" have lived with the identity so long it has become an unconscious part of their personality. I'm thinking about the Bells and O'Briens in Piedmont, James Wyatt, and the woman who crossed the playing field to insult my "C" students on Field Day at Marlinton Junior High. Pendleton County's angry rejection of Woodlands, the North Fork's bitterness over the opinions of their Franklin neighbors, and the wrenching fight over county schools all came from the myth of Appalachia and the hillbilly identity.

I never knew my Grandfather O'Brien, and since the family does not speak of him, I will never know how important Appalachian stereotypes were in his life. Being labeled a hillbilly must have done *something* to him, but how he carried that weight and how it affected his tormented life and contributed to his eventual suicide will remain a mystery. My father never struggled with the label. He took being a hillbilly to heart and spent his life backing up, apologizing for being alive. I have spent my life trying to escape his hopelessness, and of course to run from something is to be affected by it. In my life one irony seems to compound another; I was trying to escape my father's despair but hold on to him and his vision of subsistence life at the same time. As the distance between us grew, I became more like him and finally returned to his home trying to find the life he left behind. I never understood any of this as a young man. Back then, I thought I was making free-willed decisions about where to go and how to live. I thought I was shaping the kind of person I would become. Now I understand that I have been making choices from a preselected list. Looking back on all of this brings the last page of *The Great Gatsby* to mind again: it's boats against the current and the illusion of forward motion as I slip back into the past.

In a sense, I'm talking about Appalachian fatalism, a view of the world without progress, filled with people playing variations on the same roles over and over. When I became a serious reader in Morgantown, I remember encountering Camus, Sartre, T. S. Eliot, Nathanael West, and Hemingway. Their vision of an absurd world filled with people struggling unsuccessfully for dignity was more like confirmation than revelation to me. The wisecrack I made to Dave

Harbert, my phenomenologist fishing partner in Oswego, about my existentialism being Appalachian fatalism dressed up for town may not have been a joke. Then again, no one fits his or her culture exactly. Like human beings generally, my father was a complicated web of inherited traits, personal experiences, fears, frustrations, memories, and thoughts. His personality was a light show shifting and changing moment by moment. To suggest that his life, or mine, can be explained by a single fact of biography is to reduce both of us to stick figures in a child's drawing. Who knows about these things? Trying to explain yourself to yourself is a dubious enterprise.

Beaty, Becky's mother, died on January 21, 1992, while I was at that school board meeting in Circleville. I'm not sure I can explain this loss. The clear, selfless vision of family that Reverend Harry and Lula Blackhurst held was strongest in Beaty. She was our center. The spring after she died, I can remember walking up a mountain into the woods to an abandoned farm I discovered while hunting morels one spring day. There wasn't much left, a few rotting boards over a river-rock foundation, but a lilac bush bloomed in the yard each year and I would go there to cut flowers for the house. Coming down the mountain with an armload of lilacs, I thought of Beaty. The fact that she died while I was tangled up in all that turmoil made me extremely angry.

After Beaty's death, I began to have a recurring dream. In the dream, or all that I can remember of it, I'm in some kind of waiting room or terminal. I'm sitting against a wall looking down at my hands as if writing or maybe carving something with my pocketknife. The room is crowded with quiet, serious people whom I seem to know but cannot place. Each time I look up, the crowd has thinned and there is the sense that in time I'll be all alone. Waking, I always think of my father.

When my mother called in July 1995, I was filleting bass in the kitchen. It was oven-hot, and the cicadas were making a racket in the walnut tree outside. I remember this much clearly: "John, this is your mother. Your father's dying," but the rest of the conversation escapes me.

For the next two days, I was on the phone a lot. Mostly I talked with my sister Nancy, the oldest child. I remember hearing that my father was in the hospital, no longer conscious, and not expected to last the night. Rushing to Philadelphia would have been pointless; even if I had arrived before he died, he would not have known I was there. I could not understand why my mother waited so long to call. Not calling at all would have made some sense, but why wait until my father was no longer conscious?

I learned from Nancy that some members of the family would resent my presence. After talking with my brothers and sisters, she said, "We've agreed not to say anything to you while you're at the funeral." The image that jumped into my mind was of the family gathered at one end of a room while I stood alone at the other—my brothers and sisters glaring at me. As I saw it, going to the funeral would help no one, and so I started for Piedmont hoping to mark his passing in some way, and hoping to make myself feel better.

And this brings me back to where I started, in the car across the street from his small tar-paper home in Piedmont. Bach brings his exquisite argument home to no avail. I feel no better and nothing has changed.

Down the dreamlike hill into town, I park at the Bells' house, where Grandfather Bell looked through Grandmother O'Brien's face years ago. The brick house seems old and in poor repair and much too small for the elegant home I remember. In my mind the scene between my Grandfather Bell and Grandmother O'Brien is in a spotlight on center stage; it's filled with drama and significance. But how could anything so dramatic have happened on this weary street? It occurs to me that I am in the Orchard, the fancy part of Piedmont. As this small town fades away, social divisions and the desperate striving to appear as one thing rather than another seem even more absurd. My grandparents have died, but the social tensions in this small Appalachian town live on.

A boy on in-line skates glides around the corner. When he stops to look at me, I say, "Is this still the Bells' house?" He says, "Amarosas live here." The answer brings me up short. Amarosa was the man who recognized my father in the drugstore on that boyhood trip forty years ago. How can Amarosas be living in the Bells' house? The kaleidoscope of memory seems to be spinning wildly.

I walk around Piedmont. The sun has no mercy in this dying town. I walk past the empty shops with the windows boarded up, crunching glass on the sidewalk. The heat is an anvil on my back. I think, What's the name of this movie?

I stop in a beer joint—one of the few places open in Piedmont. It is cool and dark. I sit at the end of the bar, order a Stroh's beer, and look around. Half a dozen men in their thirties sit on stools eating sandwiches or drinking beer. I want to stand up and say, "I'm Red O'Brien's son and I've come back to find out about him. He died last night." I can't, of course. When the woman behind the bar comes back to ask about another beer, I whisper, "Did you know the O'Brien family?"

"The who?" she says.

I say, "My dad was from Piedmont. Jim O'Brien. He married Flora Mae Bell."

"I think I heard of Bells," she says.

"How about O'Briens? They lived up the mountain."

She stares off a moment, then says, "I don't know of any O'Briens. Not in Piedmont anyway."

I say, "See, my father just died and I wanted to find out about him. He grew up in Piedmont and I thought . . ."

The woman turns and yells, "Anybody here know an O'Brien family?" One man has heard about an O'Brien who works in the school board office in Cumberland, Maryland, but that's all.

Sipping my beer, I listen to the men talk about the mill. One man says, "They won't hire Piedmont men no more. They want this town to die." This may or may not be true, but the conviction that someone, or some organization—mill, missionaries, lumber company, coal company, in conjunction with state politicians—controls everything is Appalachian. No one seems terribly angry. It's fate or something like fate.

At the office of the *Piedmont Herald,* I ask about my grandfather. The editor, a woman in her forties, says, "We don't go back that far. O'Brien sounds Catholic. You might try the church burial records in Westernport."

Across the bridge I walk down the street and stand in front of the church I went to when the family came to visit. My business is in the rectory, but I walk into the church. The smell of incense and burning candles has not changed in all these years. I light two candles and kneel at the altar rail. The last thing my father said to me was, "Say Hail Marys." I start, "Hail Mary, full of grace, blessed art thou among women . . ." but then falter and must start over. I make it all the way through on the fourth attempt. But as hard as I try, I cannot make this mean anything to me.

In the rectory, a young priest with a brown wooden cross around his neck pages through an oversized record book. He runs his finger down one page and says, "Here, James Vincent O'Brien."

"Mine accident" is written as the official cause of death, which shocks me. Have I invented my life?

The priest says, "Calm down. That doesn't mean anything. Suicide is never the official cause of death. Mine accident is code. Look here, the burial is in late afternoon. If you'll notice, all the others are in midmorning. That's after a Requiem Mass. We can't say a Requiem for someone who has taken his own life."

I will not go to his grave, not today. I drive back up the hill to the tar-paper house to say good-bye one last time. I stare into the back-yard where my grandfather committed suicide. *After the fight with the mill foreman, he comes home, walks out into the yard, and in a burst of manic energy, kills himself three times over.* It keeps playing through my mind like a jerky filmstrip. The immensity of that anger overwhelms me.

I am thinking about summer nights in the old neighborhood. My father let us run around until just after dark most nights and then would whistle us in. Each boy had a specific whistle—two short notes followed by a long descending note, for instance. Out running the streets in the dark, we would stop and return the whistle to let him know we were all right and on the way home. Now I can't remember my whistle and it seems a terrible thing to have forgotten.

It comes down to fathers and sons. Who owes what to whom? Where does trouble begin and end? Sometimes I think my grand-father, my father, my son, and I are variations on a single personality meant to carry some dark message. The picture of my grandfather fills my mind. He is staring out beyond the frame. I mumble, "Tell me what you see."

Acknowledgments

T
HIS BOOK would not exist if it were not for my wife.
Becky has not only put up with my fits and moods, she
has typed, critiqued, and proofread various revisions
without complaint—all of this while teaching first grade. No
writer has ever had a better friend, companion, or wife.

I want to thank my family—Christopher, Shelly, Marci,
C.T., Rachel, Sean, Allison, and Jack—for standing by me
through hard times.

The support of certain friends was important—Bob and
Donna O'Connor, Lee McCarthy, and my brothers and sisters
at the Club.

I have interviewed over three hundred people in Pendleton
County, too many to try to name them all. I wish to thank
everyone who took the time to speak with me. The stories I
heard at kitchen tables, in farmhouse living rooms, in Greg
Bowers's veterinary office, and on truck rides to high pastures
remain vivid in my memory. Listening to the stories about your
lives was a rare privilege, and I will always appreciate this. I
admire Pendletonians—locals and come-heres alike. I have
done my best to write the truth as I understand it. No doubt
some people will disagree with this or that point, but I hope
fair-minded readers will appreciate my attempt at honesty. I
believe the community is rich enough and strong enough to
accept an honest portrait.

I have read well over a hundred books and scores of articles about West Virginia and Appalachia but feel especially indebted to the following: *Feud,* by Altina L. Waller;

Appalachian Mountain Religion: A History, by Deborah Vansau McCauley; *Modernizing the Mountaineer: People, Power, and Planning in Appalachia*, by David E. Whisnant; *All That Is Native and Fine: The Politics of Culture in an American Region*, also by David E. Whisnant; *Miners, Millhands, and Mountaineers: Industrialization of the Appalachian South*, by Ronald D. Eller; *Power and Powerlessness: Quiescence and Rebellion in an Appalachian Valley*, by John G. Gaventa; *Appalachia on Our Mind: The Southern Mountains and Mountaineers in the American Consciousness*, by Henry D. Shapiro; and *Who Owns Appalachia? Land Ownership and Its Impact*, by the Appalachian Land Ownership Task Force.

And I am enormously grateful to my editor at Knopf, Jon Segal. Jon's insight, tireless effort, and saintlike patience have made this book what it is.

Printed in the United States
by Baker & Taylor Publisher Services